SECRET LIVES
of the FIRST LADIES

WHAT YOUR TEACHERS NEVER TOLD YOU ABOUT THE WOMEN OF THE WHITE HOUSE

BY CORMAC O'BRIEN

PORTRAITS BY MONIKA SUTESKI

QUIRK BOOKS

Library of Congress Cataloging-in-Publication Number: 2004 112 082

ISBN: 1-59474-014-3

Printed in Singapore

Typeset in Grotesque, Caecilia, and Bickham Script

Designed by Susan Van Horn

Distributed in North America by Chronicle Books
85 Second Street
San Francisco, CA 94105

10 9 8 7 6 5 4 3 2 1

Quirk Books
215 Church Street
Philadelphia, PA 19106
www.quirkbooks.com

Dedication

For Lauren, forever and always my first lady.

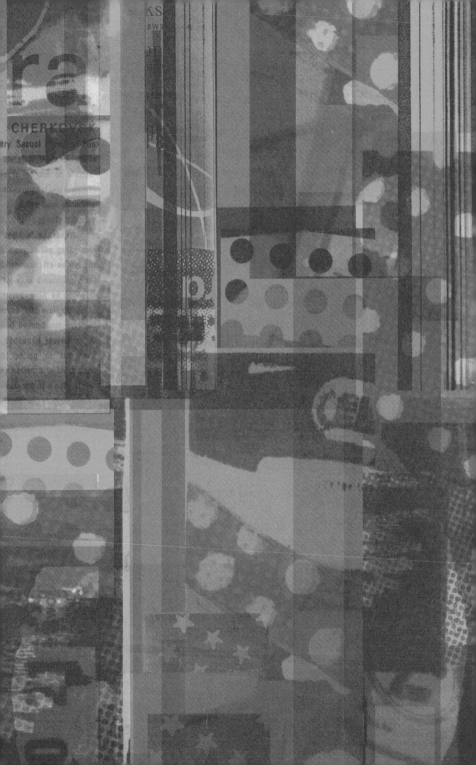

Espiscopalian 14
Presbytchan 7
Meth 6

CONTENTS

Introduction 9

Martha Washington (1789–1797) .. *Epis* X 11
Abigail Adams (1797–1801) .. *Congregationist* 18
All the Presidents' Wives: Martha Jefferson 24
Dolley Madison (1809–1817) ..... *Quaker* 25
Elizabeth Monroe (1817–1825) .... *Epis* X 32
Louisa Catherine Adams (1825–1829) .. *Catholic* 37
All the Presidents' Wives: Rachel Jackson 44
All the Presidents' Wives: Hannah Van Buren 45
Anna Harrison (1841) ...... *Pres* O 46
Letitia Christian Tyler (1841–1842) .. *Epis* X 50
Julia Gardiner Tyler (1844–1845) ... *Epis / Cath* X 54
Sarah Childress Polk (1845–1849) ... *Pres* 61
Margaret Taylor (1849–1850) ... *Epis* X 66
Abigail Fillmore (1850–1853) ... *Unitarian* 71
All the Presidents' Wives: Caroline Fillmore 77
Jane Pierce (1853–1857) .... *Congregationist* 78
Mary Todd Lincoln (1861–1865) .. *Pres* O 83
Eliza McCardle Johnson (1865–1869) .... *Meth* ✓ 92
Julia Dent Grant (1869–1877) ..... *Meth* ✓ 98
Lucy Webb Hayes (1877–1881) .... *Meth* ✓ 106
Lucretia Garfield (1881) .. *Dis of Christ* 113
All the Presidents' Wives: Ellen Herndon Arthur 119
Frances Cleveland (1886–1889, 1893–1897) .... *Pres* O 120
Caroline Harrison (1889–1892) .... *Pres* O 128
All the Presidents' Wives: Mary Harrison 135
Ida Saxton McKinley (1897–1901) ...... *Pres* O 136
All the Presidents' Wives: Alice Lee Roosevelt 143
Edith Kermit Roosevelt (1901–1909) .... *Epis* X 144
Helen Herron Taft (1909–1913) .... *Epis* X 151

CONTENTS

Ellen Axson Wilson (1913–1914) ... *Pres O* ... 159

Edith Bolling Wilson (1915–1921) ... *E.pis X ✓* ... 165

Florence Kling Harding (1921–1923) ... *Meth* ... 173

Grace Coolidge (1923–1929) ... *Congretionalist* ... 181

Lou Henry Hoover (1929–1933) ... *E.pis / Quaker X* ... 188

Eleanor Roosevelt (1933–1945) ... *E.pis X* ... 196

Bess Truman (1945–1953) ... *E.pis X* ... 204

Mamie Doud Eisenhower (1953–1961) ... *E.pis X* ... 211

Jacqueline Bouvier Kennedy (1961–1963) ... *Cath* ... 218

Lady Bird Johnson (1963–1969) ... *Epis X* ... 226

Pat Nixon (1969–1974) ... *Cath / Quaker* ... 234

Betty Ford (1974–1977) ... *E.pis X* ... 243

Rosalynn Carter (1977–1981) ... *Meth / Baptist* ... 251

All the Presidents' Wives: Jane Wyman ... 258

Nancy Reagan (1981–1989) ... *Disciples of Christ* ... 259

Barbara Bush (1989–1993) ... *Pics O* ... 267

Hillary Rodham Clinton (1993–2001) ... *Meth ✓* ... 274

Laura Bush (2001–) ... *Meth ✓* ... 282

Selected Bibliography ... 289

Index ... 291

Acknowledgments ... 296

INTRODUCTION

"I never wanted to be the president's wife, and I don't want it now. You don't quite believe me, do you? Very likely no one would—except possibly some woman who had had the job."—ELEANOR ROOSEVELT

So your husband has just been elected president of the United States. Kudos! Now it's all black-tie dinners, gourmet cooking, government-paid protection, and servants at your beck and call. Outstanding.

But hold on a minute. Your hubby is beginning a demanding relationship with the American people. He's surrounding himself with egotistical advisors who fill his harried head with harebrained schemes—and do their best to interfere with your relationship. And then there are the ubiquitous media freaks whose very paychecks depend on their ability to run roughshod all over your privacy.

On top of all that, you don't even get paid for any of this. Yippee!

Now, before you get carried away, remember: Nobody voted for *you*. It's your husband who's expected to balance the budget, fight the wars, and make foreign heads of state feel wooed and bullied at the same time. Your job is rather simpler: You are to do . . . well, whatever it is that you feel is most important. But be careful. Everyone's watching. Literally. If you want to stay home and cultivate a safe refuge for your husband, fine. Just don't appear to be a kept woman without any intellectual interests. If political activism is your thing, go crazy—as long as you don't look like a person who's exercising power that was given to her strictly because she shares a bed with the chief executive. Naturally, you're wondering how you'll know when you're verging into forbidden territory.

But don't worry—you'll know. Jane Pierce had plenty of reminders that her gloomy spiritualism made the White House feel like a morgue. When Lucy Hayes forbade alcohol of any sort in the executive mansion, she was derided as a puritanical priss. And Edith Wilson caught holy hell when she ran the executive branch of government while her husband struggled back to health from a stroke. As you'll soon find out, there is no shortage of people willing to offer instructive criticism. It's no wonder Pat Nixon said, "Being the first lady is the hardest unpaid job in the world."

Still, you have to look on the bright side: You've got one of the most vaguely defined positions in American government, giving you a very enviable freedom of purpose. Wanna tackle drug abuse? Falling literacy rates? The plight of an endangered species? Go for it. Because you can't possibly be fired. And if things get too hot to handle, you can always blame them on your powerful roommate—after all, he's the jerk who got you into this in the first place.

Finally, you're bound to achieve a certain level of immortality, a permanent place in history that allows you to be scrutinized and picked apart by books like this one. You just might find yourself enjoying the ride—provided that you keep your life in perspective. Betty Ford may have put it best: "I don't feel that because I'm first lady, I'm any different from what I was before. It can happen to anyone. After all, it *has* happened to anyone."

1 *Martha* WASHINGTON

June 2, 1731–May 22, 1802

MARRIED:

May 15, 1750 (Daniel Parke Custis); January 6, 1759 (George Washington)

PRESIDENTIAL HUSBAND:

George Washington

CHILDREN:

Daniel, Frances, John, and Martha (all with Daniel Parke Custis)

FIRST LADY:

1789–1797

ASTROLOGICAL SIGN:

Gemini

RELIGION:

Episcopalian

SOUND BITE:

"I live a very dull life here and know nothing that passes in the town—I never go to any public place, indeed I think I am more like a state prisoner than anything else."

In his twilight years, George Washington went to the newly founded capital city of the United States named for him, intent on buying a plot of land. The seller, however, wasn't keen on parting with the property and proved an obstinate negotiator. When the famous general and former president persisted, the seller snapped: "You think people take every grist that comes from you as the pure grain. What would you have been if you hadn't married the Widow Custis?!"

The impertinent fellow had a point. We tend to forget that Washington would never have become the Father of Our Country without the vast property holdings that secured his income and reputation. And that property was acquired by marrying a woman with whom he was probably never in love: Martha Dandridge Custis.

Born the eldest of eight children into modest Virginia aristocracy, Martha Dandridge was raised in a world of quintessential eighteenth-century paradoxes—a landed society of hard-partying, tobacco-growing grandees who memorized the Bible, armed themselves to the teeth, and whipped their black slaves with vigor and impunity. Her education encompassed dribs and drabs of reading

and writing combined with countless hours of domestic instruction, a curriculum tailored toward fulfilling her sole purpose in life: finding a husband, breeding heirs, and running a household of her own.

By the time Martha—at fifteen—was being paraded by her parents, John and Frances, before the eligible bachelors of Williamsburg society, she had grown into a rather pretty (if very short—she wasn't quite five feet tall) young woman who impressed everyone with her kind, agreeable nature. She was considered a catch; her duties as eldest daughter on the Dandridge's 500-acre plantation had turned her into a domestic powerhouse, and her decent education had bred a relatively refined lady. She was fond of polite conversation, music, and wearing finery that had to be ordered from England. It was enough to catch the eye of several suitors, but Martha latched on to a man she'd known her whole life: Daniel Parke Custis, her godfather (and twenty-one years her senior). After getting Daniel's notoriously irascible father to overcome his opposition to the match, the two were married in 1750.

Daniel was handsome, charming, one of the richest planters in the colony,

> Our first first lady shared a rival for her husband's affections. Many speculate that Sally Fairfax was George Washington's true love, and wealthy Martha was just a way to increase his holdings.

and dead by 1757. His passing came on the heels of two other deaths: the couple's eldest children, Daniel and Frances, were cut down in their youth by the pervasive sicknesses of the day. At twenty-six, Martha was a widow with two little brats left to raise, over 17,000 acres of land to run, and nearly 300 slaves to oversee.

Which is why she wasted no time in finding another husband. Sure, she was an immensely capable woman with a canny business sense and enormous discipline, but why make it hard on yourself when you live in a colony full of randy men squabbling over the shortage of women?

One of those men was George Washington, who possessed two problems: First, he was relatively poor, a militia colonel whose frontier heroics weren't putting any coins in his pocket; second, the love of his life—Sally Fairfax—was married to his best friend. (Oof.) Intent on developing his treasured estate, Mount Vernon, Washington wooed the wealthiest widow in Virginia, Martha Custis, whose riches were the key to becoming the influential gentleman of leisure that he wanted to become. For her part, Martha saw a certain star quality in this dashing soldier. George was tall, well built, physically brave, an outstanding horseman, well behaved, and . . . young (nine months her junior)! Who better to give her huge estate to?

After marrying in 1759, the two settled into something like domestic bliss. George used his wife's money to turn Mount Vernon into a palace, and Martha tried to forget that Sally Fairfax lived in the neighborhood. But the idyll was shattered when Martha saw her husband off to the Continental Congress in 1775, then found out that he'd been appointed commander of the rebel army (a post he accepted without her consent). So much for marital tranquility. For the next eight years of the Revolution, Martha saw her husband only during winter encampments. George made one trip to Mount Vernon throughout the war and stayed for a mere two days.

So it's hardly surprising that Martha bitched up a storm when the country that stole her husband during the war decided to borrow him again in peacetime. George had become the biggest thing since the Franklin stove, and nobody could conceive of anybody else as president of the infant republic. Though mortified at the prospect of being torn away from Mount Vernon yet again, Martha put on a game face for the trip up to the capital at New York City, cheered by throngs and rocked by thirteen-gun salutes virtually the whole way.

Once there, she was treading on new ground. As wife to the man whom many revered as a virtual monarch, she ran the risk of creating a presidential household that looked too much like European royalty. She was, after all, a Southern dame, with a natural inclination toward class consciousness and fine living. Her solution was to strike a balance between democratic simplicity, on the one hand, and official dignity, on the other. To be sure, she took to wearing extravagant clothes, rode about in a gilded coach, and began the custom of holding receptions in which lady callers were curtly welcomed. But she also cultivated a charitable demeanor to all who met her, including her husband's growing throng of enemies, and continued to embrace the role of happy domestic matron (her needlework was legendary).

In the end, Martha was allowed only a brief period of untrammeled private living with her "Pappa," as she called George. He died in 1799, two years after surrendering the presidency to John Adams and departing from public responsibility. Martha locked up their bedroom, took to sleeping alone in another part of Mount Vernon, and burned all the couple's private correspondence (a fact that has irritated curious historians ever since). She followed George to the grave in 1802. Hers was a vital role in the making of her husband and the United States, and not just on account of her wealth. Somebody had to be the first presidential spouse, and we could've done a lot worse than the generous, pragmatic, sociable Martha Washington.

ELDEST OF EIGHT . . . OR NINE?

Most history books claim that Martha Dandridge was the firstborn of eight children. But the truth isn't quite that simple. Apparently her father, John Dandridge (like so many other planter-aristocrats of his time), had a taste for mistresses. According to an obscure document written years after Martha's death, John Dandridge had an affair with a woman of African-Cherokee descent. The relationship produced Ann, a mulatto who was younger than Martha. Though little more is known about her, it is probable that Ann grew up in the Dandridge household as a slave and—when not toiling at her chores—a playmate of Martha's.

Horsing Around

Most of us perceive the Mother of Our Country as demure and retiring, but the truth about Martha is a little less refined. Remember, she grew up in a wild frontier society. At least one anecdote survives to give us some idea of her rambunctious childhood. Apparently, she once rode her horse onto the porch of her uncle's estate and scared the bejeebers out of everyone by threatening to ride her steed into the house. She was talked out of the escapade by her scandalized aunt.

THINK YOUR IN-LAWS ARE A PAIN?

Daniel Parke Custis, Martha's first husband, was loved by everybody. He was a cheerful, considerate man who wanted nothing so much as a normal, peaceful existence. And no wonder—he'd been raised by one of the angriest (and wealthiest) nut cases in all of colonial America. John Custis IV, Daniel's father, was a man whose eccentricities often bordered on insanity.

Daniel was terrified of him. John seemed to think that no woman was good enough for his son (and, hence, his fortune). He immediately opposed Daniel's match with Martha. To his credit, Daniel never gave up on his young fiancée—though he couldn't muster the courage to confront his pop, either. The situation festered. John went so far as to give some of his most expensive and treasured possessions to a common mistress in Williamsburg, as if to say that she deserved it far more than that Dandridge gold digger. He even threatened to cut Daniel out of his will altogether.

A solution was found by some of Daniel's closest friends, who managed to talk John out of opposing Martha. It is a measure of John's erratic disposition that he was so easily persuaded. We'll never know precisely what was said to him (though a common legend has it that John, one of the most prominent horticulturists of his day, was won over by word of Martha's own gardening gifts).

Martha the Murderess?

Even after his death, Martha continued to be haunted by the legacy of her father-in-law. As if to pester his son and daughter-in-law from the beyond, John Custis IV drew up a will that can only be called sadistic.

He stipulated that his illegitimate son by a slave woman, "Mulatto Jack," be freed, and that Jack inherit a handsome portion of the Parke-Custis fortune. Daniel was to care for Jack until he was of such an age as to take charge of his inheritance.

As generous as this may seem to us today, the will was a terrific headache for Daniel and Martha for one primary reason: According to the laws at the time, Mulatto Jack could not be freed except by the royal governor's consent. Which means that the will, though required by law to be carried out to the letter, was impossible to fulfill. It also meant that the young couple would need to spend a fortune on drawn-out legal battles to get the will changed. In the meantime, Mulatto

Jack—Daniel's half-brother—lived with the newlyweds in their house until a resolution could be reached.

That resolution arrived in September 1751 with Jack's death. It neatly solved the issue of the inheritance. Jack was young and, by all accounts, healthy. Of course, sickness and infirmity could creep up on anybody quickly in the eighteenth century (accounts record that he succumbed to something involving a "pain in the neck"), but one can't help but gasp at Daniel and Martha's unexpected good fortune.

Did Daniel or Martha actually kill the poor fellow? We'll never know. But given the fact that both were almost universally praised for their honesty and goodwill, it seems more likely that—if Mulatto Jack was murdered—one of their friends decided to bring the young couple's troublesome issue to a conclusion without their knowledge. Makes you wonder, though, doesn't it?

BLOWN GLASS

Martha never forgave John Custis IV and blamed her first husband's early death on his father's mind games and abuse. Shortly after Daniel died, she paid a visit to the Williamsburg mansion that had been her father-in-law's main residence and auctioned off the remainder of his valuable possessions. That is, except for his priceless collection of handblown wineglasses. Those she proceeded to smash in a spectacular act of vengeance.

LUCK BE A LADY

During the Revolutionary War, newspapers branded Martha a loyalist. It's safe to say that they were mistaken. During every winter of the war, while both sides were in quarters until the spring campaigning season began, Martha traveled from Mount Vernon to be wherever George was with his troops. She became something of a surrogate mother to the freezing, threadbare soldiers—creating bandages, mending uniforms, and so forth. She often acted as her husband's clerk, copying much of his correspondence and being trusted with military secrets. Though terribly fond of the latest fashions from overseas, she insisted on boycotting foreign finery during the war and made a point of wearing only colonial homespun. Her efforts were definitely appreciated—one regiment at Valley Forge christened themselves "Lady Washington's Dragoons."

2

Abigail ADAMS

November 11, 1744–

October 28, 1818

MARRIED:

October 25, 1764

PRESIDENTIAL HUSBAND:

John Adams

CHILDREN:

Abigail Amelia, John Quincy, Susanna, Charles, and Thomas Boylston

FIRST LADY:

1797–1801

ASTROLOGICAL SIGN:

Scorpio

RELIGION:

Congregationalist

SOUND BITE:

"Remember all men would be tyrants if they could."

When Abigail Adams brought her young son John Quincy to the crest in front of their home to watch the Battle of Bunker Hill from a distance, it was without a sense of horror. To her, the fighting was an inevitable reaction to what she considered British tyranny.

> In an age when women were expected to stay silent, Abigail Adams always spoke her mind—and always rushed to her husband's defense.

She was a patriot to the marrow of her bones and remained a passionate—and extremely eloquent—champion of all things American till her dying day.

The other two loves of her life—John Adams and politics—would help forge one of the most extraordinary relationships in American history. In an age when most women were content to take a backseat to their husbands and keep their mouths shut, Abigail gave free rein to her extraordinary intellect, forming fully one-half of a brilliant and loving partnership. And her husband wouldn't have had it any other way.

Born in Weymouth, Massachusetts, Abigail Smith seemed destined for greatness from a young age. Though persistent health problems kept her from going to school and receiving a formal education, the home-schooling she received from her well-read family more than made up for it. Hers was a child-

hood shaped by keen conversation and debate around the dinner table. She acquired a lifelong love of books, particularly poetry, and it wasn't long before she was smart enough to teach herself French.

When, at the age of fifteen, she met the feisty and successful lawyer John Adams, there seemed little indication that the two would one day be hopelessly in love. John was unimpressed, remarking that Abigail showed a disturbing "lack of candor." He would be singing a very different tune only two years later, by which time—having had a chance to spend much time together—the two had become obsessed with each other.

The newly married couple moved into a house that John had inherited, right next door to his childhood home. There, while Adams went a-lawyering throughout Boston, Abigail took to running their small farm. By 1772, there were four children to be raised: daughter Nabby and sons John Quincy, Charles, and Thomas. Abigail developed into a thrifty and efficient housewife, taking control of the household finances and making investments in land that would help support her in later, more troubled times.

Those troubled times, when they came, proved almost too much even for the resourceful and courageous Abigail. While John was off in Philadelphia during the Continental Congress, his wife struggled with maintaining the farm and with her own loneliness. The Revolutionary War made things much worse. While John struggled through diplomatic postings in Europe, Abigail passed the war years by casting musket balls, scraping money together to feed her family, hunting down whatever gossip she could about the war, and—most importantly— writing to her absent husband. The couple maintained a correspondence with each other that reads like a history of the times co-written by two lucid, well-educated lovers. They wrote movingly of their relationship, exchanged ideas and humor, and longed for the day when they'd be reunited.

That day arrived in 1784, after Abigail—implored by John to join him in Europe—decided that the perils of an ocean voyage were nothing compared to remaining away from him. After joining her husband in France, Abigail followed him to England, where he was made America's minister plenipotentiary to the Court of St. James's. Europe was the capstone to Abigail's education, a four-year course in foreign culture that widened her already considerable intellectual horizons. If it made her worldlier, it also galvanized her love of America. She blanched at the filthy streets of Paris, blushed at the theater's scantily dressed performers, was horrified by the French servant class's laziness and impertinence. In England, she grew bored with court customs and chafed at the open criticism of her husband.

But criticism, unfortunately, was something she was going to have to get used to. John Adams had acquired a reputation as a tireless promoter of liberty and an abrasive pain in the ass. His vital role in the shaping of the young republic earned him the first vice presidency, but his argumentative, headstrong nature quickly earned him enemies. Much of the criticism was directed at his haughty belief in the notion that the new country should be led by an educated elite. It was the sort of thing that many, including the eminent Thomas Jefferson, found repulsive. Abigail, always the supporter of her dear husband, merely fueled the fight by backing him 100 percent.

Once John succeeded George Washington as president, the criticism got worse. Abigail's fear of rule by popular mobs was no secret, and her influence over her husband was equally well known. She was soon being called "Mrs. President" behind her back, and mocked as a domineering aristocrat with queenly aspirations. Abigail continued to view herself as the president's partner (which she was) and struck back by commissioning pro-Adams journalism in the press. The whole messy situation left a bad taste in her mouth and convinced her that the United States might just succumb to another revolution.

Abigail was more than just the savvy sounding board for her husband's ideas. She was the sort of capable partner who made life in the political limelight a lot easier—while John embroiled himself in the business of government, his wife drew on years of experience to run a tight presidential household. The Washingtons may have lived beyond their means, but under Abigail's control, the Adamses managed to save enough of their $25,000 presidential salary to invest for retirement. It's an important fact often forgotten when taking the measure of Abigail Adams. Sure, she was the first woman to be both a presidential wife and mother (John Quincy would one day make it to the White House); the protofeminist who reminded John Adams to "remember the ladies" during the drafting of the Declaration of Independence; and the equal of her ingenious, multitalented husband. But she was also a person whose strong beliefs were forged in the cauldron of adversity, a capable, practical, hardheaded New England matriarch who appreciated the benefits of liberty so dearly purchased. By any measure, she was an extraordinary woman.

FIRST MATE

When John Adams wrote to his wife pleading for her to join him in France, Abigail was hesitant. Granted, she wished more than anything to be reunited with her husband. But she had never been away from home before and dreaded the perils of an Atlantic crossing (storms, green drinking water, cramped quarters, pirates, and so on). Nevertheless, on June 18, 1784, she and her daughter, Nabby, boarded the *Active*, bound for England, where John promised to meet them to accompany them to the Continent. They brought two servants and a cow with them.

The seasickness started almost immediately and remained for days. The passengers' condition was exacerbated by the ship's cargo of whale oil and potash, which, tossed by the ocean's waves, infused the entire vessel with a stagnant reek. Abigail and Nabby shared two tiny compartments with another woman and were forced to keep their doors open at night for ventilation, which exposed them in their nightclothes to the crew and male passengers. Oh, well. At least they were better off than the cow they'd brought, who was so badly injured by a storm that it had to be killed and tossed overboard.

The *Active* eventually made it to calmer waters, which finally meant an end to the seasickness. But Abigail had barely recovered before she started taking control of the ship. The cook, according to her, was a "lazy, dirty Negro with no more knowledge of his business than a savage." She proceeded to take him under her wing and teach him his craft and even did some of the food preparation herself. Then she moved on to the rest of the ship. Horrified by the lingering stench, she got down on her hands and knees and scrubbed the vessel from stem to stern. By the time the vessel made it to England, the captain was convinced that Abigail wanted his job.

THE ADAMS FAMILY

Abigail loved her children—perhaps to death. She wrote to her son John Quincy in 1778, after he went to Europe to begin the diplomatic career that would eventually take him to the presidency, that "I had much rather you should have found your Grave in the ocean you have crossed or any untimely death crop you in your Infant years, rather than see you an immoral profligate or a Graceless child." John Quincy would achieve greatness, but his siblings weren't quite so lucky. Being a child of such exacting parents as John and Abigail could be harsh. Charles and Thomas both died from alcoholism. Nabby was convinced by her parents to forgo the love of her life (who went on to become a successful playwright) to marry her father's secretary, Colonel William Smith, who never provided enough for his wife and family. (Nabby died at forty-eight from breast cancer.) Abigail relied on her high standards to sustain her at the darkest moments. As she wrote to her sister upon the death of Charles, "Weep with me over the grave of a poor unhappy child who cannot now add another pang to those which have pierced my heart for several years."

Turkey Talk

Abigail Adams had been raised to speak her opinion, a quality that her husband relished. But when John Adams was elected to the highest office in the land, Abigail wondered if her mouth would get her in trouble. After all, her only predecessor as first lady was Martha Washington, who—like most eighteenth-century women—had kept her place, which wasn't in the sphere of politics. Abigail wrote to her husband that she was aware of the prudence of following "Lady Washington's" example—but that she'd rather be bound, gagged, and shot like a turkey.

THE LAUNDRY ON THE HILL

John and Abigail Adams were the first presidential couple to occupy what would eventually become known as the "White House." But when they took up residence in 1799, the new structure was a far cry from the splendid landmark we know today. Much of it had yet to be finished, it was dramatically understaffed, and the mansion even lacked stairways. Abigail made the most of a bad situation, but it showed: she was forced to hang the laundry in the building's reception area (now the East Room), where every government caller could see it.

Martha Jefferson

1749–1782

By the time she met Thomas Jefferson, Martha Wayles had already been married once, to a successful lawyer named Bathurst Skelton. That union lasted only two years, and Martha was a widow at twenty. She was a ravishing young Southern belle when the future president became smitten with her, and, in addition to boasting an expansive education, she loved to play music—the quality that most endeared her to the violin-playing Jefferson. They were married in 1772. Thomas bought her a piano and arranged for lessons from a music teacher, and the two spent long hours expressing their heartfelt devotion in duets that wowed guests. Martha's health, however, wasn't nearly as extraordinary as her musical ability, and bearing six children only strained her frail physique further.

Worse, only two of the kids lived beyond infancy: Patsy and Polly. With his wife's health failing daily, the music went out of Jefferson's life in more ways than one. His responsibilities to the Virginia Assembly and Continental Congress during the Revolution often suffered so that he could be near his dying wife. According to legend, he promised her not to remarry—and remained true to his word, despite notorious flings with Maria Cosway and a slave named Sally Hemings. Indeed, if we are to believe contemporary accounts from witnesses close to Jefferson, Martha's death left him utterly devastated. By the time he became president of the United States, Martha had been gone nineteen years, forcing Jefferson to rely on his daughters and Dolley Madison to imbue the White House with female grace during his administration.

3

Dolley MADISON

May 20, 1768–July 12, 1849	
MARRIED:	
January 7, 1790 (John Todd Jr.); September 15, 1794 (James Madison)	
PRESIDENTIAL HUSBAND:	
James Madison	
CHILDREN:	
John Payne and William Temple (both with John Todd)	
FIRST LADY:	
1809–1817	
ASTROLOGICAL SIGN:	
Taurus	
RELIGION:	
Quaker	
SOUND BITE:	
"Our sex are ever losers, when they stem the torrent of public opinion."	

In July of 1849, a grateful United States said goodbye to Dolley Madison in a funeral fit for an empress. Presiding over the event was President Zachary Taylor, whose words made a fitting capstone to the life of America's "Queen Mother": "She will never be forgotten, because she was truly our first lady for a half century." It was the first use of the term "first lady," and appropriately so: for Dolley Madison was, and perhaps still is, the *suma inter pares* of presidential spouses.

Though born in North Carolina, Dolley Payne grew up on her family's plantation near Ashland, Virginia. As Quakers, the Paynes deliberately avoided participation in the Revolutionary War. The peaceful, egalitarian sect also opposed slavery, a fact that finally drove Dolley's father, John, to free his slaves in 1783 and take the family north to Philadelphia. His piety and progressive politics were rewarded with bankruptcy and humiliation: Within six years his nascent starch business went belly-up, compelling the Quaker community to disown him for fouling up his finances. He died three years later.

Fortunately for Dolley, she had already found another means of support: John Todd Jr., a fellow Quaker with a successful law practice. The two were married in 1790, had two children, and lived a comfortable life among Philadelphia's elite.

The dream soon turned into a nightmare. Yellow fever struck Philadelphia

in October of 1793, subjecting the city to a calamity of biblical proportions. Hero-ically, John Todd decided not to flee (as so many others did, including much of the federal government), and offered his legal counsel to the dying and widowed. This decision cost him his life. The Todds' youngest son, William Temple, was also struck down. Dolley succumbed to fever, but recovered.

The twenty-five-year-old widow now drew on her late husband's wealth to raise their remaining son, John Payne Todd. Dolley continued to make a splash in society and drew attention with her gregarious and kindly nature. Though largely ignorant of practical matters, she relied on legal and financial advice from a coterie of male admirers who flew to her like moths to flame. One of them was Aaron Burr, who introduced her to a friend of his named James Madison.

Madison was a genius, to be sure. He had written George Washington's speeches, impressed even the great Thomas Jefferson with his breadth of learn-ing, and contributed as much as anyone—perhaps more than anyone—to the creation of the country's Constitution. He was also a sickly, withdrawn little thing, in almost every way the opposite of the chatty, extroverted Dolley. They fell hard for each other nevertheless and were married in 1794. It was more than the

Thanks to her magnificent turbans and scandalously low-cut gowns, Dolley Madison reigned as the White House's first fashion diva.

beginning of a warm and very successful marriage; it was also the birth of a new Dolley. For, shortly after the wedding, her fellow Quakers gave her the boot for marrying outside the faith. And Dolley, free to act upon her unrestrained pro-clivities, threw off her modest Quaker duds and never looked back.

Her introduction to official government hostessing came earlier than expected when James (whom Dolley called her "little Jemmy") became secretary of state in 1801. Because both President Jefferson and Vice President Burr were wid-owers, Dolley became the de facto female voice of the administration. She rose to the occasion with gusto and panache. Dinners at the Madison residence were gay affairs indeed, thanks in large part to Dolley's gift for gab and deft social choreog-raphy. Jemmy even had her sit at the head of the table, where she could direct con-versation toward subjects that would engage all and offend none.

Such experience served her well when, in 1809, she became the first lady in title as well as practice. She had more public seasoning under her gown than any previous presidential spouse, and it showed. Schooled in the Jeffersonian tradition of entertaining, in which the aristocratic was shunned in favor of the simple and republican, Dolley knew how to throw a party. Gone were the stilted levees of her predecessors, full of bowing, humorless courtiers. At Dolley's affairs, people mingled, joked, laughed, and treated themselves to ice cream—a French delicacy that Jefferson had introduced her to. The kindly, buxom hostess could be seen everywhere, dressed to the nines and offering a smile and a handshake to senator and servant alike. While Jemmy ensconced himself in a corner to murmur over grave issues with colleagues, Dolley's schmoozing galvanized relationships and assuaged the rancor of political foes. As Henry Clay put it, "Everybody loves Mrs. Madison." (Dolley replied, "That's because Mrs. Madison loves everybody.") Such graces were indispensable not only to her husband. Dolley once got two congressmen, John Epps and John Randolph, to call off their duel over a nasty political argument.

Dolley didn't even let military conflict dampen her spirits. When war broke out in 1812 with England, the first lady found herself maligned behind her back for her pacifist Quaker background. She made a point of correcting such misrepresentations by fully and publicly supporting her husband. It worked, perhaps too well: At a victory celebration, the son of the secretary of the navy chose to lay the flag of a captured British ship at Dolley's feet, rather than at her husband's (she proceeded to blush, perhaps as a result of upstaging the diminutive president). After getting chased out of Washington by an invading British army in 1814, Dolley merely brushed the dust off her clothes, returned to a gutted capital, took up residence with Jemmy in a private home—and started entertaining again. Besides, 1815 brought peace and victory . . . and more celebrations for her victorious husband, who was now the toast of the town. She even found time to organize relief for war orphans.

After Jemmy completed his second term, the Madisons moved to his Virginia estate at Montpelier. The allure of Washington, however, never waned for Dolley. Upon her husband's death in 1836, she moved back to the capital to resume her role as First Entertainer of the land and was even granted an honorary seat in

Congress (by unanimous vote, no less). She remained at the heart of Washington society, a tangible and beloved link to the country's Founding Fathers, a doyenne who was allowed to send the second message in the new Morse code (after Samuel Morse himself, of course) and who helped President Polk lay the cornerstone of the future Washington Monument. Until her death in 1849, it was customary for newly inaugurated presidents to call on the Queen Mother and receive her blessing.

MAKING UP FOR LOST TIME

Concealed within Dolley Payne Todd the Quaker was a fashion diva just begging to bust out. And that's exactly what happened when, at twenty-six, Dolley was booted out of the Quakers for marrying James Madison. Her wardrobe soon started matching her shining personality: extravagant gowns of silk and satin, low-cut dresses to show off (often scandalously) her ample bosom, and so on. But nothing made Dolley stand out quite like her turbans. She was rarely seen at public gatherings without her head wrapped in one, its elaborate folds sporting brightly colored feathers up to a foot in height. They soon became something of a trend owing to Dolley's enormous popularity, but nobody could carry them off like the "Presidentress." Such magnificent finery came at a price, of course; she was rumored to spend a thousand dollars a year on the turbans alone.

Snuff Job

Dolley was a devout user of snuff tobacco, often interrupting a moment of socializing to sniff up a pinch from her stained fingers. Because ladies rarely embraced such a habit, most of the fellow addicts who dipped into her bejeweled snuffbox were men. And it's hardly surprising—the cleanup required after every dose could look decidedly unladylike. Dolley carried two handkerchiefs for the job: a delicate lacey thing for prep work, and a thicker one for the messy spots.

CARRYING A TORCH

As a Quaker, Dolley was brought up to despise slavery. Her father had freed all of his and even petitioned Congress to outlaw the institution. But her second husband, James Madison, was (like all good Virginia planters) a prominent slave owner. Her personal feelings on the subject remain somewhat vague. On at least one occasion, however, she seems to have forgotten the guiding principles of her childhood. At a reception she threw in 1815 to impress the new British ambassador (and to convince him that there were no hard feelings in the wake of the War of 1812), she took great care in creating a festive atmosphere—which included stationing torch-holding African slaves throughout the house to provide illumination. One appalled partyer described it as "a barbarous Egyptian display."

UP IN FLAMES

With a few painful exceptions, the initial stages of the War of 1812 went fairly well for the young United States. Then the British brought the other arm out from behind their back in 1814 and decided to get serious. That summer, they landed an army on the American coast. Its goal was clear: the federal capital at Washington. But its commander, Rear Admiral Sir George Cockburn, had an even more specific objective in mind: Dolley Madison.

Cockburn had publicly announced his intention of capturing the first lady and taking her back to England, where she was to be paraded through the streets of London as a war prize. By the time British redcoats were making a stir on the outskirts of Washington, Dolley was on her own at the White House. Jemmy had departed to be with the troops (who, incidentally, were getting their tails kicked by Cockburn's scarlet professionals). After ascending to the roof of the presidential mansion and watching the fireworks through a spyglass, Dolley decided—spurred by a letter from Jemmy urging her to flee—that it was time to get while the getting was good. She directed the servants to gather up some valuables (including a pair of beautiful red curtains and the famous Gilbert Stuart portrait of George Washington) and flee before the arrival of the enemy. During the evening of August 24, Cockburn and his party arrived at the White House looking for Dolley. They had to settle instead for the dinner she had laid out before fleeing, which they proceeded to devour. Cockburn, his prize having eluded him, settled for one of her seat cushions (so that he "could be reminded of her seat," he is rumored to have said), which he took with him before ordering that the place be torched.

The burning of the White House was an insult to every American, but Dolley took it particularly hard. Fortunately, she found a clever and stylish way to cope: Dolley took the expensive red curtains that were rescued prior to her flight from the mansion and had them made into a gorgeous new gown—to be worn, of course, at functions celebrating victory over the British.

MONEY MATTERS

Those who paid a visit to Dolley Madison during her twilight years in Washington typically left a little money somewhere in her Lafayette Square home before taking their leave. For as everybody knew, despite her legendary status and powerful friends, the capital's grand dame was a virtual pauper.

It hadn't always been so, of course. Both of her husbands had been wealthy men. But James Madison's Montpelier estate began to lose money even before his death in 1836 and would continue to drop in value long afterward. In fact, one of the primary reasons for Dolley's return to Washington after Jemmy died was to peddle his papers to Congress. Encompassing the great Madison's career, reflections, and accomplishments, the papers were surely worth $100,000. Or so she thought. In 1837, after watching the poor old widow pester everyone who would listen about getting a good price for Jemmy's memoirs, Congress finally gave her $30,000 for part of them.

It wasn't a bad sum. But Dolley's financial problems were unusually nasty, due in large part to her son John Payne Todd, who had grown up to become every mother's worst nightmare: a drunken, quarrelsome, philandering fool. Even worse, he was addicted to gambling and had a habit of losing at it. James Madison, before he died, estimated that he had lost around $40,000 to his stepson's insatiable lifestyle and stints in debtor's prison. Things just got worse once Jemmy was gone. Dolley never could say no to her son.

Fortunately, Congress could. Perhaps out of pity, they bought the rest of Madison's papers from her for $25,000 in 1847, but kept the money safe from Payne Todd by putting it in a trust fund that only Dolley could use. (Payne Todd actually had the gall to show up in Washington and threaten the managers of the trust with physical harm. His poor old ma had to beg him not to make things worse than he already had.) Sadly, the funds came only a year and a half before her death.

4 *Elizabeth* MONROE

June 30, 1768–September 23, 1830

MARRIED:
February 16, 1786

PRESIDENTIAL HUSBAND:
James Monroe

CHILDREN:
Eliza Kortright, James Spence, and Maria Hester

FIRST LADY:
1817–1825

ASTROLOGICAL SIGN:
Cancer

RELIGION:
Episcopalian

SOUND BITE:
"No comment." (All of Monroe's correspondence was burned soon after her death.)

Little is known about America's fourth first lady, largely because her correspondence was burned shortly after her death and neither her husband nor daughters wrote extensively about her during their lifetimes. This

Elizabeth Monroe suffered from a mysterious "falling sickness" that was never properly diagnosed. On one occasion, she even tumbled into a burning fireplace.

much is certain, though: She had the odious task of succeeding the legendary Dolley Madison; and, possessing none of Queen Dolley's beloved qualities, she pretty much messed things up.

Elizabeth Kortright had unlikely origins for a future American first lady. Her father, Lawrence Kortright, was a wealthy merchant and British loyalist, and he had a son (Elizabeth's brother) who wore a red uniform during the Revolution. But the Kortrights patiently ate their crow after the war and remained in New York, where they were prominent members of the mercantile elite. Elizabeth was raised with all the aristocratic trappings that her family's wealth could afford. It created in her a tendency toward snobbery that would one day bite her in her blue-blooded rear end.

By the time she was sixteen, she had become a refined, stunning, dark-haired

beauty who could have her pick of suitors. She ended up choosing James Monroe, a Virginia delegate to the Confederation Congress being held in 1785 in the temporary capital of New York City. Like most landed Virginians, Monroe had plenty of land and slaves, but very little cash—a fact that drove many of Elizabeth's friends and family to accuse her of courting beneath her station. She calmly rebuffed them and married the fellow in 1786.

The newlyweds moved to Virginia, where James started practicing law to put more money in his pocket. But the lure of politics proved irresistible, and he soon ended up serving as a U.S. Senator. Then, in 1794, the Washington administration made him minister to France, and the Monroes were off to Europe.

The new minister and his wife embraced the culture of their new French surroundings with what can only be called fanaticism. Elizabeth felt right at home among the culture and finery of the French, who soon embraced her as *la belle Americaine*. The couple enrolled their daughter Eliza in a French school, learned to speak the language fluently, and almost started regretting that they would one day have to return to America.

That day didn't come until 1797, by which time the Monroes had become as French as any Americans could ever be. Elizabeth watched her husband get elected governor of Virginia, then bore a son who died of whooping cough during infancy. It was enough for her to start pining for the courts of Europe, and she didn't have to wait long—in 1803, President Thomas Jefferson sent James back to France to negotiate the Louisiana Purchase with Napoleon.

The mission in France was just the beginning of a tour of duty that would take James to London, Madrid, and other European cities on diplomatic service. But none of them held the appeal for Elizabeth of her beloved France. In London, for instance, the Monroes were routinely sniped for being representatives of an upstart little country (although, whenever she attended the opera, the orchestra welcomed her by playing "Yankee Doodle").

After returning to America, Monroe became Virginia's governor again in 1811, then resigned to assume the role of James Madison's secretary of state. By 1816, he was important enough to realize his dreams of being president and was elected to a term that would become known as the "Era of Good Feelings" for its conspicuous lack of partisan squabbling.

"Good feelings," however, were soon lacking among the prominent members of Washington society. The cause was the presidential spouse. She was haughty, formal, and . . . well, not Dolley Madison. Elizabeth blamed her aloofness and lack of entertaining on ill health and a White House that was still recovering from its 1814 destruction, but nobody really believed her. She reversed Dolley's custom of initiating social relations with society folk and the diplomatic corps, preferring instead that they call on her. They not only failed to do so, but went so far as to boycott official presidential functions. And on those few occasions when they did attend, Elizabeth made things worse by being a no-show. Instead, she delegated White House hostess duties to her eldest daughter, Eliza. Things got bad enough to draw the attention of Monroe's cabinet, who feared the situation would mess up their relationship with Congress. Little came of it, though, and White House receptions—in which the elaborately dressed first lady, when she bothered to attend, greeted guests with a curt nod—continued to show dismal attendance. Indeed, some of those who managed to come were actually turned away by guards posted by daughter Eliza to reject those who weren't properly dressed.

Seemingly nothing that Elizabeth did could make things better. She oversaw the refurbishment of the White House, but the European-style furniture she used (much of it bought from disenfranchised French nobility) merely made the mansion look more aristocratic to American eyes. And the first lady's famous beauty (she seemed incapable of aging) just enflamed the jealousy of Washington women.

Though Elizabeth had her admirers, particularly among the European diplomats who appreciated her class-conscious refinements, she never did win the devotion of an American populace who viewed her as mysterious and unapproachable. She preceded her husband James to the grave by ten months, succumbing to the illnesses upon which she had blamed a career of public absences.

TO THE RESCUE

The Marquis de Lafayette, a young French nobleman who served in Washington's army during the Revolution, personified his native land's friendship with the United States. But when the Revolutionary concepts he fought for in the New

World came to France, they came with a lot more severity and violence. Indeed, men like Lafayette—and their families—were suddenly under attack in Revolutionary France for their aristocratic ties and soon found their necks in the guillotine. It was at the height of this bloodthirsty period, 1795, when Elizabeth Monroe performed the one public act for which she is chiefly remembered.

Her husband, then the American minister to France, learned that Lafayette's wife had been imprisoned and was slated for execution. He was powerless to act officially on her behalf, though he desperately wanted to—such an intervention would jeopardize his country's relationship with France. Monroe's wife, on the other hand, was a different matter altogether. Elizabeth agreed to visit the poor marquise, and, traveling to the prison in a coach displaying her husband's diplomatic seal, drew quite a crowd.

She entered, visited briefly, then stood and loudly proclaimed that she would call on the poor woman again tomorrow. The guards who overheard this soon spread the word, and the marquise—whose execution was scheduled for that very day—was spared indefinitely, solely on the threat that Mrs. Monroe might show up for another conversation and be horrified at the marquise's absence. Her obvious attachment to the American envoy and his wife scared off the French government, which wanted to avoid scandalizing the United States.

SECRET SICKNESS

The illnesses that always seemed to keep Elizabeth from making frequent public appearances have remained cloaked in mystery. She probably suffered from arthritis. Some historians speculate that she was also afflicted with epilepsy. Little to nothing was known about the "falling disease," as it was then called, and it was almost certainly a source of embarrassment to both Elizabeth and her husband. Perhaps this is why they remained so elusive about her health and condition. James did mention that she was prone to "convulsions," one of which she suffered while sitting before a fireplace, which left her burned after she fell into it.

5 *Louisa Catherine* ADAMS

February 12, 1775–May 15, 1852

MARRIED:

July 26, 1797

PRESIDENTIAL HUSBAND:

John Quincy Adams

CHILDREN:

George Washington, John, Charles Francis, and Louisa Catherine

FIRST LADY:

1825–1829

ASTROLOGICAL SIGN:

Aquarius

RELIGION:

Catholic (sort of)

SOUND BITE:

"Debt and meanness is the penalty imposed by the salary of an American minister."

Louisa Catherine Johnson Adams was an accomplished scholar, litterateur, and musician. But her greatest accomplishment may well be that she survived a long marriage to the most cantankerous president in American history: John Quincy Adams.

The second daughter of eight children, Louisa was born in London to an English mother and American-born father. The family lived in France between 1778 and 1783, where Louisa learned French and was influenced by the Roman Catholic faith. It wasn't long before the Johnsons realized that they had a prodigy on their hands: Louisa was a poet, a singer (despite her shyness), and could play the harp and piano with ease. Her father's mercantile wealth paid for lessons and instruction, and it seemed as if the bright girl had great expectations.

In 1795 she met another prodigy. John Quincy Adams, the son of the American vice president John Adams, was in London on a diplomatic mission and soon had eyes for the charming and beautiful Louisa. He was the most well traveled young man in all the United States and boasted a towering intellect to boot. But grace with the opposite sex was not one of John Quincy's many gifts, and his courtship of Louisa was so clumsy that it took the poor girl weeks just to figure out that he was interested in her. By May of 1796, she had spent enough time

with him to overlook his nerdier qualities, and she consented to marry him.

JQA responded by postponing the wedding indefinitely, offering a window into the chaotic heap of neuroses that clouded his mind. Like all Adamses, he was preoccupied with money (or, more specifically, the lack thereof) and insisted on waiting until he was sure of his financial future (a day that would never come, actually). That, and the fact that he possessed a conspicuous lack of sensitivity toward people, began to wear on Louisa's patience. She wrote him a series of letters that pleaded and fumed, until JQA finally consented to meet at the altar in July of 1797.

But there wasn't much of a honeymoon. The marriage was difficult from day one and rarely got better. For his part, JQA found his financial fears confirmed upon the discovery that his new father-in-law, Joshua Johnson, had in fact

While visiting New York in 1807, Louisa Adams's infant son was snatched from her arms by a thief (she gave chase and eventually recovered the baby).

become bankrupt, leaving Mr. and Mrs. John Quincy Adams with little to live on beyond his meager diplomat's salary. It was the sort of mishap that stuck in JQA's craw, never to come loose, and fueled his already frightful predilection toward irritability and depression. Louisa soon found herself married to a man who found fault in everybody. And despite his own parents' equitable relationship, he firmly believed in the subservience of the fairer sex, even when they were brilliant, gifted, and vivacious (like his wife).

If Louisa hoped things would improve in 1801, when John Quincy was recalled home from his diplomatic circuit in Europe, she was sorely disappointed. Upon meeting her famously uncompromising in-laws in Quincy, Massachusetts, poor Louisa found herself lacking. Former First Lady Abigail Adams, who had opposed her son's marriage to an "English woman," was particularly hard, finding fault in all that Louisa tried to do. Born and bred of European wealth, Louisa was jolted by the frugality and homespun self-reliance of New England: "Had I stepped into Noah's Ark, I do not think I would have been more utterly astonished."

She would've preferred almost anywhere else—say, Washington, for example. Which is where she was off to in 1803 when John Quincy got elected to the Senate. The American capital was a breath of fresh air, not the least because the remnants of her own family lived there. She went horse riding whenever possible, took trips to the racetrack, and tried to ignore the beating her husband was taking in the political arena (the unscrupulous combat of politics would always depress her). She couldn't have known that, soon enough, it would all come to an end—and that she would find herself in a place that made New England look like paradise.

In 1809, President James Madison appointed John Quincy Adams minister to Russia. No one consulted Louisa about the momentous move, and that made her angry. But what really sent her reeling was the fact that her husband, in his infinite capacity for cruelty, had made arrangements for their two eldest sons to stay behind in America. Louisa would have to face the rigors of a frozen foreign land without even the company of her beloved George and John. Only little Charles Francis would make the journey. It was a blow from which she never truly recovered. She did not see the United States again for over eight years.

When James Monroe appointed JQA secretary of state in 1817, it was an invitation to start looking forward to the White House. The State Department had always been viewed as grooming for the top dog position, and few secretaries of state could look back upon a career as impressive as John Quincy's. He threw his hat into the ring in 1824, and Louisa—for the first time in her life—began playing a vital role in his professional career. For years, she and her husband had butted heads over women's rights, raising the children, even where to live (JQA preferred summering in Quincy, much to Louisa's chagrin), but now she lent her keen mind and charm to John Quincy's cause. She threw elaborate and outstandingly successful parties, delighted everyone with her music and poetry, and generally compensated for her husband's surliness. Her greatest coup was a bash celebrating the anniversary of Andrew Jackson's victory over the British in the War of 1812. Not only was it remembered as the party of the decade, but it craftily drew attention away from Jackson, who was JQA's principal opponent for the presidency, and onto John Quincy himself. It all worked. Despite a hotly contested and controversial election, JQA became the country's next chief executive.

The next four years were enough to make Louisa wonder whether all her efforts on John Quincy's behalf had been a terrible mistake. Virtually every one of the president's policies was vehemently contested, and the poor slob soon became a lame duck. He sank into a new nadir of grumpiness, abated only by regular swims in the Potomac (usually in the nude) and long moments of gardening, his new love. Louisa responded with feelings of estrangement and depression. They sat silently at dinners, each engrossed in their own reading material. Louisa began referring to the White House as "a dull and stately prison."

Which is why she was overjoyed to leave it in 1829. Sick to death of official squabbling and calumny, she looked forward to a life without politics. Naturally, JQA spoiled the moment by winning a seat in the House of Representatives. Louisa's dread notwithstanding, his years there would become the zenith of his long and distinguished career, seeing him earn the nickname "Old Man Eloquent" by consistently championing such hot-button topics as abolitionism. And Louisa found herself swept up into it. She became as devoted to ending slavery as her husband and finally discovered her own voice, as well—particularly on the issue of women's rights. Such passions brought the two together, doing wonders for a partnership that had rarely been a pleasant one. Their last years together were probably the best of their marriage.

Having utterly spent himself on strenuous efforts in Congress, John Quincy finally collapsed in February of 1848—fittingly, right on the floor of the House of Representatives. He was dead two days later. Louisa lived only for another four years; upon her death in 1852, she was buried next to her husband in Quincy, Massachusetts. In an unprecedented honor for an American woman, both houses of Congress adjourned for a day of mourning.

It cannot be said that Louisa and JQA didn't love each other. They certainly did, as numerous tender letters attest. But their differences in temperament and outlook wore heavily on both of them. Louisa, in particular, suffered long bouts of depression that made her physically ill. And her outstanding intellectual and creative gifts were underappreciated by a husband who spent too many years looking at her as an underling or appendage. It is sad and telling that her 1840 autobiography was entitled *Adventures of a Nobody*.

MOTHER LOAD

During her childbearing years, Louisa suffered so many miscarriages and still-births that, out of eleven pregnancies, only three children lived to adulthood. Granted, pregnancy was fraught with hazards in the early eighteenth century, but such a record would be hard to bear for a woman of any era.

For those of her offspring who managed to live long enough, life could be pretty harsh. The Adams line seemed cursed. In 1807, Charles Francis, still an infant, was snatched from the arms of his maid in the streets of New York City. Louisa and the maid ran after the thief, who tore off with the babe and disappeared around a corner. He was found only after the two women went house to house, banging on doors. The culprit eventually emerged and gave Charles back, insisting that the little tyke was so beautiful, he wanted to show him to his wife. Louisa's first child, George (delivered by an intoxicated midwife whose oafish ministrations left poor Louisa with a gammy leg for weeks), ended up throwing himself off a steamer in 1829. And then there's John, who died of alcoholism. When you combine all this with a perpetually aloof and disagreeable husband, it's little wonder that Louisa was depressed so often.

FACE-OFF

Louisa and John Quincy fought over many things—including makeup. While in Europe, Louisa followed the latest fashion and took to wearing rouge, which, her husband argued, made her look more like a strumpet than a diplomat's wife. He actually wiped it off her face on at least one occasion. A determined Louisa finally got fed up and, while getting ready for an appearance at court, insisted that JQA shut up and deal with it. She was wearing rouge, and that was that. John Quincy stormed out of the house, boarded the carriage, and left without her.

FROM RUSSIA WITH LOVE

Louisa hated life in Russia. The schedule of court appearances and balls kept her and John Quincy out to the wee hours almost every night, the winters were appalling (and long), and the hired help was hopeless (their Russian household had a revolving door for servants, who were constantly caught loafing around or stealing things). When she received word from her husband in December of 1814 to pack everything up and join him in Paris, it came as a godsend.

But it also came as a shock. After all, she would have to sell most of their possessions, then trek clear across Europe with her young son Charles Francis and a few servants, all without the husband who was accustomed to handling things without her. It was a daunting prospect.

She had no idea.

Their journey westward began in February in arctic temperatures that froze all their provisions solid. Only melting them with candles made them eatable. They got lost several times amidst the snow-clad vistas, traveling in a horse-drawn sled that often broke down. Crossing frozen rivers meant that men had to proceed ahead of them, using poles to probe for weak spots. Their lodgings along the way were deplorable, and the servants didn't make things any easier—Louisa began to worry very seriously about getting robbed and abandoned.

They eventually arrived in Berlin and prevailed upon friendships that had been made on previous visits during JQA's extensive diplomatic travels. But the trip ahead was going to be just as dangerous, if not more so; Napoleon had made his triumphant return to France and set all of Europe scurrying to arms. Louisa's party passed through corpse-strewn battlefields, ever watchful for marauding troops.

By the time they reached France, the martial tension had come to a head, and French armies were everywhere. Louisa, abandoned by her servants (who were afraid of being drafted), now relied for her and Charles's safety on a fourteen-year-old Prussian boy, their only escort. Louisa borrowed her son's toy sword, displaying it in the window of the carriage after learning that those with military hardware were less likely to be bothered by marching brigades. It worked, but only most of the time—she had to rely on craftier measures to reach Paris, including passing herself off as Napoleon's sister to crowds of soldiers.

At long last, after a six-week odyssey, Louisa and Charles Francis arrived in Paris. They were welcomed by an astonished John Quincy Adams, who listened to every word of his wife's incredible account with pride and admiration. Louisa's heroics were soon the stuff of diplomatic legend, and she became the lady of the hour. The journey remains the most memorable chapter of her life, and one of the most harrowing ordeals suffered by any American first lady.

Rachel Jackson

1767–1828

Andrew Jackson's wife was a devout Christian who had no desire whatsoever to be first lady. As it happened, she never had to be. She passed away after her husband had won the very contentious 1828 presidential campaign against John Quincy Adams—a campaign in which Rachel's name, much more than Andrew's, was dragged through the mud with merciless glee by political opponents. It was one hell of a way to spend the last year of a life that had seen plenty of hardship.

Rachel had married a man named Lewis Robards when she was seventeen, and she came to regret her decision almost immediately. Robards was an insanely jealous man who tended to erupt whenever his sociable wife exchanged even the smallest pleasantries with other men—including Andrew Jackson. It turns out that Robards had every reason to worry about Jackson, who had taken a particular shine to Rachel. Moreover, Rachel had taken a shine to Jackson. Arguments and threats ensued, and the two men almost settled the issue with a duel. When Robards became even more combustive than usual, Rachel decided she'd had enough and fled south to Spanish territory (escorted, significantly, by Jackson). Robards finally decided to cut his estranged wife loose and arranged for a divorce. Rachel then married Jackson in the summer of 1791—only to discover that her divorce wasn't officially final before her second wedding, making her a bigamist and an adulterer. Oops.

Rachel and Andrew settled the confusion by remarrying after the divorce was finalized, but the damage had been done—damage that Jackson's opponents whipped into a scandal years later in 1828. Though the experience had humbled her and made her obsessively pious, Rachel was pilloried in the press as a wanton woman, and her husband was cast as a wife-stealer. Fat lot of good it did John Quincy Adams, who lost the election anyway. As for Rachel, she died shortly before Christmas 1828, spared from the fate of assuming the first lady role that she dreaded.

Hannah Van Buren

1783–1819

Hannah Van Buren was born in Kinderhook, New York, the same home-town of the man she would one day marry: future president Martin Van Buren. We know that Hannah spoke Dutch at least as well as English (a trait shared by Martin), that she was the sort of modest, charitable Christian that was revered at the time, and that she was a member of the local First Presbyterian Church—which she joined only because there weren't any local churches of the Dutch Reformed variety. Aside from these spare facts (and that she died some eighteen years before her husband became president of the United States), historians know very little about her. Interestingly, Martin himself hardly helped—in the autobiography he wrote late in life, he failed to mention Hannah a single time. That's right: Martin Van Buren wrote an autobiography in which his only wife simply didn't rank as important enough to mention. Oy.

6

Anna

HARRISON

July 25, 1775–February 25, 1864

MARRIED:

November 25, 1795

PRESIDENTIAL HUSBAND:

William Henry Harrison

CHILDREN:

Elizabeth Bassett, John Cleves Symmes, Lucy Singleton, William Henry Jr., John Scott, Benjamin, Mary Symmes, Carter Bassett, Anna Tuthill, and James Findlay

FIRST LADY:

1841

ASTROLOGICAL SIGN:

Leo

RELIGION:

Presbyterian

SOUND BITE:

"I hope my dear, you will always bear upon your mind that you are born to die and we know not how soon death may overtake us, it will be little consequence if we are rightly prepared for the event" (to son William).

Anna Tuthill Symmes Harrison never wanted to be first lady. In fact, she never wanted her husband to be president, and for good reason: By the time he was elected to the position, they were both getting too old for such shenanigans. Her husband, William Henry Harrison, should've listened to her—after only a month in office, he was dead, and Anna never even got to step foot in the White House.

Raising a family in frontier America wasn't easy. In the end, Anna Harrison outlived nine of her ten children.

Anna was born in Sussex County, New Jersey, the second daughter of John Cleves Symmes and Anna Tuthill Symmes. She never knew her mother, who died a year after she was born, and John took the girl to be raised by her maternal grandparents on Long Island while he fought the British during the Revolution. She was given the finest formal education that money could buy and soon developed into a pious,

learned, level-headed young woman.

At nineteen, when she moved to the Northwest Territory to join her father and his third wife, Anna was running behind schedule in the husband-finding department (in those days, it was common for ladies to marry at sixteen or seventeen). She soon found a candidate on a trip to Lexington, Kentucky, where she met a dashing young army captain named William Henry Harrison. The two fell deeply in love—much to the chagrin of Anna's father, who didn't think that young William's officer salary was sufficient to support his daughter. The young lovers sidestepped the problem by getting married while her father was away. John, incensed, didn't speak to his son-in-law for weeks afterward.

William soon went about proving what he was made of. After serving as secretary and delegate to the House of Representatives for the Northwest Territory, he was appointed territorial governor of Indiana. Then, in 1811, he became a war hero after slaughtering a slew of Indians at the Battle of Tippecanoe. His name was on the lips of important people all over the country, and in 1816 he was elected to the House of Representatives. From there, his career in politics really took off, from positions in the Ohio and U.S. Senates to a gig as America's first minister to Colombia.

But while William was off being important, Anna stayed home and did the real work: running a household and raising a throng of children. Life on the frontier was no picnic, and Anna had to draw on all her faith, education, and strength of character to endure what can only be called the unendurable. Though William had become a man of significance, he never earned enough money to make his vast family very comfortable. Grouseland, the family mansion in Vincennes, Indiana, was as much a fort as it was a home. The comforts of civilization were rare and dearly purchased, and hostile Indians filled the countryside. By 1840, six of Anne's children had succumbed to the grim realities of frontier life.

Little wonder, then, that the embattled woman looked forward to her husband's retirement, when he could be with her all the time. William, however, had other ideas. In 1836, he ran for president. Anna was delighted when he lost, only to find her worst fear come true in 1840, when he won. She wept openly, terrified that the demands of the White House would rob her of the last years of her husband's life. While she stayed in Indiana awaiting better weather to travel,

William—sixty-eight years old—proceeded to Washington to give his inaugural address without her. The new president spoke for an incredible hour and forty-five minutes, all while suffering frigid weather without gloves or a hat. The ordeal paved the way for pneumonia, which killed him on April 4, 1841. Anna's grim prediction had come true.

She had planned on making the trip east in May. During Harrison's single month as president, their widowed daughter-in-law, Jane Irwin Harrison, had filled the role of White House hostess. Anna remains the only first lady to have never stepped foot in the executive mansion (besides Martha Washington, of course, whose reign came before the house was built).

In the end, the worries that Anna's father had about William's failure to provide for her came true. The late president left his poor wife saddled with debt, much of which had to be paid off by the $25,000 pension voted her by a sympathetic Congress. For the rest of her long life, she lived in relative poverty.

TURNIP TALE

When Anna was still an infant, her father, John Symmes, decided to take her to Long Island to be raised by her grandparents. But that was easier said than done—the Revolutionary War was raging, and John would have to pass through enemy lines to get his little daughter to safety. According to legend, he donned a British uniform, bundled Anna into a sack, and, upon being questioned by curious British soldiers, explained that his precious cargo was in fact a bag of turnips, bound for the kitchen of the British commander on Long Island. The troops let him pass, and Anna was delivered safely.

PRESIDENTIAL GENES

That Anna outlived nine of her ten children is horrific and astonishing. But consider all the grandchildren she ended up with—one estimate puts the total at forty-eight. Moreover, one of those grandchildren, Benjamin Harrison (born to Anna's son John Scott) would one day go on to become president of the United States. Anna is the only first lady to be both a wife and grandmother to an American president.

7

Letitia Christian
TYLER

November 12, 1790–
September 10, 1842

MARRIED:
March 29, 1813

PRESIDENTIAL HUSBAND:
John Tyler

CHILDREN:
Mary, Robert, John Jr., Letitia, Elizabeth, Anne Contesse, Alice, and Tazewell

FIRST LADY:
1841–1842

ASTROLOGICAL SIGN:
Scorpio

RELIGION:
Episcopalian

SOUND BITE:
"Because I am ill is no reason why the young people should not enjoy themselves."

John Tyler was the first vice president to become president while in office. He was also the first president to have his wife die during his term, the first to get remarried while in the White

> As first lady, Letitia Tyler rarely made public appearances. Even during raucous parties, she would remain upstairs in her bedroom, confined to her wheelchair and reading the Bible.

House, and the first to have two first ladies during his stint as chief executive. One of those wives went on to become a famous figure in the annals of American history.

Letitia Christian Tyler is the other one.

Such anonymity can be traced to her upbringing. She was born the seventh of twelve children near Richmond, Virginia, to Robert Christian, a wealthy planter, and Mary Brown Christian. Like most women of the Old South, she learned that grace and beauty could get her far—as could keeping her mouth shut on matters that were considered the province of men. As a result, she evolved into a quintessential belle: pious, polite, reserved, and as good at avoiding public conversation in weighty matters as she was at knitting.

Around 1808, she met fellow Virginian John Tyler. A law student of keen intelligence and ambition, Tyler was struck by Letitia's delicate good looks and agreeable demeanor. He was also nearly put off by her obsession with propriety—the guy didn't dare even kiss her hand until three weeks before their wedding in 1813.

The couple soon made up for lost time. By 1830, Letitia had given birth to nine children. Her brood's education and welfare would be Letitia's highest priority, followed by the running of her family's plantation home. Husband John could contribute little beyond his seed to the Tyler family experience, as he was off making a name for himself. After serving in the War of 1812, he was elected to the House of Representatives and the Virginia legislature. Soon enough, he became governor of Virginia, and then went up to the U.S. Senate.

Tyler was a man of principle, however, a quality that usually gets politicians into trouble. By 1836, he had pissed off both the Democrats and Whigs by voting his conscience and felt compelled to resign his seat in the Senate. He and Letitia moved the family to Williamsburg, Virginia.

It was there, in 1839, that Letitia suffered her first stroke. Running after a brood of children and keeping the slaves in line had taken their toll, and Letitia's health would never be the same. The religion to which she had always turned in good times and bad now began to obsess her, and—wheelchair bound—Letitia spent nearly all her time in her bedroom, devouring the Bible. She continued to exert a tremendous influence on domestic affairs, but now had to rely on others to carry out her instructions. John, elected to the vice presidency in 1840, planned on remaining in Williamsburg to avoid the discomfort of moving his wife to Washington.

Death intervened—specifically, President William Henry Harrison's. Letitia now had no choice but to accompany her husband to Washington. But this was long before the days of government laws mandating wheelchair access—the new first lady found herself imprisoned by a mansion that afforded her little maneuverability. As a result, official hostessing duties were delegated to her daughter-in-law Priscilla. The first lady herself rarely made public appearances, preferring—even during White House parties—to remain upstairs with her Bible. A demure and bashful person to begin with, her crippled condition made Letitia all the more willing to remain out of sight. Official Washington never really got to know her, and many wondered if the president's spouse really existed at all. Only a major event like the White House wedding of her third daughter, Elizabeth, brought her down from her second-story sanctuary. It was one of the very few occasions in which Mrs. Tyler made a public appearance.

Any opportunities to know her vanished in 1842, when she suffered another stroke. She died on September 10. Sadly, she had to spend her last months on earth watching her beloved husband become one of the most alienated presidents in American history, a man whose policies made Congress boil with rage—including his Whig party associates, who abandoned him.

Her funeral—the first of a sitting presidential spouse—captured the attention of all Washington and the nation, swept up by a tragedy they had never known before. The people's eyes, however, were soon drawn to a Long Island socialite who stole the president's heart and took the capital by storm . . . .

MISTRESS WITH A HEART

Letitia was a woman of her time and place; in other words, she believed in owning slaves and couldn't imagine living without them. Not that she didn't consider their welfare, of course. Her heart went out especially to her fellow women: Letitia insisted that the female slaves not work in the field, and all of them were given household chores. We can only assume that such splendid generosity downgraded their roiling hatred to simmering resentment.

"A" FOR EFFORT

During John Tyler's term as governor of Virginia between 1825 and 1827, Letitia struggled with a tiny entertainment budget. She and her husband, like all plantation aristocrats, tended to be cash-poor despite their real estate holdings, and Tyler's paltry salary didn't make things any easier. Letitia attempted to remedy the situation in a rather imaginative, if pathetic, way. Intending to inspire sympathy from the Virginia legislature, she invited some lawmakers to the Tyler home for a dinner party. The fare was anything but sumptuous: ham, bread, and whiskey. If any of the guests were appropriately moved, they didn't show it: The Tylers were not voted any more money, and Letitia didn't throw any more parties for state legislators.

8

Julia Gardiner
TYLER

May 4, 1820–July 10, 1889

MARRIED:

June 26, 1844

PRESIDENTIAL HUSBAND:

John Tyler

CHILDREN:

David Gardiner, John Alexander, Julia, Lachlan, Lyon Gardiner, Robert Fitzwalter, and Pearl

FIRST LADY:

1844–1845

ASTROLOGICAL SIGN:

Taurus

RELIGION:

Episcopalian, then Catholic

SOUND BITE:

"What dinner parties of the usual kind in country or city would not appear dull to me after all those brilliant ones we gave at the White House!"

Julia Gardiner's marriage to President John Tyler began with a bang—literally. On February 28, 1844, the two were sailing down the Potomac aboard the United States Navy vessel *Princeton*, along with plenty of other important

> **Talk about excess: Julia Tyler never traveled anywhere without her twelve "ladies-in-waiting" (nicknamed "The Vestal Virgins" by a critical press).**

Washington folk. Getting so many stuffed shirts onto one ship was the handiwork of Dolley Madison, whose presence still dominated the capital's social scene. It was a gala event, full of toasts, laughter, bad political jokes, and . . . slaughter. One of the gunboat's cannons accidentally exploded, cutting a handful of partygoers to shreds with chunks of hot flying iron. Upon discovering that her father was among the slain, Julia fainted—right into the arms of President Tyler. It was the loss of her father that finally convinced the young Julia to accept the widowed chief executive's standing offer of marriage, and the two got hitched the following June.

Tyler wasn't the only man chasing Julia's skirts. She had attracted countless suitors, many of them nearly as powerful as the president. It's hardly surprising:

Julia had spent her entire life preparing for a career in coquetry. Born on her family's private island off the coast of Long Island to David Gardiner, a lawyer, and Juliana McLachlan Gardiner, a rich heiress, Julia was schooled in refinement at one of New York City's most prestigious academies for moneyed young ladies. As a teen, she became accustomed to all the stuff that wealth could purchase—including the fashionable grand tour of Europe, where she learned to appreciate the way in which men looked at her. She was even presented to the French court by her parents and gathered up a string of slavering male admirers who were heartbroken at her return to America. A buxom, dark-eyed beauty, the fun-loving Julia combined a natural flirtatiousness with graceful and educated manners, and set out to take advantage of all that her elevated station in life could bring her.

Which, of course, brought her to Washington, where all manner of powerful men awaited her charms. During the early 1840s, Daddy took Julia and her sister on visits to the capital, where he rented out a space large enough to entertain all the fellows who came a-calling on the now-sensational Gardiner girls. Julia turned down proposals from all of them (including a Supreme Court justice), but adored the attention all the same. In 1842, she met the president, thirty years her senior and still mourning the loss of his wife, Letitia. By the following February, Tyler's grief had abated enough for him to start showing a conspicuous interest in the young Long Island siren. After dinner and cards, the nation's leader threw caution (and propriety) to the wind, showered Julia with attention while scandalized guests looked on, and chased her through the White House like a smitten schoolboy.

Julia proved as cool as a cucumber, however, and took particular interest in making the randy old man wait as long as possible for his amorous reward. His marriage proposal, made at a Washington's Birthday ball, was turned down—Julia answered "no" three times, each time striking him in the face with the tassel that dangled from her festive cap. Tyler ended up proposing yet again, and left it an open invitation. And so it went, until the poor girl's father was rudely eviscerated on the deck of the *Princeton* in 1844.

Their wedding that summer was conducted in secret, in part to alleviate the alarm of Tyler's children from his previous marriage. At least one of them, Letitia Tyler Semple (who was virtually the same age as Julia), would never forgive Julia for taking her mother's place. For her part, Julia—now the first lady and, at twenty-four, the youngest up to that time—drank in the celebrity of her new role with relish. She had reached the big time, and she made the most of it. In addition to traveling about town in a four-horse carriage, she totally refurbished the White House with her family's money and decked out the mansion's staff in garish new livery. Those in Washington who preferred republican austerity were most alarmed, however, by the first lady's coterie of ladies-in-waiting. This was simply unheard of and smacked wildly of courtly excess. Dubbed the "Vestal Virgins" by a critical press, Julia's twelve female companions accompanied her everywhere. At White House levees, they lined up on either side of Julia, who sat crowned upon an elevated dais like some goddess descended from Mount Olympus.

It all had to come to an end, of course, and—after taking advantage of her influence to get executive appointments for a slew of her kinfolk—Julia said goodbye to White House glitz in 1845. In typical Julia style, she did so with as much pomp as possible. At her Grand Finale Ball, held on February 18, 1845, 3,000 guests got hammered on a virtual ocean of champagne while the outgoing president's spouse danced with ambassadors from nearly every European nation. It was one of the most lavish nights in Washington history.

After retiring to Tyler's Sherwood Forest estate in Virginia, Julia continued to bear children for her seemingly inexhaustible husband (John fathered his last of fifteen children when he was seventy years old, for crying out loud). The couple also took up the Southern cause. Tyler, an avowed states' rights man, was openly sympathetic to his native Dixie, and Julia, though born a Yankee, followed suit—and with a vengeance. Though both had wanted the Southern states to avoid secession, they nevertheless threw their lot in with the Confederacy when the Civil War broke out in 1861. Tyler went to serve in the Confederate Congress, where he died in January of 1862. Julia, left a widow at forty-one with a brood of children to raise, continued to support the cause of the Confederacy with a passion.

Money, however, became the consuming issue of her life. Her late husband's lousy investments hadn't left her much cash in the pot, and as the South's fortunes waned, so did Julia's. With Sherwood Forest in decline, she determined to relocate herself and her children up north to her mother's home on Staten Island, a journey during wartime that required them to travel to New York via

Confederate-friendly Bermuda. Once there, she had to fight for the possession of the Staten Island house with her brother David, a staunch Unionist who no longer had any sympathies for his rebel sister. Though she would eventually win custody of the estate after the war, things had definitely gone south for her (pun intended). Her children were mocked and assaulted for their Confederate loyalties, and Julia was forced to send them overseas to be educated. Efforts to either maintain or sell her extensive Southern properties brought her plenty of grief and precious little profit.

In 1872, "Mrs. Ex-Presidentress" (as Julia insisted on calling herself) had the gall to move back to the capital, drawn, despite her precarious financial situation, to the city's social scene. There, she became a Catholic and fought to get a first lady's pension from Congress. Despite their better judgment, they eventually gave it to her. The socialite who had grown up on Long Island, ruled over Washington, played the Southern belle at Sherwood Forest, and battled for a home on Staten Island chose Richmond, Virginia, to live out her final years. True to form, until she died there in 1889 of a stroke, Julia dominated the city's elite, a prima donna till the end.

HOW TO SUCCEED IN ADVERTISING

Julia's parents weren't just thinking about their daughter's worldliness when they decided to take her to Europe in 1839. Their primary motivation was getting her the hell out of town. Julia had recently scandalized Long Island by committing what everyone, especially Mr. and Mrs. Gardiner, considered a disastrous faux pas.

It all started when a New York City dry goods company, Bogert and Macamly's, approached Julia about doing a little bit of advertising. Flattered, the curious nineteen-year-old agreed. The result was a colorfully designed handbill showing the precise likeness of Julia strolling before the company's storefront. "I'll purchase at Bogert and Macamly's, No. 86 Ninth Avenue," proclaimed the copy. "Their Goods are Beautiful and Astonishingly Cheap." The advertisement's caption read, "The Rose of Long Island."

Julia was delighted. Her parents were not. The daughter of a prominent Long Island family had been used in what was one of the very first examples of celebrity-driven promotion in the nation's history. Girls of breeding simply did not do this. It was akin to prostitution. Desperate to get Julia away from the scene until the storm of embarrassment blew over, the Gardiners whisked their now-famous little girl off to Europe.

POLKA DOT

Though many Washingtonians were disgusted with Julia's aristocratic excesses as first lady, she still managed to have plenty of admirers. And no wonder: F. W. Thomas, one of the countless men who found Julia irresistible, was a reporter for the *New York Herald*. Julia took him on as a sort of press agent, and Thomas gleefully complied, ensuring the first lady a steady stream of fawning journalism.

But Thomas wasn't the only friend that Julia had in the publishing industry. Mrs. Tyler was a legendary dancer. She was particularly gifted at waltzes and had single-handedly introduced the polka to Washington society (it went on to become quite the rage). So famous were her skills on the dance floor that a New York music publisher printed "The Julia Waltzes," so that the masses might dance to the first lady's favorite tunes.

CHIEF CONCERN

It was Julia Gardiner Tyler who first got the marine band to play "Hail to the Chief" upon the president's arrival at social functions.

Confederate Widow

When one considers that Julia was New York born and bred, her efforts on behalf of the South seem remarkable, to say the least. She always embraced her husband's political ideas as her own, and states' rights—as well as slavery—was no exception. In 1853, Julia took umbrage with a letter from prominent British ladies to their counterparts in the American South that pleaded for an end to slavery. She penned a response that appeared in numerous newspapers, leaving little doubt as to what its author thought of such a notion. In addition to harping on the usual nonsense about the welfare of blacks under white domination, she denounced Harriet Beecher Stowe's *Uncle Tom's Cabin* and went so far as to claim that slaves "live sumptuously" when compared to lower-class Brits.

Her ardor for her adopted region never waned, even during her sojourns to the North during the Civil War, where she lobbied against President Lincoln, handed out pro-Southern pamphlets, and struggled to ease the plight of Confederate prisoners of war. (It galled her no end that, in her absence, Sherwood Forest was turned into a school for African-American children.) Little wonder that she and her kids suffered attacks after the war by fellow Staten Islanders.

A SIXTH SENSE?

In January 1862, Julia awoke from a dream in which her husband, away in Richmond at the Confederate Congress, was mortally ill. She promptly traveled to see him, only to discover that he was quite fit. Just days later, however, he fell ill and soon died.

It wasn't Julia's only encounter with the unexplainable. She continued to profess an ability to foresee the future in her dreams and is rumored, on one occasion, to have hosted a séance in which the table levitated.

9 Sarah Childress
POLK

September 4, 1803–
August 14, 1891

MARRIED:
January 1, 1824

PRESIDENTIAL HUSBAND:
James K. Polk

CHILDREN:
None

FIRST LADY:
1845–1849

ASTROLOGICAL SIGN:
Virgo

RELIGION:
Presbyterian

SOUND BITE:
"To dance in [the White House] would be . . . respectful neither to the house nor to the office."

With no children to look after, Sarah Childress Polk was free to devote her extraordinary mind and energies to the career of her husband, James Knox Polk. It was an arrangement that suited them both perfectly—until James worked himself to death, leaving Sarah decades with little more to do than miss him.

Sarah was born the third of six children near Murfreesboro, Tennessee. Her father, Joel Childress, succeeded at everything from plantation owner to tavern keep, acquiring a large-enough fortune to send Sarah to some of the finest schools in the country. Her liberal education gave Sarah a love of reading and conversation that lasted a lifetime and earned the respect of all who encountered her.

Her keenest admirer was a stern little fellow named James Polk, who met Sarah in 1820. She eventually accepted his proposal of marriage, but—significantly—on one condition: that he make something of himself by winning a seat in the Tennessee legislature. He soon did, and the two were married, cementing a partnership in politics that would take them all the way to the White House.

James was all business, a tight-lipped man who liked almost nothing except working hard and getting ahead. He stammered through conversations that were about anything but politics and lacked the social graces that earned so many of

the great men of the age a place in history. Thankfully, his bride made up for all that. In addition to being just as dedicated and organized as James, Sarah was charming, elegant, and witty. She had a gift for intelligent gab, adorned herself in finery that was beautiful without being showy, and stuck piously to the strictures of her Presbyterian faith. Such qualities allowed her to get away with much that normally would've been considered unladylike for the age. She preferred the company of men, for instance, eschewing the fluffy chitchat of her fellow women for the heady talk of the men's parlor. Though she typically sided with her husband on major issues, she was not afraid to disagree with him, even in public. It wasn't long before Sarah became just as popular in powerful circles as her husband, helping James win a seat in the United States House of Representatives (where he eventually became Speaker) and a term as governor of Tennessee.

Sarah Polk did a terrific job of managing her husband's finances. Of course, slave labor made the task a simple one.

With the support of giants like former president Andrew Jackson, James won the Democratic party's presidential nomination in 1844. But Mrs. Polk, whose organizational and social skills did much to get her husband where he was, had begun to attract the rancor of some—especially women—who thought she was spending too much time debating and not enough time in the kitchen. Sarah brushed them off with a feisty retort: "If I get to the White House, I expect to live on $25,000 a year and I will neither keep house nor make butter." Stick that in your bread oven.

The intrepid Sarah did indeed make it to the White House, and she was true to her word. The new first lady distanced herself from her whimsical and profligate predecessor, Julia Tyler, by entertaining often and tastefully, entirely within the president's salary (indeed, she managed to squirrel a fair amount of it away for retirement). And she steered clear of the kitchen, spending much of her time gleaning newspapers and reading speeches for her husband, who often relied on her as a private secretary. In fact, as the spouse of a president who rarely consulted his cabinet, Sarah was the second most important figure in the administration. As James himself later admitted, "None but Sarah knew so intimately my private affairs." The first lady actively championed the administration's expansionist policies, held lavish dinners to win support for the war against Mexico, and never missed church on Sunday (James, though a Methodist, acquiesced to being dragged to his wife's Presbyterian services).

James had promised from the beginning that he would seek only one term as president. It was a good thing, too—no president ever slaved so hard at the job. After surrendering the White House to Zachary Taylor, he and Sarah retired to Nashville. There, having exhausted himself with four years of relentless effort, James died in 1849. Tragically, something in Sarah died with him. The man to whom she had been wife, partner, friend, counselor, and secretary was gone. She had been the fuel beneath his rising star, and no first lady before her had exercised such direct influence. For the next forty-two years, she did virtually nothing. Secluded within the home that she converted into a temple to her husband, she never ventured out except to attend church. During the Civil War, she continued to be an absentee landlord to a piece of her late husband's Mississippi property, declared her neutrality, entertained officers from both the North and the South, and eventually sought comfort in the care of a grandniece. She died in 1891. Though a pension granted to her by Congress helped ease her final years a bit, the money could probably have been put to better use somewhere else— the fact is, Sarah Polk never really needed any help from anyone.

SAHARA SARAH

Sarah Polk took her Presbyterian faith very seriously. Church attendance on Sundays was mandatory—those impious souls who made the mistake of calling on the first couple on the Sabbath were promptly invited to join the Polks at church. Indeed, one hapless Austrian minister who came to the White House on a Sunday intending to present his credentials was simply turned away.

But Sarah's spirituality wasn't reserved for only one day of the week. While first lady, she forbade dancing and card-playing in the executive mansion at all times. Her reputation preceded her—at the inaugural ball for her husband, the band stopped playing as soon as the Polks entered the room (they struck up again after the new president and his wife left). In truth, Sarah loved gathering people by the piano, but only to sing hymns. The thing that really rankled Washingtonians, however, was Sarah's ban on hard liquor. Those politicians and socialites who'd been accustomed to enduring White House events by gulping down whiskey-spiked punch had only glasses of wine to get them through the hours of tedious small talk and insincerities. It wasn't long before the mistress of such a dry house became widely known as "Sahara Sarah."

THE CHEAPEST LABOR OF ALL

Sarah's choice to ban hard alcohol at the White House was an expensive one. After all, whiskey at the time was cheap—wine wasn't. All the more reason to be impressed by her stewardship of the mansion's resources, which brought her well under the Polks' $25,000 salary. How did she manage to make ends meet?

In a word, slaves. Most of the White House duties during the Polk adminis-tration were performed by African slaves, who—we need not point out—weren't in the habit of lining up for a paycheck at the end of the month. Sarah's views on what many called the "hated institution" were alarmingly straightforward (the one thing she had in common with her predecessor, Julia Tyler). "The writers of the Declaration of Independence were mistaken when they affirmed that all men are created equal," she once pointed out to her husband. "There are those men toiling in the heat of the sun, while you are writing, and I am sitting here, fanning myself, in this house as airy and delightful as a palace, surrounded with every comfort. Those men did not choose such a lot in life, neither did we ask for ours; we are created for these places." One wonders how eager she would've been to express her opinion had one of "those men" been present to contest her theory.

Margaret TAYLOR

September 21, 1788–
August 18, 1852

MARRIED:
June 21, 1810

PRESIDENTIAL HUSBAND:
Zachary Taylor

CHILDREN:
Ann Margaret Mackall, Sarah Knox, Octavia Pannel, Margaret Smith, Mary Elizabeth, and Richard

FIRST LADY:
1849–1850

ASTROLOGICAL SIGN:
Virgo

RELIGION:
Episcopalian

SOUND BITE:
"A plot to deprive me of his society, and shorten his life by unnecessary care and responsibility" (referring to her husband's nomination for president by the Whig Party).

o accurate portrait has survived of Margaret Mackall Smith Taylor. We can imagine, however, what her face would've looked like: careworn and streaked with wrinkles from years of life as an army bride and from worrying

> **As her husband campaigned to be president, Margaret Taylor prayed every night for his defeat. The powers that be weren't listening.**

over her husband's presidency, which she dreaded far more than any of the frontier hazards that shaped her character and outlook on life.

There was nothing in Margaret's upbringing to indicate that she was destined for a life of military postings in the wilds of America. Born in Calvert County, Maryland, she was the daughter of Ann Mackall and Walter Smith, a former officer in the Revolution whose plantation wealth bought him access to the elite society of the slave-owning East. In 1809, she met Zachary Taylor, an officer in the army. By 1810 he was a captain, and they were married.

Zachary was also from a good family and was given over 300 acres of prime

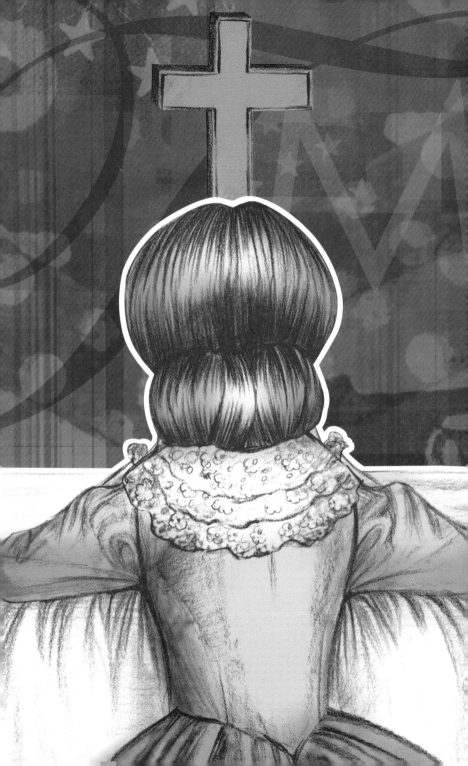

Kentucky land from his father as a wedding present. The newlyweds had every reason to expect an easy life together.

But while Taylor was an officer, he hadn't gone to West Point, and couldn't expect to merely shoot up through the ranks. In fact, for the next forty years or so, he was at the whim of superior officers who had a hell of a lot of territory to patrol. As a result, he and Margaret were moved from one remote place on the frontier to another, racking up hundreds of miles of travel through the fringes of a vast country. From the forests of Minnesota to the swamps of Florida, the Taylors became experts at roughing it in style. In crowded tents and ramshackle cabins, Margaret raised her children, saw to her husband's needs, learned how to use a gun, and still found time to make life a little easier for the enlisted men under Zachary's command. In 1820, fever claimed two young daughters, but Margaret— long since acclimated to the dangerous world into which she had married— merely kept on trucking. The surviving children, when they were of sufficient age, were sent east for their schooling, and Margaret continued to draw on her innate strength of character to get her through the separations and the lack of amenities. In 1840, Zach was stationed in Baton Rouge, and Margaret turned their new digs—a mansion that had once housed Spanish aristocrats—into the sort of home they'd never been able to enjoy. It was like a reward for all the hardships they'd been through.

The relative domestic bliss came to an end in 1845, however, when Zach was ordered to the front in the war with Mexico. Margaret was furious at the prospect of losing his company, but she had no idea just how great a cost the war would exact: Zachary survived, but became a national hero. Now Margaret would have to share him with the entire United States.

Called "Old Rough and Ready" for his willingness to share in his men's hardships, General Taylor was as apolitical as he was a hard-fighting soldier. But that didn't stop the Whig Party from wooing him for a presidential run. He answered the call to duty, and took the Whigs up on their offer. Margaret was crushed. After keeping her peace through decades of discomfort, she had finally had enough. She wanted to spend her waning years with her husband in the retirement she believed he had earned. To her, a presidential term was like a death sentence, sure to squeeze the last bit of life out of the old soldier she'd loved and stood by since 1810. She prayed every night for his defeat in the 1848 election.

The powers that be weren't listening. Old Rough and Ready became the next president of the United States, and Margaret quietly prepared herself for the next—and, as it would turn out, final—sacrifice on behalf of her country. To ease the frustration she felt at having lost her husband to the executive branch, she attended church. Every day. (Apparently, the Almighty's inability to arrange a Taylor defeat in 1848 hadn't spoiled His relationship with the new first lady.) Besides this, she did very little. Virtually all hostessing responsibilities were turned over to twenty-five-year-old daughter Betty, while Margaret busied herself with needlework and the occasional social visit. Few first ladies have ever been so reluctant to embrace the role. During the presidential campaign, Taylor's opponents portrayed his wife as a sort of mid-nineteenth century version of white trash—a pipe-smoking, firewood-stacking, uncouth little frontier troll who had no right being the spouse of a national leader. The truth couldn't have been further from the image: Margaret was an Eastern lady born and bred, a well-heeled woman who'd spent nearly as much time in urbane settings such as Philadelphia and New York as she had within bow-shot of hostile Native Americans. But her self-imposed anonymity in the White House did nothing to correct the public myth. (It didn't help that her better half had a habit of dressing like a refugee and spat tobacco juice all over the executive mansion as if he were still campaigning against Seminoles in the Florida back country. Those wondering what real frontier behavior looked like needed to look no further than the president himself.)

Forty long years of trudging behind her soldier-husband was starting to take its toll. Margaret had been prone to sickness long before becoming first lady, and she seemed to get only worse with time. But it was Zachary that everyone should've been worried about. On July 4, 1850, President Taylor attended a bout of long-winded public presentations to celebrate the nation's birth. Exhausted by the oppressive heat, he retired to the White House, where he washed down a bowl of cherries with iced milk. He soon became sicker than a dog. On July 9, he died. Margaret, imploding with grief, had to be literally torn from her husband's corpse while she wailed about the quickness of his passing and the horrible fact that they'd not exchanged any final sentiments before the end. Her grisly prediction of presidential tragedy had come true.

Numbed by the catastrophe, Margaret packed up and left the capital with little fanfare. She spent most of her final two years of life in Mississippi with Betty, the daughter who'd been her surrogate first lady. When she died in 1852, any hope that the nation—and posterity—had of getting to know her better died with her.

Smoke and Mirrors

Being a war hero and all, Zachary Taylor proved a difficult target for his enemies in the 1848 election. So, naturally, they took aim at his wife, ripping her apart as illiterate, crude, vulgar, and generally uncivilized. A cartoon was published in which Margaret was seen sitting by a fire in a log cabin smoking a long corncob pipe—the sort of thing that ladies simply weren't supposed to do. In fact, Mrs. Taylor hated tobacco smoke, claiming that it literally made her ill (Zachary was forbidden to smoke in her presence, and generally avoided smoking altogether, preferring instead to take his tobacco between his cheek and gum).

CHARACTER ASSASSINATION

Zachary's untimely death hit his wife like a ton of bricks. Margaret, saddened to the point of hysteria, pawed the preserving ice from his corpse on several occasions to gaze upon his frozen face, and refused to attend his memorial service, preferring instead to remain in bed, where she quaked and shuddered with grief. She also did something else: She refused to have him embalmed. Such an unorthodox demand raised eyebrows, and a rumor soon started circulating that Margaret had avoided embalming to prevent anyone from learning that she had poisoned her husband. Her tremendous depression notwithstanding, the rumor persisted and acquired the weight of fact. Not until more than 140 years later, when historians convinced Taylor's descendants to exhume his remains, was the notion finally put to rest. In 1991, a Kentucky medical examiner subjected a bit of Taylor's hair to laboratory scrutiny, concluding that Old Rough and Ready had not in fact been poisoned.

11 *Abigail* FILLMORE

March 13, 1798–March 30, 1853

MARRIED:

February 5, 1826

PRESIDENTIAL HUSBAND:

Millard Fillmore

CHILDREN:

Millard Powers and Mary
Abigail

FIRST LADY:

1850–1853

ASTROLOGICAL SIGN:

Pisces

RELIGION:

Unitarian

SOUND BITE:

"Take pains, my dear little boy,
that every letter we receive
from you is written better than
the last one" (in a letter to her
son Millard Jr.).

Abigail Powers Fillmore was a rare bird indeed: a mid-nineteenth-century woman who actually worked for a living. Self-educated and self-made, she introduced Millard Fillmore to a world of learning that rescued him from ignorant obscurity and forged him into presidential material. But Abigail, for all her smarts, did little to advance the cause of her gender in an age when women were still expected to play second fiddle. And her intellect and ability went mostly unused during her years as first lady.

Lemuel Powers, a Baptist clergyman, died when his daughter Abigail was only two years old. He left his family little money but plenty of books, and young Abigail spent most of her childhood in the Finger Lakes region of New York State reading as many of them as she could. It wasn't long before she found her true calling: By the age of sixteen, she was a dedicated schoolmarm.

A few years later, at an academy in New Hope, New York, she met the man who would become her most famous pupil. Millard Fillmore was the son of a dirt farmer, apprenticed to a clothmaker, and pretty clueless. But the eighteen-year-old possessed several qualities that set his elder teacher's heart a-fluttering: He was a strapping blue-eyed looker with a ferocious eagerness to learn. As Abigail

welcomed him into a world of literature, geography, and history, the two fell in love, united by their mutual excitement for self-betterment through education. Millard proved an apt pupil indeed, and took up some teaching of his own while studying law.

Though engaged in 1819, the two wouldn't be married until 1826—and not because of shyness or second thoughts. Apparently, Abigail's family felt a little underwhelmed by Fillmore's impoverished background, a fact that only drove him to study harder and get jobs teaching law even as he continued to learn it himself. After a seven-year engagement, during which the two love-birds saw very little of each other, Millard felt confident enough in himself to screw his in-laws' criticism, and he married his bride (ironically, in the home of Abigail's brother).

Abigail Powers met her future husband in the classroom—*her* classroom, to be exact. Millard Fillmore was one of her prize pupils.

Mrs. Fillmore continued to teach until 1828, when her life was changed forever by the birth of a son and the beginning of her husband's political career. Saddled with a baby to rear, she gave up her classroom teaching, saw her husband off to a seat in the state legislature in Albany, and spent a lot of time writing letters to him about missing his company. She got him back in 1830, only to lose him again in 1832—this time to Washington, after Fillmore was elected to the U.S. Congress.

By this time, Abigail had another child and—despite living comfortably in their new Buffalo, New York, home—was getting a little tired of living apart from her husband. But Buffalo was a better place to raise and educate children at the time, and she didn't consider it prudent to make a move to the nation's capital. It wasn't until 1836, when Millard got reelected to Congress, that Abigail made the move south to join him. Even then, the kids were left in Buffalo with relatives and would see very little of their parents over the next six years.

It was hardly an ideal state of affairs, and Abigail assuaged her angst at being separated from her children by throwing herself into the business of being a Washington wife. Ever the student, she availed herself of the city's galleries and lecture halls, went to a few concerts, and boned up on all the most important political issues of the day so as to offer useful advice to Millard (he listened keenly to every word and rarely made a decision without her input). She followed the same routine in Albany after 1847, when Fillmore secured the New York State comptroller position. But while she endeared herself to all in high circles, Abigail found most of the pomp and ceremony an utter bore. It had become obvious to her that she shared two loves: her husband and her books. And while she played the role of political consort as well as anyone, it was intellectual pursuits that occupied her mind most of the time.

Millard hit the big time in 1848, securing the vice presidential nod on the Whig ticket with Mexican War hero Zachary Taylor. Abigail, however, was troubled by the development. Going back to Washington meant more dinner parties and insipid political conversation with overdressed divas. It also meant moving the family's prodigious library (again), and the prospect of arranging it all was too much for her. Even worse, her health had been steadily deteriorating for years—bronchial problems and persistent headaches were taking their toll, making public appearances even more irksome. As a result, she said goodbye to her veep husband in 1849 and shuffled off to Buffalo.

Abigail was in a state of morbid depression when she received word in 1850 of President Taylor's death. Alone and ill in Buffalo and feeling sorry for herself, she had even started experiencing premonitions of death. Now, suddenly, Millard was president, and she would have to be her nation's first lady.

Not surprisingly, Abigail didn't relish the idea. She continued to advise Millard on everything—including the Fugitive Slave Bill of 1850, which she insisted he not sign (he did anyway, hurting his popularity in the North and probably dooming his reelection). But the endless stream of receptions took its toll, forcing her to socialize with elites who made her feel inadequate even as her declining health made it increasingly difficult to stand through it all. Like many first ladies before and after her, she ended up delegating much of the first ladying to someone else—in this case, daughter Abby, who picked up the slack with aplomb. Abigail started spending as much of her time as possible in the sanctuary she'd created within the White House: a library where, surrounded by her books, she could receive intellectual visitors and sit at her piano, which she had taught herself to play.

A light appeared at the end of the tunnel in 1852, when Fillmore lost reelection to Franklin Pierce. Abigail found it difficult to conceal her glee at the prospect of returning to Buffalo and retiring with Millard, who still had plenty of law-practicing years in him. The following March, this most bookish of first ladies was escorted to Pierce's inauguration by two of her favorite authors: Washington Irving and William Makepeace Thackeray. She and her fellow litterateurs watched Fillmore surrender the executive reins to Pierce, fighting the chilly weather by making witty banter. She couldn't have known it at the time, but another presence had joined the conversation: a pneumonia bug. Three weeks later, it claimed her life.

Abigail did get to Buffalo again, but had to settle for a plot in Forest Lawn Cemetery. As for the man she helped elevate to the highest office in the land, he went on to marry again in 1858 to an Albany widow named Caroline McIntosh, whose wealth allowed Millard to live in style until his death in 1874.

BAD TRIP

In 1842, Abigail was taking a walk in Buffalo when she came upon a section of uneven sidewalk. Heedless, she badly twisted her ankle—and proceeded to keep walking on it for days afterward. It was a bad idea. The ankle healed improperly, forcing her to get around on crutches for another two years. The injury would give her pain for the rest of her days and made standing for long periods impossible, accounting for much of her unsociability at White House events once she became first lady.

No Feminist

Abigail Fillmore must have been an inspiration to many women of her time. She had risen from humble beginnings on the New York frontier to become a learned, extremely well-read professional who didn't need to rely on a man's financial help (at least at first). Among the people most impressed by her were a group of prominent Washington citizens, who, in 1840, invited her to speak at the dedication of a new building. Abigail dismissed the generous and very unusual offer as absurd, insisting that women had no place making public speeches.

MAKING BOOK

Over the years, Abigail and Millard Fillmore acquired a private library of over 4,000 books, an astounding collection for the time (especially for folks who were never rich). Nothing made Mrs. Fillmore light up like the purchase of a new book—indeed, her husband never neglected to buy a few more for her during his travels to such cities as New York, Albany, and Washington.

Which is why Abigail was horrified, upon becoming first lady, to discover that the White House had none. An executive mansion without a library was an outrage, and she wasn't going to let it stand. With her insistence, Millard got $2,000 from Congress to start a book collection for the library, and Abigail personally oversaw the purchase of every volume. She got maps, reference works, histories, and some novels, all of which were housed in the second floor parlor-turned-library. She then completed the room's decor with a piano, to which she would retire when looking for an escape from her pain and the cares of political hostessing. It was the beginning of the official White House library and the act for which Abigail Fillmore is principally remembered.

Caroline Fillmore
1813–1881

Having once been married to a self-made teacher, Millard Fillmore decided the second time around to go for the big money. Five years after the death of his first wife, Abigail, the former President married a fifty-two-year-old widow named Caroline McIntosh, a finishing school graduate with a personal fortune whose precise amount remains a matter of conjecture.

What is certain is that she was loaded. Born in New Jersey and once married to a very successful merchant in Troy, New York, Caroline was just as fragile and retiring as she was rich. She was also careful: The marriage to Fillmore came with a prenup that kept the McIntosh money in her name. Millard's job was to invest it wisely, which he appears to have done until his death in 1874. After moving into a gigantic and rambling mansion appropriate to their standing, the former President and his second wife became the center of Buffalo society, entertaining lavishly and often. If many suspected that Fillmore married for money, it seems certain that Caroline married for nobler reasons. Her devotion to Fillmore was obvious to anyone who saw the inside of her enormous home, which she decorated with an astounding number of busts and portraits of the thirteenth president.

Jane PIERCE

March 12, 1806–December 2, 1863

MARRIED:

November 19, 1834

PRESIDENTIAL HUSBAND:

Franklin Pierce

CHILDREN:

Franklin Jr., Frank Robert, and Benjamin

FIRST LADY:

1853–1857

ASTROLOGICAL SIGN:

Pisces

RELIGION:

Congregationalist

SOUND BITE:

"Oh, how I wish he was out of political life! How much better it would be for him on every account!" (referring to her husband).

Jane Means Appleton Pierce hated politics with a passion—upon discovering that her husband had secured the Democratic nomination for president, she fainted. But being married to a career politician was the least of her worries. The powers that be had Jane in the crosshairs from her birth, and the poor woman's life reads like a Greek tragedy.

Jane Pierce became known as the "Shadow of the White House." She rarely left her bedroom and penned countless letters to her deceased son, begging for his forgiveness.

She was born to a well-off New England family who'd done well in the textile industry. But Jane's father, Jesse Appleton, was no seamster. In addition to being president of Bowdoin College, he was a Congregationalist minister—and seems to have taken his calling a bit too seriously, fasting on behalf of the Lord until his ill-fed physique up and died in 1819. Jane's mother, Elizabeth Means Appleton, moved the family to Amherst, New Hampshire, and continued raising her six children with a Calvinist severity that would've made her late husband proud.

Jane was child number three and swallowed every morbid morsel of her parents' stern religiosity, blossoming into a melancholy, jittery little thing with

plenty of suspicions and virtually no self-confidence. Her constitution followed suit: anxiety, bronchial problems, and tuberculosis (probably inherited from her father) played havoc with her health. She found what solace she could in books, becoming a devoted and accomplished student.

She met Franklin Pierce, a member of the United States House of Representatives and a fellow New Hampshirite, in 1826. That the two began a romantic relationship is proof positive that opposites do indeed attract. Gregarious and vain, Franklin was nothing like his withdrawn, pious consort. And there was plenty more about him that set the teeth of Jane's family to grinding: Like all good Jacksonian Democrats, Pierce believed in states' rights and the constitutional protection of slavery; he was a congressman, which meant he dabbled in . . . well, politics, which was demeaning; and, finally, he liked to drink and drink and drink.

Jane stood by her man through an eight-year courtship, during which she fended off attacks on Franklin's character from her family and—watching her beau serve in the New Hampshire legislature and the United States Senate—developed a disgust for politics that only made the former task more difficult. The two married in 1834, by which time Jane had developed an intense desire to see Franklin make a living at almost anything but his chosen profession. He stuck to his guns, however, and Jane often stayed away from Washington to be in New Hampshire with her family. There, in 1836, she had their first child. He died within days.

Things only got worse when Franklin became a U.S. senator the next year. By 1842, however, he began taking pity on his beleaguered wife and resigned his seat. After moving to Concord, Pierce opened a law practice, stopped drinking, and even turned down an offer from President James Polk to become U.S. attorney general. It was the closest thing to happiness that Jane had ever known. The Fates, however, had merely taken a coffee break. They got busy again in 1843, killing off Jane's second son with typhus at the tender age of four. She now held on to the third, Benjamin, with something like desperation, having to guard him from danger alone when Franklin volunteered to fight in the Mexican War in 1846.

After he returned safely, it appeared as though the star-crossed Pierces had once again put their troubles behind them and entered a period of domestic tranquility. But the operative word here is "appeared." Plenty of Franklin's friends thought he had a presidential run in him, and—unbeknownst to his blissfully ignorant wife—he agreed. Having given Jane every impression that his days in politics were over, Franklin surreptitiously schemed with fellow Democrats to make a run for the White House in 1852.

As you've probably guessed, he succeeded. And you can imagine how Jane reacted to his nomination.

Disaster struck again just weeks before Franklin's inauguration. The Pierces were traveling in New England with their only remaining child, eleven-year-old Bennie. Their train jumped the rails, and—right before Jane's eyes—the back of Bennie's head was torn off by flying debris.

Needless to say, the damage to Jane's psyche was incalculably huge. Her sons were gone, her husband had deceived her, and now she faced the prospect of becoming the nation's first lady in a city based upon the banal bustle of politics that turned her stomach.

Ascribing Bennie's death to the whim of the Almighty (who, in Jane's increasingly hysterical imagination, had done away with the boy in order to free up all of Franklin's time for his enormous new responsibility), Jane became a living specter. She missed her husband's inaugural and had to be convinced to go to the White House to join her husband after a fortnight of deep depression. Once there, she turned the mansion into a tomb, complete with black mourning bunting. She dressed in black, turned over all hostessing duties to her aunt, and sat upstairs in a cloud of doom while a married couple from New Hampshire with hotel experience was hired to attend to the day-to-day necessities of the household. Two years would pass before she found the strength to join her husband at White House social events, and her appearances were anything but cheery. She had truly become, as everyone began to call her, the "Shadow of the White House."

By the end of Franklin's administration, Jane was in serious need of a vacation. But even as the couple toured Europe and the Caribbean, she carried with her a lock of Bennie's hair in a little box to remind her of the calamity that gave her life shape. They returned to New Hampshire, where they watched the country make a slippery descent into civil war. It was in the midst of that conflict, in 1863, that Jane's tuberculosis finally took her, ending the misery that had been her life. A bereft Franklin gave in to the alcoholism with which he had struggled for his entire adult life and eventually died from it.

AND THE BAND PLAYED ON—NOT!

Jane was nothing if not pious. She insisted on having Franklin read to the White House staff every day from the Bible, as well as lead a hymn sing-along, and she prayed several times every day (like Margaret Taylor, she prayed every night for her husband's defeat before his election—and, just as in Margaret's case, the Almighty took no notice). Even Saturday nights were reserved for prayer. She put an end to the Saturday Marine Corps Band concerts that had become popular in the White House, insisting that they interrupted her pre-Sabbath supplications to the Lord.

P.S. TAP THREE TIMES IF YOU GET THIS . . .

You might be wondering how Jane spent all those hours in the White House while other people ran the household. Interestingly enough, she spent many of them writing letters to Bennie. Whether he was able to read them in the beyond is anyone's guess, but one wonders if he would've bothered, given their mordantly depressing nature. Jane had convinced herself that her last son's horrific death had been the deliberate act of a divine power who, in addition to allowing Franklin room to be president, disapproved of the boy's parents. As a result, she penned note after note asking for her son's forgiveness for not paying enough attention to him while he was alive—a fact that's all the more tragic when you consider that she had in fact doted on him.

Honeymooners

During his term as president, Franklin Pierce lived two lives: In one, he read scripture in the White House and spoke reverently of an unforgiving religion; in the second, he acted upon his love of socializing and taverns, fleeing the White House and his ghastly wife to get drunk and slap shoulders with the boys. It was a clear and dramatic example of how different the two Pierces were. They ended up taking different sides right to the bitter end. While Franklin was a "doughface" (a Northerner with Southern sympathies), Jane abhorred slavery and advocated war during the crisis of Southern secession. It is truly amazing that the marriage held together at all.

13 *Mary Todd*
LINCOLN

December 13, 1818–July 16, 1882

MARRIED:
November 4, 1842

PRESIDENTIAL HUSBAND:
Abraham Lincoln

CHILDREN:
Robert Todd, Edward Baker,
William Wallace, and Thomas

FIRST LADY:
1861–1865

ASTROLOGICAL SIGN:
Sagittarius

RELIGION:
Presbyterian

SOUND BITE:
"What a world of anguish this
is—and how I have been made
to suffer!"

In 1864, during her husband Abe's re-election campaign, Mary Todd Lincoln fretted. It wasn't just that she wished the best for Lincoln and the war-torn country. Her immediate concern was the exposure of a secret she'd kept from the president for years: Mary had run up a very serious amount of debt from clothing purchases. Should Abe win, she could sit on them for awhile until some way of paying them off could be found. But should he lose, the couple's transformation into ordinary citizens would leave her no option but to tell him. And that worried her terribly.

Purchasing the latest fashions with reckless abandon was a manifestation of one of Mary's defining traits: the belief that being first lady came with certain entitlements—one of which was the right to look the part.

Being the spouse of a president had been a goal of Mary's since her Kentucky youth. Born the third daughter of seven children to Robert Smith Todd and Eliza Parker Todd, Mary was a quintessential Lexington belle. Her prominent family bought her the finest education of the day, schooling her in everything from music and dance to mathematics and geography. Blessed with an extraordinary intellect, she quickly absorbed it all—her French was flawless, her wit razor-sharp, and she earned a reputation as a gregarious young lady who never shied from expressing her opinions or throwing herself into an argument. Lively,

literate, and whip-smart, she was clearly destined for great things.

And she knew it. Such confidence gave her an edge that became serrated with feelings of resentment and anger, the result of clashes with her insensitive stepmother (her biological mother died when Mary was only six). The thorny family situation gave her the impetus to make a life of her own. After teaching for a spell, she moved to Springfield, Illinois, where she met Abraham Lincoln in 1839.

There were plenty of things about this lanky lawyer that Mary wasn't crazy

In an attempt to communicate with the dead, Mary Todd Lincoln hosted numerous séances at the White House.

about: he was sloppy as hell and often absentminded; he was born of poverty and lacked many of the social graces that were important to the aristocratic Mary; and he certainly was no looker. But he was profoundly smart, honest almost to a fault, and positively glowing with potential. Determined to find a man who was going places, the notoriously flirtatious Mary passed up a long line of suitors to be with Abe (including Abe's political opponent Stephen Douglas), certain that he was destined for greatness. After a troubled courtship in which jealousies and misunderstandings nearly ended the relationship, the two were married in 1842.

Abe traveled often on the law circuit, leaving Mary to carry on alone much of the time. While she soon became known as a lavish entertainer, she also became known as a temperamental witch—especially to household servants, who often simply took off rather than cope with Mary's explosions. Such confusing turns of temper would become legendary, as would her husband's capacity for patiently enduring them. Though the two possessed tremendously different personalities, they were undoubtedly in love. Which was a good thing, because they'd need it in the coming years.

Though Lincoln was elected to the United States Congress in 1846, his political career eventually began to fizzle, much to Mary's chagrin. If Abe was eager to climb the political ladder, Mary was even more so, and she began to involve herself in her husband's campaigning with a gusto that was quite rare for the age. Worldly, social, and very well educated, she was perfectly suited for the role and effectively stumped on Abe's behalf. Her efforts paid off during the Lincoln-Douglas debates of 1858, which truly put Abe on the map. In 1860, the new Republican party nominated him for the presidency, touching off a firestorm of controversy throughout the country as tensions over the extension of slavery put the South on the brink of secession. Though Abe was no abolitionist, he was staunchly against slavery's progress in western territories and states, and his election blew up into a civil war.

The conflict compelled Lincoln and his family to skulk into Washington like human contraband, dodging the threat of assassination. It was a somewhat ignominious start, but Mary had arrived at last—she had bet on the right horse and couldn't wait to cash in on her winnings. First on the list was the White House itself: It needed refurbishing badly, and Mary rose to the occasion. And then some. In fact, she blew through the $20,000 congressional appropriation with alarming ease, scandalizing her husband by overspending on curtains and furniture while a struggling war effort had trouble getting rifles and uniforms to the front. Then she began making trips to New York and Philadelphia to go on shopping sprees for every garish gown and headdress that she could lay her hands on. The press followed, recording every purchase (and inventing a few). It wasn't long before the country began to sour on the new first lady.

It wasn't only the lavish spending in wartime that alienated people. Having been an integral part of Abe's political career for years, Mary soon realized upon entering the White House that her husband no longer needed her advice as much as he once had. Men surrounded him now, strangers who developed a hostile relationship with Mary. She returned the hostility in spades, accusing the cabinet of self-interested behavior and even disloyalty. The administration became a cockpit of sparring egos. Even the servants were put off, labeling Mary the "hellcat" for her intemperate behavior and resigning with disturbing regularity.

Things really went haywire when, in 1862, Willie—Mary's favorite son—died of typhoid fever. If she was already hotheaded and abrasive, she now became utterly unmanageable. The shopping sprees continued apace (though now Mary favored black gowns), her rants became more frequent (fueled by an increasingly hostile press), and even Abe's seemingly infinite reservoir of patience was starting to run thin. Mary turned to spiritualism in the hopes that séances could reach Willie's spirit. Tension mixed with mordant melancholia, arguments and rumors dominated White House life, and Lincoln's cabinet members loathed and feared the first lady by turns.

But beneath all the erratic behavior and hysteria remained an intelligent, compassionate woman. Mary was at least twice as ardent about freeing the slaves as her husband had ever been, and posterity can thank her virtually as much as Abe for the 1863 Emancipation Proclamation. By 1864, her worries about debt notwithstanding, Mary believed in her heart of hearts that her husband's reelection was the only hope for the country (though, unlike the president, she favored a policy of fierce retribution for the South upon the conclusion of the war). But she, more than anyone else, had recognized the wrinkles of stress on Abraham Lincoln's face. And as her husband's policies were vindicated by a resounding 1864 presidential victory, Mary had an acute premonition of his death—a feeling of doom that she simply couldn't shake.

Her premonition, of course, came true on April 14, 1865. The hopes and dreams of a lifetime went up in smoke with the bullet from John Wilkes Booth's pistol, and Mary's penchant for irrational behavior made the tragedy even worse. She secluded herself in the bedrooms of the unprotected White House while vandals and souvenir-seekers ran off with the mansion's tablecloths and silverware. Former vice president Andrew Johnson, now chief executive, wondered what to do about getting Lincoln's widow to vacate the executive mansion, unaware that she was convinced of his complicity in the plot to murder her husband. To Johnson's irritation, it took her nearly a month to leave the White House.

She moved with her two remaining sons to Chicago, there to begin a post-presidential life that was even more miserably sensational than her years as first lady. Saddled with debts, she offered her late husband's paraphernalia in exchange for financial relief. Maddened by a persistently hostile press (which found an ally in William Herndon, an old law partner of Abe's, who propagated rumors that Lincoln had been in love with another woman), she wrote enraged letters to newspapers and lobbied politicians to defend her, mostly in vain. Racked by pain, she made long sojourns to Europe, where spas offered physical relief and foreign crowds offered anonymity. But tragedy and mishap thwarted peace at virtually every turn: youngest son Tad died from a protracted illness in 1871; an Illinois court judged her insane in 1875, based on evidence enthusiastically provided by eldest son Robert; and severe maladies—migraine headaches, back pain, diabetes fueled by a taste for sweets—began to rob her of her sight and even her ability to sleep at night.

Through it all, she fought a long and arduous battle to secure a pension from Congress. It was the defining struggle of her life, pitting her reputation and sense of entitlement against a government and country that were trying their best to forget her. She won out in 1870 but, true to form, started fighting to have it increased. She won that battle, too—just months before her degenerating body finally called it quits. She was buried in Springfield, Illinois, beside her husband—the one man who never stopped believing in her and who never lost the capacity to shrug off her impossible eccentricities.

SOUTHERN BELLE

As first lady, Mary Lincoln was a devout Unionist and abolitionist. Her best friend from the White House years till the end of her life was a former slave named Elizabeth Keckly, a talented seamstress whose creations were a treasured part of Mary's wardrobe. Mrs. Lincoln even invited African Americans into the White House as guests (including the great Frederick Douglass), the first presidential spouse to do so. But hailing from Kentucky and speaking with a Southern drawl didn't put her in good stead with many Northerners, and baseless rumors of Mary's Southern sympathies raged during the Civil War. Mary's family didn't make things any easier on her: she had three half brothers fighting for Dixie. It was a rather awkward situation, and Mary didn't always handle it with the delicacy it required. When the Confederate husband of half sister Emilie Todd Helm died in the war, the first lady actually draped black mourning bunting throughout the White House, infuriating Northerners who spent a lot of time reading casualty lists from the front.

GREEN-EYED MONSTERS

Jealousy was a part of Mary and Abe's relationship from day one. Indeed, it very nearly prevented them from getting married in the first place. In January of 1841,

Abe was late in picking up Mary for a party. After discovering that she had left without him, he showed up at the party himself, only to witness her flirting with another suitor. An argument ensued, the courtship was called off, and Lincoln became utterly despondent. Only the intervention of mutual friends brought the two back together after a year of silence and separation.

CASH OUT

When Mary overspent the congressional appropriation for the White House furnishings within months of moving into the mansion, Abe lost his cool. "It would stink in the nostrils of the American people," he fumed, "to have it said that the President of the United States had approved a bill overrunning an appropriation of $20,000 for flub dubs, for this damned old house, when the soldiers cannot have blankets." He even considered paying the balance out of his own pocket, a threat that chilled Mary to the bone. She responded by selling off excess manure purchased for the White House grounds and by letting some of the mansion's staff go to cut back on expenses. She even had the gall to petition the government for a salary when she began running the kitchen herself, the only time a first lady tried to get her fingers into the government's till for services rendered. (Not surprisingly, they turned her down.)

Abe didn't know the half of it. Though Mary's infamous shopping excursions for gaudy clothes had been thrillingly covered by newspaper reporters, the fact that she wasn't paying for many of her purchases was largely a secret. As Mary ran up tens of thousands of dollars in department store debt, the president remained blissfully ignorant, immersed in the enormous burdens of his office. His assassination brought financial reality crashing down on Mary's head. Suddenly a widow, with legions of merchants expecting payments, she would spend much of her remaining years trying to make ends meet—a problem that many women of the day in her situation would've solved by remarrying, something Mary seems not to have even considered. Nearly two and a half years after Abe's murder, she inherited $36,000 from the settlement of his estate. But rather than make things easier for her, it seemed merely to galvanize her desire to create monetary security.

She tried everything: selling off stocks, coaxing politicians and other influential folks with Abe's possessions (for example, walking sticks) to create a retirement fund for her, and, of course, aggressively petitioning Congress for a pension that she fully believed she deserved. But nothing highlights her desperation quite like the clothing sale she arranged in 1867 with the help of friend Lizzie Keckly in New York City. "Mrs. Lincoln's Second-Hand Clothing Sale" was billed as an opportunity to buy some of the former first lady's garish gowns at bargain prices. Mary and Lizzie expected to make a killing. They were way off—virtually nobody showed up.

No Mama's Boy

After Abe's assassination, Mary's relationship with her eldest son, Robert, began to deteriorate. He seems to have agreed with the rest of the world that his mother was difficult, unpredictable, and, as time went by, weirder and weirder. To be fair, Mary tried to make amends. Despite her financial worries, she showered Robert and his family with gifts and even sold her Chicago pad to him at a bargain price. It did little to tighten their relationship, however, and Robert grew truly alarmed with his mother's eccentricities as time went by. She was paranoid, sickly, delusional. When she ran naked one night into a hotel elevator, Robert decided that enough was enough.

He moved quickly. After hiring men to track Mary, he swore out a warrant against her on the basis that she was insane. In 1875, she was taken into custody and put on trial. Robert paid a handful of doctors to back up his case, and, before an all-male jury, Mary was judged legally incompetent. (Even Mary's defense was sympathetic to Robert—he provided his mother's lawyer himself, a man who refused to call a single witness). Mary was consigned to an asylum in Batavia, Illinois, immediately after recovering from a suicide attempt she made with poison.

She proved her capacity for lucid thought by getting herself released in under a year with the help of Myra Bradwell, one of the most famous female attorneys of the age. Hell hath no fury, ta-da, ta-da, and Mary went after her traitor son with a vengeance. She regained control of her property, cut Robert out of everything, and even demanded—and received—every penny she ever gave him. Robert responded by joining the likes of William Herndon in publicly lambasting Mary as a profligate lunatic. And so it went.

The awful irony is this: After settling her score with her son and getting Congress to award her a handsome pension, Mary's death cruelly evened the tally. Robert inherited some $84,000 from his beloved mother's estate.

GETTING INTO THE SPIRIT

According to an old story, Abe Lincoln once directed his wife's attention to an asylum that could be seen from the White House, telling her that she would end up there if she didn't master her grief over Willie's death. The boy's demise certainly had an awful impact on both Mary and Abe's lives—they were, by all accounts, doting parents who took more than the usual interest in their children's company. Abe bore up under the strain in his own quiet way, throwing his energies into winning the Civil War. Mary, however, reacted rather differently. Like Jane Pierce before her, she became an avid spiritualist, believing that the souls of the dead walked among the living like gossamer beings who could be contacted with the right amount of effort. That effort, of course, was provided by quacks who had perfected the sleight of hand necessary to convince patsies like Mary Lincoln that deceased persons were noisily trying to interact with them in a mysterious mode of communication that included tapping sticks and jumping tables. In rooms darkened to conceal the mischievous reality, spiritualists held séances in which elaborately fashioned hoaxes (often performed with the help of a hidden colleague) made it appear as if spirits had come calling. Mary ate it up and even claimed to have dreams in which little Willie appeared at the foot of her bed.

Any hopes of Mary seeing through the charade were dashed when a prominent Georgetown spiritualist claimed to have divined precisely what the first lady wanted to hear: that Abe's cabinet was a bunch of selfish crooks who couldn't be trusted. Oh, what vision! Surely, Mary thought, this whole spiritualism thing was on to something. She found plenty of fellow believers on her trips to Europe and embraced the cult for the rest of her days. Sadly, it was used as evidence against her in the court that ended up sentencing her to an asylum. Discerning men of education—like Mary's son Robert—apparently didn't think spiritualism held much water.

14

Eliza McCardle

JOHNSON

October 4, 1810–January 15, 1876

MARRIED:

May 17, 1827

PRESIDENTIAL HUSBAND:

Andrew Johnson

CHILDREN:

Martha, Charles, Mary, Robert, and Andrew Jr.

FIRST LADY:

1865–1869

ASTROLOGICAL SIGN:

Libra

RELIGION:

Methodist

SOUND BITE:

"I do not like this public life at all. I often wish the time would come when we could return to where I feel we best belong."

Eliza McCardle Johnson was the quintessential supermom whose family always came first. And, when you consider the Civil War, alcoholism, and controversial politics that dominated the lives of her loved ones, it was a demanding role indeed.

Penny-pinching First Lady Eliza Johnson bought cows to provide the White House with fresh milk. (They grazed on the lawns out back.)

Eliza was born the only child of John McCardle and Sarah Phillips in Greeneville, Tennessee. John was a shoemaker who left his little family virtually nothing upon his death in 1826. Eliza and her mother made ends meet by making quilts and sandals.

As it happened, the man she ended up falling in love with was quite handy with a needle, as well. Andrew Johnson, two years her senior, was a tailor's apprentice who came from an even poorer background than Eliza had. They were married when Eliza was sixteen, bought a small two-room house in nearby Warrensburg, and set about trying to put some distance between themselves and the poverty line.

They succeeded. Andrew ran his tailoring business out of the front room of

their house and made a tidy profit. But he was almost completely uneducated, a fact that needed to be corrected if he was ever to make something more of himself. Eliza came to the rescue. Though her own education was anything but complete, she had spent some time at the Rhea Academy in Greeneville during her youth, which made her a virtual scholar compared to her husband. As Andrew stitched and sewed in the front room, Eliza read to him, taught him to improve his writing during breaks, and encouraged him to read on his own. He was an eager student, and she a capable teacher—by 1828, after acquiring some public experience in a debating society, Andrew had enough basic learning to enter local politics. He was on his way.

While he never gave up tailoring, Andrew rose quickly up the political ladder, and came to prefer it to needlework as a means of making money. Eliza busied herself with domestic chores at home and raising their five children while Andrew went off to wherever his public career took him: Nashville, for the state legislature; Washington, for the United States House of Representatives; and, in 1853, back to Nashville to become governor.

By this time, Eliza had managed her husband's income with enough savvy to buy a decent house with a farm and a large handful of slaves. But she had also acquired something else: tuberculosis. She now had another, more ominous reason to stay home while Andrew went a-politicking. When he went off to Washington in 1857 to take a seat in the Senate, she remained in Tennessee with the kids, the slaves, the farm, and her ugly coughing spells.

By the time Eliza got up the strength to join her husband in the national capital for a time, the country's mounting crises cut the visit short. She journeyed to Washington in 1860, only to hightail it with Andrew back to Tennessee in 1861 at the outbreak of the Civil War.

Andrew Johnson was unique: a senator from the South who supported the Union. Such views didn't exactly win him any popularity contests in Tennessee, and his penchant for angry debate only made things worse. President Lincoln made him military governor of the state in 1862, putting the irascible Johnson in charge of a region split by warring factions and battling armies. From his Nashville capital, Andrew presided over an uneasy occupation, surrounded by Southern sympathizers who viewed him as a traitor and plotted his death.

Things weren't any easier for Eliza. In 1862, she insisted on remaining at the Johnson homestead in the east of Tennessee and only barely escaped with her life from Confederate forces. She made the best of a tense life in Nashville after joining her husband there, trying to do her all for a family surrounded by hostile mobs.

Her life would soon become even more stressful. Impressed by Johnson's forceful rule over Tennessee, Lincoln made the contentious tailor his vice presidential partner in the 1864 election. Her husband's rise to the second-highest office in the land didn't sit well with Eliza at all, who was already pining for the simpler days when he was making suits in the front room. Lincoln's assassination the following April nearly undid her, and not only because Andrew was now the president of a fractured nation—he was also a marked man, and she knew it.

Nearly four months would pass before the new first lady could get her tubercular husk of a body out to Washington to join her spouse. Once there, she chose a room right across from Andrew's office and proceeded to spend much of what remained of the next four years sitting in it. While fretting over the possibility of her husband's assassination, she read, sewed, and took great comfort in the presence of her family, virtually all of whom moved into the White House to be with her and the president.

But she wasn't crazy about her gig as first lady. She shunned reporters, made almost no public appearances due to her ill health, and turned over hostessing duties to daughter Martha, who pleased all visitors with her attention to domestic detail and simple country charm. Eliza aided her husband by tending to his wardrobe (he was too busy to be the tailor himself), overlooking his diet, gathering newspaper clippings (one pile for good news, one for bad), calming his infamous temper, and maintaining complete faith in his ability to do the right thing. When he was impeached in 1868 by a Congress disgusted with his lackluster reconstruction program for the South, Eliza never wavered in her support for him. When he was acquitted, it surprised her not in the least.

Despite all her sitting around, Eliza's frail form continued to disintegrate, and she was delighted to say goodbye to the White House in 1869. But Andrew wasn't satisfied with going back to fixing pants and got back into the politics that annoyed Eliza so. In 1875, after getting a seat in the United States Senate, Andrew felt he had vindicated himself before the American people after his impeachment fiasco. Then, just months later, he died in Washington. It was a great blow to Eliza, back in Tennessee, who—her undying support notwithstanding—had always looked forward to a retirement with Andrew that looked more like the simple, nonpolitical life they'd once enjoyed. She followed him to the grave less than six months later, perhaps scolding herself for having given him an education all those years ago that allowed him to aim higher than a tailor's shop.

Country Roads, Take Me Home . . .

Nothing quite exposes the dangerously absurd situation that many people found themselves in during the Civil War than the predicament of Eliza Johnson. In 1862, just a month after Andrew was appointed military governor of the explosive mess that was Tennessee, she found herself in the eastern part of that state, bedridden and in hostile territory. Acting on instructions from the Confederate government, the Southern commander in Eliza's region issued orders that all Union sympathizers must vacate the area within thirty-six hours. Eliza mustered the strength to inform him that her condition made compliance with such a rude dictate utterly impossible, and the general allowed her a few months' reprieve. In September, Eliza got out of bed and started the journey west across the mountains and out of Confederate territory to Nashville, where her husband waited. Joining Eliza were her children Charles, Andrew Jr., and Mary (as well as Mary's husband, Daniel Stover), all of whom were considered enemy aliens in their own state, at least until they could get to the part of it that was controlled by Andrew and the Union forces.

The trip took a month. They were frequently hounded and questioned by Confederate soldiers, often forcing them to take a circuitous route, and had such difficulty finding shelter from unsympathetic homesteads that, on one occasion, the refugees were forced to escape foul weather in an abandoned shed near a railroad line. Despite her awful health, Eliza maintained her matriarchal role throughout, watching over her children and keeping the goal of Nashville in everybody's mind. They reached the city—and a relieved Andrew Johnson—on October 12, 1862.

SETTING SONS

If the Civil War made life hard on Eliza, her own sons certainly didn't make it any easier. She made two trips from Tennessee during the war, both on account of her son Robert. The first was to Illinois—Robert was scandalizing his army unit by regularly drinking himself positively stupid, and mother thought it wise to talk him down in person. His inebriate habits continued, until Eliza felt it was time to get him some serious medical help, which she sought in Massachusetts. For all her efforts, Robert was a lost cause. He continued to hit the bottle in the White House while serving as his father's secretary and was eventually sent on a diplomatic posting to Africa. He committed suicide in 1869.

Eldest son Charles, also a Union soldier and enthusiastic tippler, spared his liver from further damage by suffering a mortal riding accident in 1863. Even in-laws had a rough time in the Johnson family: daughter Mary's husband, Daniel Stover, died from tuberculosis in 1864. No wonder the first lady insisted on having her surviving family members around her in the White House. At this rate, she didn't know how much longer they'd be alive.

HOME SWEET HOME

Of all the responsibilities that Eliza left to her daughter Martha Patterson while first lady, none was as demanding as the refurbishment of the White House. In the weeks following Abraham Lincoln's assassination, souvenir-seekers ransacked the mansion, running off with curtains, furniture, silver, and china. The Johnsons inherited a wreck. Fortunately, Congress pitied the first family enough to grant them a $30,000 appropriation for furnishings and repairs. And, in dramatic contrast to Mary Lincoln, Martha stuck to her budget—and still managed to create a home that wowed visitors with its tasteful decor. She even bought cows, which grazed on the White House property and provided fresh milk every day. Eliza may not have been the most active first lady in history, but she sure did have a gift for delegating.

15

Julia Dent GRANT

January 26, 1826–
December 14, 1902

MARRIED:
August 22, 1848

PRESIDENTIAL HUSBAND:
Ulysses S. Grant

CHILDREN:
Frederick Dent, Ulysses Jr.,
Emilie, Wrenshall, and Jesse
Root

FIRST LADY:
1869–1877

ASTROLOGICAL SIGN:
Aquarius

RELIGION:
Methodist

SOUND BITE:
"Dear Washington, how I love
you, with your beautiful, broad,
generous streets and blue
skies! The sun shines always
there for me."

On a summer day in 1875, President Ulysses S. Grant returned to the White House after personally mailing a letter. His wife, Julia, confronted him, knowing that the letter must have been very important and irritated that "Ulys" hadn't let her in on what it said. Amused by her agitation, Grant calmly

> After being whacked by an oar as a child, Julia Grant never saw straight again. She could barely cross a room without bumping into furniture.

told her that he'd written the Republican Party, explaining that he had no intention of seeking a third term.

"I know you too well," said the president to Julia after she exploded at him for not telling her first. He knew her well indeed—for Julia would've torn the thing to shreds had she been given half a chance. She simply loved being first lady too much to let her husband spoil the party without a fight.

Julia Dent Grant also loved her husband, their occasional squabbles notwithstanding. By the time she met him in 1844, she wasn't the prettiest of the Dents' eight children. But she was an accomplished dancer and horsewoman, could carry a tune, and charmed everybody with her good humor and smiling demeanor. Julia

was full of vim and vigor, a quality that endeared her to the soldiers stationed near her family's lavish Missouri estate. But of all the officers with whom she danced, none caught her eye like the one courtier who, ironically, refused to step onto the dance floor: Ulysses Grant (he would remain a lifelong wallflower).

The feeling was mutual. Grant was smitten by the ebullient Julia and began calling on her often. But if the sound of wedding bells was in the air, at least one concerned party had developed selective hearing. Julia's father, Frederick Dent, didn't like the thought of his daughter getting hitched to an army officer. Dent had raised his children in the sort of aristocratic splendor that a large homestead could offer, and he wondered how a guy in uniform could possibly do better. Then there was the issue of slavery: Ulysses frowned on the institution, while Dent utterly relied on it. The two also argued over the looming war with Mexico. Though Ulysses wore a uniform, he saw the conflict for what it was: naked aggression against a weaker country. Dent, an ardent expansionist, thought Ulysses was being silly. As for Julia, she wanted to have her cake and eat it too, admiring her beau's progressive and courageous views while continuing to savor the life that African slave labor could provide.

Of course, the war with Mexico became a reality, and Ulysses had to answer the call to duty, regardless of his feelings on the subject. He managed to get in a proposal of marriage before he went south in 1845, but a surly Mr. Dent insisted that the wedding wait until the war's conclusion. Julia did her part by putting ugly images of her betrothed's battlefield mutilation out of her mind for three long years. When Ulys returned in one piece in 1848, the couple made it official, the opinion of Frederick Dent be damned.

For the new Mrs. Grant, it was the beginning of a difficult army life that was full of long journeys that took her far afield. Her posh upbringing had left her lacking in many of the domestic skills, but she did her part and acquired a great deal of experience (not to mention toughness) along the way. Ulys was away from her and their children often, and Julia traveled to him with the kids whenever she could. It was a trying beginning for a family, but she loved her husband dearly and made it work.

But it wasn't working for Ulys. Long separations from his wife and little ones were starting to make him depressed, and he began complementing his fantasies of leaving the army with large quantities of whiskey. His fantasies came true in 1854 when the military, alarmed by his intoxicated stunts, offered him the option of resigning. He was overjoyed.

Until, that is, he realized just how hard it was to make a living in the civilian world. After toiling over a plot of land that Grant had aptly dubbed "Hardscrabble," he tried his hand at everything from rent collection to selling cordwood on the street. But Julia, who had never experienced poverty like this in her life, showed her true colors by bearing up under the strain and never, ever losing her faith in Ulys—who, she continued to earnestly believe, was destined for great things (often to the ridicule of friends).

She was right, of course. But it took a nightmarishly bloody civil war to prove it. In 1860, the Grants were living in Galena, Illinois, after an increasingly desperate Ulys was given a job in his brothers' leather goods shop. Southern secession changed everything the following year, however, and Grant got back into the uniform that would make him a national icon. He rose quickly from a trainer of troops to a battlefield commander, and a list of vital and uncanny victories earned his name a privileged place in White House conversations. Indeed, by 1864 he was already being considered a presidential candidate. He settled for commander in chief of the Union armies instead.

For Julia, her husband's wartime greatness was the fulfillment of all her predictions—and the vindication of years of hardship. She moved to Washington, now the lady of the most powerful soldier on the continent, and took to political society like a fish to water. It was a pleasant change of pace indeed from the years spent eating in military messes and writing letters home for amputated soldiers. Grant's star continued to rise after the war—the title "General in Chief" was created specifically for him, and Julia soaked up every minute of the couple's blossoming celebrity.

By the time Ulys ran for president in 1868, Julia had called Washington her home for four years and relished the notion of staying for another four. She got her wish—upon completing his oath of office at the inaugural in 1869, Grant turned to his beaming wife and said, "And now, my dear, I hope you are satisfied."

Oh, was she ever. After Mary Lincoln's peripatetic emotions and Eliza Johnson's mysterious anonymity, Julia Grant's infectious enthusiasm was a breath of fresh air for the capital and the country. The Gilded Age had begun with a bang, and sitting at its center was the regal first couple, hobnobbing with rich financiers and captains of industry like Renaissance royalty.

It was all so glittery and charming that few people, including those in the press, seemed to care that much about the corruption that racked the administration. In the summer of 1869, Abel Corbin—the president's brother-in-law—took part in a sordid scheme to corner the gold market. Grant squelched the plan at the last minute, but word soon leaked that the first lady herself may have made a profit on the scam. Scandal struck again when Julia's own brother, John Dent, was accused of benefiting from Secretary of War William Belknap's illegal finagling of Indian trading funds.

But Julia never let any of it, including the accusations of nepotism (which were true), trip her up. Through two terms as first lady, she actively advised her husband, thrived as first entertainer of the land, schmoozed with newspaper reporters (she was the first first lady to issue press releases), and adored every minute of it. Which is why, of course, she reacted with horror to Grant's reluctance to seek a third term. She had to be pried from the White House like an oyster from its shell, and, upon boarding the train that took her and Ulys away from her beloved Washington, she collapsed into a seat and wept like a baby.

The Grants were soon off on a two-year world tour—if Julia couldn't be first lady anymore, she could at least be received like royalty from Westminster to Egypt to India. She and Ulys were still riding the wave, surfing on all the fawning praise and expensive living to which they'd become addicted. But the wave hit a rocky shore not long after returning to the United States. Once again, Ulys found himself having to find employment in the private sphere; and he proved just as unlucky at it as he had been back in his Hardscrabble days. He joined up with a brokerage firm that went bust and, with memories of privation flashing in their minds, the Grants started selling off many of the gewgaws they'd accumulated through their years as heads of state. The former president took to writing articles on the Civil War and, eventually, his memoirs.

It was a stroke of brilliance and just in the nick of time. For Ulys proved to be an extraordinary writer—who had throat cancer. His sickness was an awful blow to Julia, but Grant finished his magnum opus before he died in 1885. It became a best seller, and Julia never had to worry about the specter of poverty again.

In fact, Julia became a wealthy woman indeed. In addition to the royalties from her late husband's masterpiece, she was granted a pension from Congress and made some very lucrative real estate deals. The money did more than restore her to the lifestyle to which she'd always aspired—it allowed her to move back to Washington (after selling her place in New York City), where she fought for women's suffrage and reigned as the nation's Queen Mother, just like Dolley Madison had. She even gave writing a go, composing her memoirs (they would be published long after her death). After living long enough to see the dawn of the new century, she died an esteemed national figure in 1902.

SPECIAL SIGHT

Julia Dent Grant was slightly cross-eyed her entire life. It never stopped her from being a tomboy in her youth, or—remarkably—from developing into an accomplished equestrienne. But her vision was anything but perfect, and it led to some embarrassing moments. At the gala fetes she was fond of throwing while first lady, rooms crowded with guests could be quite a challenge—she had a habit of standing still in a corner to avoid bumping into people who were either doubled by her vision or not seen clearly enough. When she did manage to move, she did so in a noticeably sideways gait that some likened to the motion of a crab, and she often knocked into furniture. During the Civil War, she seriously considered having surgery to correct it. Her adoring Ulysses forbade it, reminding her that he'd fallen in love with Julia as she was, crossed eyes and all. She never did have the operation.

PSYCHEDELIC

The squinting, cross-eyed Julia may not have been able to see too well, but, according to family legend, she had vision of a very different sort. Julia always believed that she had psychic abilities. And, truth be told, she had reason to.

On April 14, 1865, a strange man knocked at Julia's Washington residence with an invitation from First Lady Mary Lincoln for the Grants to join the president and her at Ford's Theater that evening to see the play *Our American Cousin*. Something about the messenger struck Julia as odd, and she immediately suspected mischief (or worse). Frantic, she whipped off a note to Ulys insisting that he get ready to leave town that very evening. Just hours later, Julia was having lunch at a local restaurant when she noticed the man who'd delivered her invitation sitting nearby—with another man who seemed interested in what Julia was saying to her fellow diners. Having become thoroughly paranoid, she breathed a sigh of relief when her husband showed up at the train station that evening. The two left the city and, next morning, were in a Philadelphia restaurant when word reached them by telegram that Abe Lincoln had been murdered—in Ford's Theater. As investigations later revealed, Ulysses Grant had indeed been targeted by the ring of assassins—one of whom, Julia believed, was the man who delivered her invitation from Mary Lincoln.

FIREBIRD

Julia's "sight" saved her and Ulys's lives on another occasion. While the couple was visiting Chicago in 1871, Mrs. Grant had a vision about a huge, terrifying bird with smoke billowing from its wings. Though the Grants were preparing to make an appearance at a reception, Julia insisted they cancel and get the heck out of town. Ulys obliged, and they left—just in time to escape the great Chicago fire.

Black and Blue

Though Julia Dent married a man opposed to slavery, she was slow to give up her reliance on the institution that had been such an integral part of her upbringing. In fact, while her husband was doing his part to defeat the Confederacy during the Civil War, Julia often traveled to see him—with her slaves in tow. Of course, while in free territory, she had the good sense to lease them. But it was only after the issue became a bit thorny for Ulys's reputation that she gave them up altogether.

HAREBRAINED HOSTESS

Like all first ladies who loved the job, Julia Dent Grant was an avid entertainer. Her social functions became legendary not only for their twenty- or thirty-course meals prepared by an Italian chef, but also for the fact that all were welcome: working-class folks rubbed shoulders with some of the richest robber barons in the nation. But the first lady had a rather lousy memory, a fault that can cause quite a bit of trouble at political functions. Names, opinions, voting records, and the like were hard for her to remember. As a result, she often had White House staffers strategically placed about her whose job it was to whisper facts into her ears as important people approached to say hello (people who, of course, Julia often couldn't make out properly with her bad eyesight). Unfortunately, Ulys didn't make it any easier on Julia and often teased her—or, worse, fed her false information that could end in embarrassment.

FRIGID FESTIVITIES

Grant's second inaugural ball in March 1873 was held in a makeshift structure built specifically for the occasion and aptly dubbed the "Muslin Palace" for its garish decor. Julia showed up in a truly gorgeous brocade gown made from material given her by the emperor of China—garb that, resplendent as it was, couldn't protect her from the cold. And Julia wasn't the only one shivering, for the evening was unduly chilly. Many partygoers took off early for warmer lodgings, and those who remained skipped the punch and opted for coffee. The occasion took a tragic turn when, among the thinning crowd of guests bundled in shawls and overcoats, a woman fell to the floor. She had died from a bronchial condition exacerbated by the temperature.

WHEN A CIGAR IS JUST A CIGAR

Julia had very few restrictions for her White House social gatherings. But one of them, which she enforced ruthlessly, was no smoking. She hated tobacco smoke—an intriguing fact when you consider that she married one of the most ardent cigar aficionados in the country. It was always a bone of contention between Mr. and Mrs. Grant, and the latter was not above finding her husband's stash and simply throwing it in the trash. She never succeeded in driving the point home, however, as evidenced by Ulys's death from throat cancer.

16

Lucy Webb
HAYES

August 28, 1831–June 25, 1889

MARRIED:

December 30, 1852

PRESIDENTIAL HUSBAND:

Rutherford B. Hayes

CHILDREN:

Birchard Austin, Webb Cook, Rutherford Platt, Joseph Thompson, George Crook, Fanny, Scott Russell, and Manning Force

FIRST LADY:

1877–1881

ASTROLOGICAL SIGN:

Virgo

RELIGION:

Methodist

SOUND BITE:

"Home missions seek to protect our own land from imported heathenism."

Lucy Webb Hayes became first lady during an exciting time for American women. All across the country, they were taking charge—of their careers, their right to vote, their education, and their drunken menfolk. And plenty of

> Lucy Hayes banned alcohol, card-playing, and dancing from the White House. Even pool was out—the mansion's billiard room became a home for plants.

them looked to Lucy for guidance and leadership. But while Mrs. Hayes embodied much of what the nation was beginning to call the "new woman," she was also content to act like the older variety, and stopped short of becoming the revolutionary icon that so many of her fellow women urged her to be.

Lucy was born the only daughter of three children in Chillicothe, Ohio, to James Webb and Maria Cook. Her parents were devout temperance advocates, instilling in Lucy a lifelong suspicion of demon rum. They also instilled in her a desire for self-betterment and, fortunately, had the money to make it happen. James Webb, a successful physician, left his family plenty of cash when he died of cholera in 1833 and much of it paid for Lucy's classes at Ohio Wesleyan Uni-

versity and Cincinnati Wesleyan Female College. Her schooling covered not only the basics (literature, history, geography, etc.), but also a large dose of Methodist morality in which self-scouring discipline became a daily habit. Her religious, teetotaling father would've been proud.

She met fellow Ohioan Rutherford B. Hayes in 1846 when she was a student at Ohio Wesleyan. But at fifteen, she was too young to start courting (even back then), and their romantic association didn't begin until after they met again in 1850. During their engagement, Lucy had her first experiences with charitable work—helping impoverished families, a cause that would come to define her life. She and Rutherford married in 1852.

While Rutherford set up his law practice in the years that followed, Lucy was busy with the domestic responsibilities that were the lot of every housewife. She also spent a great deal of time socializing with her family and in-laws and began having children in November of 1853. But babies weren't the only things growing inside her. She was also developing ideas about the burgeoning women's movement and the cause of abolitionism. Her father had worked to free his slaves and died an ardent opponent of the "hated institution." Lucy had inherited those ideas, and she now began to take a great interest in the Republicans, the first political party in America to directly take on slavery. Her enthusiasm was infectious, particularly to her husband—Rutherford began to attend lectures with her and to consider a life in politics.

But circumstances drove him to make a very different sort of career change. At the outbreak of the Civil War, Rutherford became an officer of Ohio troops. For the next four years, he saw more than his fair share of action and got wounded on several occasions. Life wasn't a walk in the park for Lucy, either, who found herself—like so many soldiers' wives—balancing a family with worries over her husband's welfare. She went to be with him when she could (which, on at least one occasion, meant renting out their Cincinnati home), sewed and mended uniforms, tended to the wounded (including her husband), and did some of it within cannon shot of Confederate armies. Under such dire circumstances, she continued to have children: two sons, both of whom were dead before their third year.

At the end of the war, Rutherford's battlefield heroics were rewarded with a seat in the United States Congress. Lucy went to visit him in 1866 and was never the same again. The heated political issues of the time electrified her, giving her expansive, well-educated brain a feast of delectable debates to chew on. To her growing list of progressive concerns she added the plight of freed slaves. Like all radical Republicans, she was sickened by President Andrew Johnson's anemic Reconstruction program, which seemed hardly sympathetic to the realities of African Americans. Lucy was comfortable in the cauldron of contention over these and other issues and felt as if politics had become her home.

Rutherford felt the same way and went on to become governor of Ohio in 1868. His wife—galvanized by the fire of war, tantalized by the potential of political change—dove into the role of active governor's spouse with relish. With a new infant daughter to care for (Fanny, born in 1867), Lucy's homemaking duties were as demanding as ever. But she still found time to assert her views on Rutherford's legislation programs and championed everything from prison reform to helping veterans' orphans. To her, politics had become the family business. It had been she who had gotten Rutherford into it all in the first place, and she continued to look upon his career as partly hers. When the couple tried to retire from public life after two terms in the governor's mansion, they only felt bored. Rutherford got elected to a third term in 1875, setting himself up for a presidential run. He won the presidential race the following year.

Well, sort of. The election of 1876 between Hayes and Democratic opponent Samuel Tilden was too close to call at first, requiring a congressionally appointed committee to sort things out. They eventually went with Hayes, though the popular vote had (barely) gone to Tilden. As if to ease national tensions over the election, Rutherford promised in his inaugural address to limit himself to a single term. Many of those who listened to him in the audience, however, had come to see his wife. Suffragists and temperance devotees, they looked upon the modestly adorned woman who sat next to Rutherford on that afternoon as the woman of the hour, a fellow fighter in the trenches of progress who could finally make a difference from her perch in the White House.

Many of them would be sorely disappointed. Lucy Hayes was the first presidential spouse to have a college degree and had attracted attention for her work in human welfare causes. But there was another side to her, as well: the severe Methodist who looked down upon anything that might smack of immodest behavior. She dressed the part, wearing her hair in a simple bun, doing without jewelry, and covering her décolletage with lace. It was a manifestation of her concern for propriety—try as they might, neither the suffragettes nor the temperance unions could get the first lady to officially join their causes or publicly espouse their agendas. She sided with her husband on the subject of giving women the vote—education and a career were fine, but the political decision-making was, as far as Lucy was concerned, the province of men. And while she and Rutherford ran a dry White House, Lucy stopped short of preaching to others about their drinking habits. It was a matter of individual choice, and that was that.

Nevertheless, those Americans of an evangelical bent thought she was the best thing since the King James Bible—and for good reason. In addition to banning alcohol of every sort from the executive mansion, Lucy and Rutherford prayed. And prayed and prayed and prayed. They also sang gospel hymns every night. They were pious, to be sure, and lots of people likened them to a couple of washcloths come to wipe the sinful residue from previous administrations who'd sullied the White House with booze, vanity, and worse.

Not that Lucy didn't entertain. With the help of family members (notably Rutherford's niece Emily Platt), the first lady oversaw an ambitious social schedule. And she still managed to find time to visit educational institutions, preaching the value of school for both sexes, and to accompany the president on tours of the country that offered average Americans a look at their first couple.

Having completed Rutherford's promised single term, the Hayeses returned to Ohio, where Lucy divided her time between church, family, and being president of the Woman's Home Missionary Society. For much of her adult life, she had suffered from headaches and rheumatism that childbirth only exacerbated. She soldiered on, despite the pain, until her death in 1889. Though she had intelligence, grace, and a big heart, it was Lucy's teetotaling that posterity remembers most—the portrait of her that hangs in the White House was commissioned toward the end of her first lady years by none other than the Women's Christian Temperance Union.

LEMONADE LUCY

Before leaving the White House toward the end of his second term, Ulysses Grant was thoughtful enough to stock the mansion's wine cellar so that the incoming Hayeses wouldn't have to worry about it.

What a waste.

The only occasion on which alcohol was served at the White House during the Hayes administration was in 1877, when a group of Russians came visiting. Lucy and Rutherford had to be talked into making an exception to their dry policy by staff members who were worried about offending the Russian guests. After that, nary a drop of the stuff was served for any reason. In truth, the ban on liquor was at least as much Rutherford's idea as it was his wife's. But Lucy caught most of the flack for it. A story appeared in the press in which the first lady became agitated at the sight of a glass of red beverage, only to be told by her husband that it was lemonade with a squished berry in it. From then on, she was commonly referred to as "Lemonade Lucy," and the press had a field day.

LAST CHANCE

It wasn't only the newspapers that poked fun at the Hayeses' dry policy. A tavern opened up for business not far from the White House and called itself—for the benefit of those passing by on their way to a White House social event—the "Last Chance."

GOOD LORD!

Lucy and her husband were some seriously pious folks. During their administration, the White House became a virtual house of worship: daily prayers (usually held in Abigail Fillmore's beloved library), Bible readings, and hymn sing-alongs dominated the calendar. Card playing and dancing were banned altogether. Even pool was out—the mansion's billiard room became a home for plants.

ONWARD CHRISTIAN SOLDIERS

Though organizations like the Women's Christian Temperance Union tried to get Mrs. Hayes on their rolls to no avail, Lucy did end up joining one nifty little sorority:

The Woman's Home Missionary Society of the Methodist Episcopal Church, devoted to maintaining the integrity of America's Christian culture in the wake of increasing immigration. Indeed, she became its first president in 1880. In addition to steering the society away from attaching itself to the women's suffrage movement, Lucy made a series of speeches that, while (sadly) in step with the times, have since become notorious. According to her, the boatloads of folks coming into the United States from such "less enlightened" places as southern and eastern Europe were "sadly lacking in education and religion" and "by no means well fitted for the citizenship of a republic." Even African Americans, on whose behalf she had spoken out at the end of the Civil War, were becoming a nuisance to Lucy. After all, "well-informed and conscientious observers" had pointed out that blacks reproduce at a higher rate, while the "proportion of the ignorant and unchristian does not diminish." Should they keep spawning like this, she warned, they'd exceed the total number of citizens in the United States by the end of the nineteenth century!

See what a college education can do?

Lucretia
GARFIELD

April 19, 1832–March 14, 1918

MARRIED:

November 11, 1858

PRESIDENTIAL HUSBAND:

James A. Garfield

CHILDREN:

Eliza Arabella, Harry Augustus, James Rudolph, Mary, Irwin McDowell, Abram, and Edward

FIRST LADY:

1881

ASTROLOGICAL SIGN:

Aries

RELIGION:

Disciples of Christ

SOUND BITE:

"If your [children] cost you what they do me, you would not sigh for more, I am sure" (to her husband).

James Garfield once wrote, "I have been wonderfully blessed in the discretion of my wife," and truer words were never written. Lucretia Rudolph Garfield was the epitome of discretion—and forgiveness. And in her husband, she had plenty of excuses to be neither.

"Crete," as she would come to be called by Garfield, was born in Garrettsville, Ohio, to a carpenter named Zebulon Rudolph and his wife, Arabella Mason Rudolph. Besides being of humble origins, the Rudolphs' most distinguishing characteristic seems to have been a conspicuous lack of affection, both for each other and their children. Lucretia found escape from her loveless childhood (as well as from frequent illnesses) by reading a lot and became a very intelligent young woman by the time she began thinking of college. She entered Western Reserve Eclectic Institute in Hiram in 1850 and became a teacher after graduation.

But she had picked up something besides book learning in school: an attraction for fellow student James Garfield. And it was to have as great an impact on her life as any college degree. Like Lucretia, James was a member of the Disciples of Christ and an intellectual who lit up during conversations over the fine arts. From 1853 the two struck up a lively and increasingly intimate correspondence

while he went east to attend Williams College. By the time he returned to Ohio in 1856, also to become a teacher, the young couple had been engaged for nearly two years.

Of course, they hadn't seen much of each other thus far—which was probably just as well, for their face time lacked all of the warmth that defined their letters, a fact that began to worry them both. Having no clue as to how properly romantic people went about expressing their feelings to each other, Lucretia seemed to James a rather cold fish. He, on the other hand, was as hot as a coal stove and not nearly as choosy as his betrothed about where (or with whom) he shared the warmth. Both at Williams and back in Ohio, James carried on with at least several different women, putting a strain on the engagement that almost broke it to pieces. Crete, perhaps out of a sense of guilt for her withdrawn nature,

> James Garfield's many infidelities pushed his wife, Lucretia, to the brink of devastation. On several occasions, he even tried to introduce Lucretia to his mistresses.

expressed hurt and chided James, but always stood by her choice to marry him—which she did, against all the odds, in 1858.

Wedding vows changed nothing, however, and the marriage quickly faltered. James had become a preacher, which took up much of his time, and when he became involved in state politics, he was home even less. Crete continued to see evidence of his cheating heart, but did little beyond sulking about it. Interestingly, death, destruction, and illness would conspire to patch things up between them. When the Civil War broke out, James left his wife and infant daughter Eliza (born in 1860) to lead troops against the Confederacy. He returned on sick leave in 1862 and was changed by the experience of spending precious time with Crete and their little girl before going back to the hell of combat. Eliza's tragic death the following year from diphtheria brought the spouses even closer, and their relationship began to resemble a loving marriage.

Not that James stopped sleeping around. Elected in 1863 to the United States House of Representatives, he went to Washington, where he eventually met—and fell in love with—a widow named Lucia Gilbert Calhoun, a reporter from New York. Crete visited her husband in 1864 and was confronted by the horrible news. She reacted with that combination of emotions that makes her such a strange and compelling figure: sympathy for her husband's confusion and regret, hurtful anger at his callous misstep, and affirmation of the high regard in which she continually held him. Whether intentionally or not, James was chafing at the bonds of marriage—and his wife was shoring them up with astonishing patience.

The Calhoun affair would be the final and most trying challenge that Crete and her wayward husband would face on the road to a compassionate union. On the advice of his wife, James went to New York City to end the relationship with his mistress and to gather all their love letters for destruction. He returned a new man, determined to make his marriage work. Lucretia chose to forgive him, and the two celebrated their clean slate with a four-month vacation to Europe.

As time went by, Crete continued to participate in her husband's desire for a large family. The kids kept coming, Garfield became a big shot in Congress, and Crete made as many visits to local libraries as her growing brood would allow (she once likened the raising of children to spending time with "young barbarians"). She continued to spend time in intellectual endeavors—reading (she was an expert at Greek and Latin), attending lectures and political debates, and going to concerts with James. Unlike most congressional wives, she had only a tepid desire to make the Washington social scene and preferred the company of books to the gossip and flummery of capital parties. The Garfields bought a house in Washington in 1869, and Crete shuttled back and forth between it and their Ohio farm to see to the education of their growing children.

James was steadily climbing the rungs of the Republican ladder and was elected to the United States Senate in 1880. The party nominated him for president the same year, and he beat fellow Civil War veteran Winfield Scott Hancock in the election. More a bookworm than a socialite, the new first lady enlisted the help of the secretary of state's wife, Mrs. James Blaine, to organize White House events. Crete dressed as plainly as her predecessor, Mrs. Hayes, but broke with Lemonade Lucy's ban on alcohol, considering many of the current temperance arguments wholly inane. She was much more at home advising James, which she did with regularity and verve. "You will never have anything from these men but their assured contempt," she wrote her husband, referring to the Stalwarts, the more conservative opposition branch of the Republican Party, "until you fight them dead." Such advice was typical of Crete, and she played an active role in cabinet appointments and dismissals. The president understood the worth of his savvy wife's input and rarely made a decision without her.

Theirs was a tight and effective presidential partnership. But it lasted only four months. Charles Guiteau, who'd been turned down by the Garfield administration for a consulship in Paris, decided to vent his rage by shooting the president. He did so on July 2, 1881, condemning James Garfield to a bed he would occupy for some eighty days before finally perishing. Crete, who'd just recovered from a bout of malaria when her husband was shot, sat by his side through it all, ignoring the grim predictions of the doctors who probed the president's wound for a bullet they wouldn't find until the autopsy. It was a marvelously inspired vigil that impressed the country.

So much so, in fact, that the nation rewarded the widowed Mrs. Garfield with cash, and lots of it. Crete received $360,000 from a sympathy-driven subscription campaign, $50,000 from Congress for her grief, and an annual $5,000 pension on top of it. Assassination may have taken from her the husband she toiled so long to forgive, but it also made her a rich woman. She eventually retired to sunny Pasadena, California, where she headed up literary societies and, after the outbreak of World War I, joined the local Red Cross at age eighty-five. She never married again. (Can you blame her?)

THE LAST STRAW

James Garfield admitted to friends that he was never meant for holy matrimony and that he married Lucretia more out of a sense of honor than anything else. Crete knew this, of course, and voiced her concern on more than a few occasions. "There are hours," she once wrote to James, "when my heart almost breaks with the cruel thought that our marriage is based upon the cold stern word duty." James did nothing to ease her fears: "It was probably a great mistake that we had ever tried married life." That his wife would insist on enduring his dalliances is simply remarkable, especially since there were so many of them. He struck up a relationship at Williams with a sycophant named Rebecca Selleck and continued to send letters to her after returning to Ohio. Then there was Kate Chase, daughter of the secretary of the treasury, in whose company James was often seen during a long visit to Washington in 1862. Perhaps the worst part about it all is that Garfield tried to fight his guilt by blunt and indelicate honesty—he often spoke openly to Crete about the women he was with and tried on several occasions to introduce them to her. The humiliation was sometimes too much for her to bear—during their engagement in 1857, Crete took a teaching job in Cleveland just to get away from Hiram, where the mockery of their relationship had begun to drive her crazy.

Murderer with a Heart

When Charles Guiteau shot James Garfield on July 2, 1881, it was in fact the second time he'd approached the president with the intent to kill. The first had occurred on June 18. And, though she couldn't have known it at the time, it was Crete who inadvertently saved her husband's life.

Shortly after becoming first lady, Crete contracted a very nasty case of malaria. Her severe condition worried the bejeebers out of James, much of whose time was taken up fretting over her fate. Indeed, some people in the government began to worry that the administration had virtually stalled. By the middle of June, however, she began to make a heroic comeback, and James rented a cottage on the New Jersey shore in which she could complete her recuperation. It was on the station platform, while waiting for the train to Jersey, that the two were first approached by Guiteau. But as the assassin later admitted, he couldn't go through with it: "Mrs. Garfield looked so thin, and she clung so tenderly to the president's arm, that I did not have the heart to fire on him." Too bad she wasn't there on July 2 to pull at Guiteau's heartstrings again.

Ellen Herndon Arthur
1837–1880

The future wife of the twenty-first U.S. president, Chester Arthur, was born and raised in Virginia, the daughter of naval officer William Lewis Herndon and his wife, Frances Elizabeth Hansbrough Herndon. Ellen's family boasted wealth and fame—her father's exploits as an explorer and his tragic death at sea earned him a monument at the U.S. Naval Academy in Annapolis. Ellen ran into Chester Arthur in New York City during a visit to her widowed mother and, after a brief courtship, agreed to marry the Republican-machine politician in 1859. Though she loved Arthur and eventually bore him three children, she soon felt like a fish out of water—cosmopolitan New York was thrilling, but it was Yankee country, a fact that caused no small amount of trouble for her after the outbreak of the Civil War. Chastised for her Confederate sympathies by her in-laws and separated from her family by the battle lines, Ellen sank into a depression that didn't abate completely until the war's conclusion in 1865. Her primary concern thereafter became Arthur's habit of disappearing for long stretches of time on party business. The situation made her consider a separation, but she decided instead to devote her efforts to her other love, music. In fact, it was while returning home from an opera performance in January of 1880 that she caught a very nasty bug, fell into a coma, and never woke up. Away in Albany on business when it happened, Arthur didn't even have a chance to say good-bye to her.

18

Frances

CLEVELAND

July 21, 1864–October 29, 1947

MARRIED:

June 2, 1886

PRESIDENTIAL HUSBAND:

Grover Cleveland

CHILDREN:

Ruth, Esther, Marion, Richard
Folsom, and Francis Grover

FIRST LADY:

1886–1889, 1893–1897

ASTROLOGICAL SIGN:

Cancer

RELIGION:

Presbyterian

SOUND BITE:

"I can wish the women of our
country no better blessing than
that their homes and their lives
may be as happy and that their
husbands may be as kind and
attentive, considerate and
affectionate, as mine."

One of the first gifts that Grover Cleveland ever gave to his future bride Frances Folsom was a baby carriage—for her to ride in. Twenty-seven years her senior, Cleveland first got to know Frances as a doting "uncle" and surro-

> **Frances Cleveland was the White House's first media star. Countless advertisers used her face and name to promote their products.**

gate father, the only president who could honestly claim that his wife was wearing diapers when they first met. When she became a woman, "Frank" inspired a very different sort of affection from Grover—an affection that would bring his legendary bachelorhood to an end and that would make Frank one of the most popular first ladies in American history.

Their very long relationship began in Buffalo, New York, with tragedy. Frances's father, Oscar Folsom, died in a buggy accident in 1875. Folsom's friend and law partner Grover Cleveland became administrator of his estate and unofficial guardian of his daughter. "Uncle Cleve," as the girl would come to call him, became a close friend to his late partner's wife, Emma, and a generous provider

to little Frank. Attentive and well-off financially, Grover paid for his ward's education at private schools, academies, and, eventually, Wells College, which she entered in 1882.

Frank had become a tall, dark-haired, blue-eyed beauty with a graceful demeanor and precocious intellect. At Wells, she majored in French, German, and driving the boys crazy. Though twice engaged, Frank seemed almost bored with the frothing young stallions who carried her books across the quad. She seemed to want something more: "When I marry, it must be someone more than a year older than I am, someone I can look up to and respect." Like Uncle Cleve, perhaps? For his part, Grover kept up a lively correspondence with his pretty charge and, as she blossomed into a lively and erudite woman, became prouder by the moment.

As for what happened next, there's no point in beating around the bush: Grover realized he was hot for the woman who'd been like a daughter to him. But by the time Frank was looking forward to graduation, Grover already had a mistress—and her name was the United States.

After rising through the ranks of the Buffalo political machine, Grover became governor of New York and, in 1884, won the presidential election on the Democratic ticket. A painfully honest workaholic, he was the first confirmed bachelor president since James Buchanan and a man—in his late forties—who didn't think much of marriage. But he thought very much of Frank Folsom—a fact he managed to conceal beneath a veneer of tireless political labor (despite one off-the-cuff remark that he was "waiting for his wife to grow up"). But when the president invited Emma and Frank Folsom to pay a visit to the White House, all of Washington started buzzing. Was the chief executive planning on putting his single days behind him? Wouldn't the widow Folsom make a charming wife and first lady? And that darling Frank, what a glamorous stepdaughter she'd make . . . .

Grover did indeed propose in August of 1885, but not to his old friend Emma. His engagement to young Frances was cloaked in the darkness of government secrecy, and, having secured a "yes" from the blushing bride-to-be, he sent her and her mother off on a tour of Europe. The press was left to make their own assumptions—which they did, following the Folsoms to Europe and anticipating a wedding on their return.

They got it, of course, but the wrong Folsom was wearing white. The surprise merely heightened the national sense of excitement. Cleveland was the first sitting president to have his wedding ceremony in the White House, and the public (barred from the mansion's interior) gathered in throngs outside to be part of it. It was more than the beginning of a marriage—it was the beginning of a love affair between the new first lady and her adoring people.

The newlyweds escaped to rural Maryland for their honeymoon, where they got a taste of what they were in for. For a week, they were hounded by hungry reporters. Frank had become an overnight sensation. She was beautiful, young (at twenty-one, the youngest of all our first ladies), fluent in foreign languages, extremely well educated, modest, forthright, and even musically talented (not only did Frank play the piano, but opera star Adelina Patti would later tell the first lady that she had the voice to go professional). And those were just her bad qualities. Frank became an unofficial champion for women's education and professionalism, sponsored a charity that made clothing for the poor, devoted time and energy to helping African Americans, and accepted a seat on the board of her alma mater, Wells College—a position she would hold for fifty years. As soon as she became first lady, special Saturday receptions were held at the White House for working women to attend (try to imagine this happening nowadays). Her White House events were exceedingly popular, drawing rich and poor alike, and Frank came to embody the administration's willingness to reach out. Smiling, enthusiastic, and sincere, the first lady shook hands until her palm was black and she needed to soothe her arm in ice.

Could this woman do any wrong? No. Which is why her husband's opponents made up stuff to cast the administration in a bad light. During her engagement to the president, Frank was rudely introduced to her husband's scandalous past by a cartoon that made reference to the fact that Grover had admitted to fathering an illegitimate child by a Buffalo woman named Maria Halpin. It hardly caused a hiccup in their relationship. But in 1888, as Grover struggled for reelection, the opposition pulled out all the stops and spread a false rumor that the president frequently got drunk and beat his poor wife. Until now, Frank had been treated like a darling by the country and press. But she assumed the hatred of the newspapers that was consuming her husband and retaliated in print. It did her and Grover no good—Benjamin Harrison won the 1888 election.

"Now, Jerry," the outgoing first lady told a White House servant in 1889, "I want you to take good care of all the furniture and ornaments in the house . . . . We are coming back just four years from today." Astonishingly, Frank was right. The Clevelands moved to New York City, where the limelight continued to shine upon them. Their first child, Ruth, had a candy bar named after her: Baby Ruth. But when Grover got back into the presidential race in 1892, he did it with a vengeance. And he won reelection largely because his wife was so popular.

Since 1886, Frank Cleveland had become America's goddess and the Republican Party's bane. Advertisers used her image to sell everything from soap to arsenic-based curatives; few homes in the nation were without a framed likeness of her on the mantel; Republican strategists openly admitted that a bachelor Cleveland would be much easier to beat than one married to the beloved "Frankie"; and the Democratic Party produced buttons, posters, and plates featuring Frank's portrait above her husband's and his running mate's to garner votes. Not even Dolley Madison had enjoyed such celebrity. It was unprecedented, and it was powerful. Cleveland won the election.

But as the old saying goes, "Be careful what you wish for." Frances was no longer the shining ingenue that she was during her husband's first term. She now had children to look after—children whose celebrity required her to make unpopular choices to secure their safety. Grover wasn't quite what he used to be, either. Confronted with a crippling economic crisis, the president relied on stale fiscal policies that only made things worse and angered the growing legions of poor. During their first term in the White House, the Clevelands chose to spend their private time (outside of the social season) in a private home in which they sought sanctuary from the hated press. Now, they did it again, fleeing the scrutiny of newspapermen who, starved for stories, simply made them up. It was a hard time for the first couple, but Frank ran the household like she always had—with intelligence, grace, and imagination. In addition to bearing her second child, Esther, the first lady oversaw a social schedule that welcomed common working-class visitors as well as the queen of Spain. A beautiful bond had been formed with the staff by the end of the administration, a bond that both the servants and the first lady were loath to break—at the completion of Cleveland's second term, Frank broke down in tears while saying good-bye to the mansion's employees.

She and Grover bought a place in the New Jersey countryside, ideal for quiet family time. Though retirement suited them both well, tragedy was waiting on the horizon. In 1903, the famous "Baby Ruth" died from diphtheria. Grover himself followed suit in 1908, leaving Frank with four kids. And $250,000. With cash like that, it's no wonder she never accepted an annual pension from Congress. Besides, she was still young and full of marrying potential. In 1913, she married Thomas Preston Jr., a scholar who could measure up to her high intellectual standards. Preston eventually became a professor of archaeology at Princeton, while Frank spent her time in charity, leading the Women's University Club that she helped found, and making speeches during World War I to help the war effort. When she died peacefully in her sleep in 1947, Grover got her back—Frank was buried next to him in Princeton.

HONEYMOON HAVOC

After arriving in Deer Park, Maryland, with his stunning new bride, Grover soon learned the price he'd have to pay for taking such an interesting and attractive woman as his wife. Reporters swamped the area in scores and proceeded to do whatever they thought necessary to get a peek at the celebrated newlyweds. Like Peeping Toms, they camped as close to the honeymooners' cottage as possible, scanning the structure with spyglasses in the hopes of scoring a prurient view. Waitstaff were stopped and interviewed on their way to the couple so that readers could discover what Frank and Grover were eating and drinking. The situation developed into a media circus that the president seemed powerless to stop. Not that he didn't try. Local hotels and taverns were persuaded to turn away reporters looking for a room, and security guards were charged with forcing reporters to move on—which they did, to other places that offered just as good a view. Though Frank—young, naive, and new to the limelight—endured it with a sense of humor, her husband wasn't nearly as forgiving. He ended up calling the whole fiasco "a colossal impertinence."

THE PRICE OF CELEBRITY

Though predecessors like Dolley Madison and Julia Tyler enjoyed a popular status with the American people, the nationwide explosion of interest in Frank Cleveland was something new. She was the first presidential media star, a fact that had some odd and even dangerous manifestations. For one thing, the papers insisted on referring to the first lady as "Frankie"—a nickname she always hated (though called "Frank" by her family from an early age, she always preferred "Frances"). And, despite the efforts of her and her cynical husband, innumerable advertisers got away with using her name and image to sell their products. One enterprising merchant even had the first lady's initials stitched onto his luggage and sold them on the street. But nothing better illustrates the preposterous situation in which she found herself than the time she attended an event in St. Louis. Upon seeing the first lady's parasol, the crowd grew frenzied and rushed the podium. As eager fans scaled a wall to get a look at her, the curiosity grew to a fever pitch until a barricade was stormed and eventually smashed to pieces. Though Frank escaped physical harm, the debacle galvanized her and Grover's fear of the public's mania—and, more importantly, the newspapers' gift for whipping it up.

BURYING THE BUSTLE

During Frances's first term as first lady, two Washington reporters found themselves hard up for a story during the slow summer season. So they invented one. According to the fiction they printed, the first lady—whose fashion choices always sold copies—decided to stop wearing the bustle, a frame worn at the time to expand the backside of a woman's skirt. In fact, Frances had decided to do no such thing. But once the story was printed, virtually every woman in the country stopped wearing bustles—and the first lady, confronted with a *fait accompli*, decided to follow suit. It spelled the demise of a clothing trend that had dominated women's fashion for years.

BABY RUTH

The media coverage that dominated the presidencies of Grover Cleveland eventually took a toll on his family life. Between Grover's two terms, Frank gave birth to a little girl—their first child—named Ruth. Like everything else that was part of the Clevelands, little Ruth became a sensation. A candy bar was named after her, of course, but that was just the tip of the iceberg. After winning the presidency for a second time, in 1892, Grover and Frances found that their child's safety was being threatened by the celebrity that dogged the family. When Frank saw little Ruth being handled by a crowd of tourists who'd come to visit the White House, red flags started going up all over the place. On another occasion, a visitor to the mansion actually tried to clip a bit of hair from Ruth. It was more than Frank was willing to bear—the White House grounds were closed to the public, leading to speculation that the first family was hiding some mental or physical defect in Baby Ruth. Nothing could be further from the truth, of course, but that didn't stop the newspapers from spreading rumors.

Blind Faith

Late in life, Frank Cleveland began to suffer from blindness. But her mind and courage were such that merely accepting her fate passively was out of the question. She quickly learned Braille and not just for her own convenience—Frances spent a great deal of time transcribing literature into Braille for others with the affliction, a project she continued to do even after surgery successfully removed her cataracts.

OUT OF SIGHT, OUT OF MIND

During the presidency of Harry Truman, an aged Frank paid a visit, along with other Washington notables, to the White House. There she met General Dwight Eisenhower, who had recently become one of the most famous men in history by defeating Hitler's Germany in the Second World War. But if his name had long since become a household word, Frank's had not—especially since she remarried after the death of her presidential husband, Grover Cleveland. Now going by the name Frances Preston, she approached the general and was greeted with what can only be called a letdown. "And where did you live in Washington, ma'am?" asked the clueless war hero. Her response embarrassed him mightily: "In the White House."

19

Caroline

HARRISON

October 1, 1832–October 25, 1892

MARRIED:

October 20, 1853

PRESIDENTIAL HUSBAND:

Benjamin Harrison

CHILDREN:

Russell Lord and Mary Scott

FIRST LADY:

1889–1892

ASTROLOGICAL SIGN:

Libra

RELIGION:

Presbyterian

SOUND BITE:

"Very few people understand to what straits the President's family has been put at times for lack of accommodations."

Caroline Lavinia Scott Harrison served as first lady after—and before—one of the most popular women ever to occupy the White House. The country simply didn't take to her like it did to Frank Cleveland. Mrs. Harrison was plump, grandmotherly, and exceedingly

> **Carrie Harrison helped bring electric lights to the White House. But she feared electrocution so much that she refused to touch the switches!**

domestic, all of which played a role in forging her relatively bland public image. But underneath the white-haired, matronly exterior dwelled a dynamic side to Mrs. Harrison for which she was never properly credited: a savvy activist who finally put the stamp of the White House on women's issues.

"Carrie" was born into a large Presbyterian family in Oxford, Ohio, one of five children of Mary Potts Neal Scott and Dr. John Witherspoon Scott. Her father, a minister and professor, was a devout believer in the power of education, and Carrie ended up studying at a school he founded—Oxford Female Institute. While there, she met a fellow Presbyterian named Benjamin Harrison, who was attending what would come to be known as Miami University in Ohio. He was a stern, sober-minded student who, true to his faith, refused to dance—none of which

dissuaded Carrie from falling for him (at parties, Ben usually watched from the sidelines while his gal broke the Presbyterian ban on hitting the dance floor). Carrie was more than just an eager, well-read student; she had grown into a vivacious and sincere young woman with a sly sense of humor and a gift for disarming people with it. The two kept their engagement a secret, not least on account of the alarm it would've caused to Carrie's religious and proper father, and managed to keep up a lively courtship that spanned their two campuses.

After being married by Dr. Scott in 1853, the Harrisons embarked upon their new life together—in poverty. After teaching during her senior year in college, Carrie became a full-time homemaker, while Ben struggled to make a law practice. After being admitted to the bar in 1854 (the same year that Carrie gave birth to their first child, Russell), the family moved to Indianapolis, Indiana, and things began to get easier for them. Through the rest of the decade, Ben's practice picked up and he became active in the Republican Party. Carrie, meanwhile, began to develop the willingness to join things that would characterize her later years. She taught Sunday school at the local church, sang in the choir, raised money for charities, and still found time to raise their two children and indulge her artistic side by painting watercolors.

The Civil War would offer more clubs to become a part of. While Ben raised a regiment of Indiana soldiers and went off to lead them for the Union, his wife did her part by nursing the wounded, joining the Ladies' Patriotic Association to raise money for the Northern cause, working for the Ladies' Sanitary Committee (another war-related society), and helping lead the Indianapolis Orphans' Asylum (on whose board she would serve until the end of her life). She had become an inspiration to women of her time, a devoted wife and mother whose happy attachment to hearth and home never got in the way of her tireless efforts to make a difference in the wider world around her.

Peace just brought more happiness and prosperity. While her husband earned piles of cash at his law firm (enough to get them a palatial new house), Carrie continued to set an example in Indianapolis society, joining classes to study art and literature, throwing her energies into the local missionary society, and even helping to create the "Impromptu Club," whose members gathered to discuss books. It was perfect training to become a real political wife—which Carrie did in 1880, when Ben got elected to the United States Senate.

His victory, however, came with a price. During his 1880 campaign, Carrie slipped on some ice and suffered a painful fall. From then on, her health would always be in question. After the Harrisons moved to Washington, capital socializing would be hampered for Mrs. Harrison during long bouts of illness. But her husband's career was on a roll, and in 1888 the Republicans nominated him for the presidency. And Carrie wasn't the type to let her health get in the way of progress.

In a political campaign that pitted her against the Venus of American politics, Frances Cleveland, Carrie was sold to the people as a proper, well-educated lady who'd been a teacher and who embodied all of the foremost qualities of a Christian. It didn't work, of course, but her husband was elected anyway by a nation eager for a changing of the guard. But the fight was a tough one, and Carrie got fed up with all the press coverage that accompanied it. "If there's any privacy to be found in the White House," she proclaimed after Ben's victory, "I propose to find it and preserve it."

Yeah, right. In fact, privacy wasn't the only thing in short supply at the White House—space was another. With the new first couple came their very copious family, a clan that ran the gamut from "Baby McKee," Carrie's grandson, to the first lady's ninety-year-old father. They inundated the mansion's paltry, dilapidated living space like an invading horde, and Carrie decided to do something about it: lobby Congress for a drastic expansion. But members of Congress didn't have to live in the White House, and the old building looked just dandy from Capitol Hill. So they gave the administration enough money for a modest refurbishment. Carrie did all the redecorating that she could, when she wasn't devoting time to her list of charities, which included the Garfield Hospital and the Washington City Orphan Asylum.

Indeed, Carrie continued to throw her energies into good works and causes. Unlike the several equally well-educated first ladies who came before her, she had no problem whatsoever attaching her esteemed name to the advancement of women. She helped raise money for the Women's Medical Fund of Johns Hopkins University—an organization that provided money to the school on the strict condition that it offer full equality to female students. She got her husband to hire Alice Sanger, the first woman stenographer ever to draw a paycheck in the

White House. She became the first president-general of the new Daughters of the American Revolution, a club she intended to use as a vanguard in the struggle for women's suffrage and rights. And she did it all while advising her husband, seeing to her brood of children and grandchildren, and becoming a celebrated presidential hostess—one whose gift for seeing to every detail led the press to label her a domestic diva while virtually ignoring her other roles.

Carrie offered another asset to the administration, too, and an important one: she compensated for her husband's legendary frostiness. Labeled the "White House Iceberg," Benjamin Harrison had a frigid demeanor that tended to freeze out friends and foes alike, and Carrie's warm, ingratiating manner and sense of humor were appreciated very much indeed during the Harrison years. Unfortunately, even she had a hard time bearing up under the severe sickness that overcame her in 1892. Whether tuberculosis, cancer, or something else (historians continue to speculate), Carrie's long history of bad health began to exact its final toll during her husband's bid for reelection. It was a morbid campaigning season: her death in October of that year inspired respectful silence from both her husband's and Grover Cleveland's camp, smothering nearly all of the stumping spirit that usually accompanied presidential contests. When Ben lost, media star Frank Cleveland was restored to the first ladyship, exiling Carrie Harrison to a humble place in history. She deserved better.

ANIMAL HOUSE

When men ran for president in the late nineteenth century, it was customary for them to conduct what was called a "front-porch campaign." That meant that they stayed at home and received crowds there, giving speeches and press statements whenever enough people showed up. Benjamin Harrison's 1888 front-porch campaign hit his wife like a train. Droves of curious voters visited their Indianapolis home, turning it into a wreck—furniture was broken, the fence around the property was busted apart, and the home's carpeting was worn straight through to the floor. Carrie, a stickler for hostessing details, did her best to feed as many guests as she could, all while watching her beloved homestead fall apart. Though it nearly did her in, her response was characteristically humorous. Looking at the damage that surrounded her, she quipped, "Well, it's either the White House or the poorhouse with us now."

SHOCK TO THE SYSTEM

Carrie Harrison's desire to overhaul the White House was shared by plenty of other people in Washington. The sorry fact was that, by the beginning of the Harrison administration, the old landmark was in dire need of care and modernization. In fact, the idea of relocating the presidential living space to another Washington building altogether was bandied about seriously for months. The first lady did the most with the funds given her by Congress, installing, among other things, a switchboard to accommodate more than one phone and the first White House electric lights. The lights, however, were a rather newfangled sort of thing and, frankly, put the fear of God into the first family. When White House usher Ike Hoover failed to turn them off at night himself, they tended to remain on all night—neither Carrie, the president, nor any member of their large family trusted the system enough to touch a light switch themselves, convinced that they'd get a fatal jolt by doing so.

Daughter of the Revolution

Carrie Harrison played an active role in decorating her surroundings, and she was the first first lady to bring a Christmas tree into the White House. But she also participated in another first, and one that was considerably more important: She was the first presidential spouse to deliver a speech in public that she herself had written. Though there was already a Sons of the American Revolution, the organization excluded females from joining. Which, naturally, inspired the Daughters of the American Revolution, a patriotic group that sought to celebrate and emulate the inspiring actions of the women who'd been a part of the nation's founding generation. Carrie Harrison was the group's first president-general and didn't mince words in her first speech. "Since this society has been organized and so much thought and reading directed to the early struggles of this country," the first lady proclaimed, "it has been made plain that much of its success was due to . . . women of that era . . . I feel sure that their daughters can perpetuate a society worthy the cause and worthy themselves." You go, girl.

PRESIDENTIAL PAINTER

Caroline Harrison's first love may in fact have been art. She developed a love of painting, on canvas and on porcelain, long before reaching the White House, and even had a kiln of her own to finish the china on which she would work. The duties of first lady didn't stop her, and she continued to indulge her tastes. Having moved into a mansion in which history leaped at her from every corner, Carrie felt inspired to go through the building's closets. There she found pieces of china and other tableware that had been collected by her predecessors, and she arranged for their display in the White House in a cabinet she had specially built for the purpose. Though flowers (particularly orchids) became something of an obsession as she reorganized the greenhouses and filled the mansion with plants, it was her original artwork that made a sensation. Carrie designed a line of china for the Harrison administration which featured the nation's arms (on which guests would have their food served at functions) and even produced souvenir china for tourists with her own characteristic symbol: a shamrock. But perhaps her most endearing piece was created for none other than her own grandson, Benjamin McKee. For him, she decorated a porcelain bathtub with gorgeous magnolia blossoms.

THROWING RICE AT UNCLE BEN

Some four years after Carrie's death, Benjamin Harrison took another bride: his late wife's niece, Mary Scott Lord Dimmick. Mary had been indispensable to Carrie in the White House, helping out with hostessing and secretarial duties. But Harrison's children, Russell and Mary, were thunderstruck by their father's choice and refused to attend the wedding. It was a rift that never healed, and the former president eventually had the two taken out of his will.

Mary Harrison
1858–1948

Though she had never been a first lady, Benjamin Harrison's second wife was no stranger to the White House. To begin with, Mary and Benjamin were already family when they decided to tie the knot: she was the niece of Harrison's former wife Caroline, and had served as secretary during her aunt's years as first lady. Four years after Caroline's death, former president Harrison decided to transform Mary from a niece by marriage into his wife. Harrison's two children were disgusted by the notion that their first cousin had suddenly become their stepmother, and—scared off by the prospect of intolerably awkward Thanksgiving dinners—remained irrevocably estranged from their father and his younger bride. After Harrison died in 1901, Mary found herself in the strange position of being a presidential widow who had never been first lady. Her situation proved a bit too thorny for members of Congress—in 1909, they voted against the bill that would have awarded her the sort of pension payment given to other presidential widows.

20

Ida Saxton
McKINLEY

June 8, 1847–May 26, 1907

MARRIED:

January 25, 1871

PRESIDENTIAL HUSBAND:

William McKinley

CHILDREN:

Katherine and Ida

FIRST LADY:

1897–1901

ASTROLOGICAL SIGN:

Gemini

RELIGION:

Presbyterian

SOUND BITE:

"Oh, Major, they will kill you, they will kill you!" (to her husband after his presidential victory).

At William McKinley's inaugural ball in 1897, his wife, Ida, made a memorable entrance. Resplendent in a gown of white satin, the new first lady appeared before the admiring crowd—and promptly passed out cold. To the

> Confined to bed rest for most of her husband's presidency, Ida McKinley passed the time by crocheting some 3,500 pairs of slippers.

befuddlement of the party's guests, the president picked her up, made an exit with little fanfare and no explanation, and took her home.

Few people at the ball could have known it at the time, but McKinley's nonchalance was more than just a means of coping with an embarrassing situation. Such calm had long since become a habit—indeed, Ida's spell hardly came as a surprise to him that evening. For Ida McKinley was a spectacularly sick woman.

It hadn't always been that way. When the future president began courting her in 1870, he considered himself the luckiest fellow in Canton, Ohio. Ida was the envy of almost every young woman: brilliant, beautiful, and full of infectious energy. Her father, James Asbury Saxton, was rich. Ida had gone to the finest schools, had been to Europe, and had even acquired real business experience as an employee in her father's bank. Canton society was her oyster, and she had the

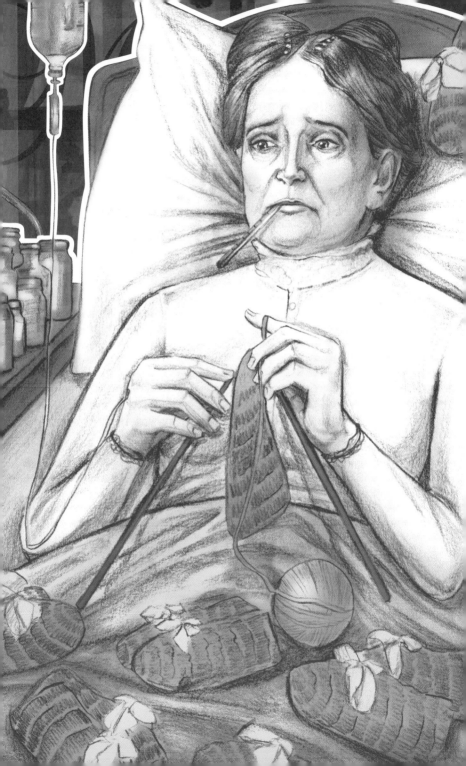

pick of the litter when it came to suitors.

She picked attorney William McKinley, who impressed everyone (including, conveniently, Ida's father) with his service in the Civil War, his ambition, and his recent election as county prosecutor. After tying the knot in a service that included two ministers (Ida was a Presbyterian, while William was a Methodist), the couple moved into a house that had been given to them by Ida's father, and settled into a married life that can truly be called blissful. They soon had a little daughter, Katie, who became the hub around which Mrs. McKinley's life revolved, and William earned a good living with his practice.

Then, just two years into the marriage, everything went to hell in a hay bale for Ida. Shortly after suffering the death of her beloved mother, Kate Saxton, she gave birth to another daughter in a delivery that was long, difficult, and exceptionally painful. Worse, Ida seemed incapable of recovering from the event and became chained to her bed, complaining constantly of headaches, weakness, stomach troubles, and an assortment of other ills. The new child—fittingly named Ida—wasn't any better off than her mother. Frail and sickly, the baby died in August of 1873, less than five months after she was born.

If the horrors of 1873 were hard on Ida, they soon became a veritable curse to her surviving daughter. Mrs. McKinley became protective to a fault with little Katie, smothering her with paranoia and instilling in her a sense of God-fearing doom that was entirely unnatural for a young child. Tragically, none of this helped: Katie was taken by typhoid fever in 1875.

This, for all intents and purposes, brought about the end of the Ida Saxton whom William McKinley had originally married. The death of Katie turned Ida into a different person—and it wasn't a change for the better. Gone was the vivacious belle who had set Canton society ablaze with her blue eyes and laughter. The doppelgänger who took her place was a convulsively ill, self-centered shell who seemed to age years with every moment.

And just what was the nature of her affliction(s)? Ida complained of everything from dizzying migraines to severe digestive problems, while historians have managed to diagnose phlebitis, cancer, and nearly everything in between. The most popular theory is that Ida McKinley suffered from "the falling sickness," otherwise known as epilepsy. Two things, however, are certain: doctors could do little for her beyond sedation, using narcotics to put her in a state of semiconsciousness that made her look like the undead; and her husband, bound to his decaying wife by a sublime sense of duty, became, in a fashion, her slave.

From 1876, while serving several terms in the United States House of Representatives, William continued to grow as a force in the Republican Party even as he made a daily—indeed, sometimes hourly—habit of looking to his wife's needs. Though he had secured the aid of a nurse, McKinley felt obliged to indulge Ida's every whim. If she felt neglected at receptions, he took time away from political talk to be with her; if she needed more thread for her needlework while he busied himself with government work, he got up to fetch some for her; and if he returned from running errands after being gone a little longer than he'd anticipated, he comforted her while she wept in frustration. Heck, he even let her win at cards.

Ida's state seemed to get better after 1891, when William became governor of Ohio. She had always been headstrong, even in the "before-time" that preceded the deaths of her daughters. Now she relied on that quality to rise to the occasion, or at least try. Conscious of her condition and its toll on her husband, Ida went through a slew of doctors in search of a cure and maintained her enthusiasm for William's success, whatever it might mean for their time together. But people were beginning to catch on to her vulnerability and erratic, needy behavior. And the Republicans, keen on getting William into the White House, wondered if his wife was really up to it.

Though it was widely believed by doctors and those close to Ida that she probably suffered from epilepsy, the word itself was never, ever uttered to outsiders. Such was the alarm that the "falling sickness" inspired at the time, and it may have played a role in concealing the truth about Mrs. McKinley during the 1896 presidential campaign. But another, more important factor helped William during the contest: His heroic devotion to Ida was universally seen as a touching and admirable quality in a would-be president. Countless people had seen how close the couple was and how McKinley made a habit of taking time out from his professional cares to see to his beloved Ida.

The bond got them both through a difficult presidency that witnessed the Spanish-American War. William continued to play his dual role as politician/caretaker, a double burden that got only heavier as the first lady's condition worsened: seizures, headaches, even terrible menstrual cycles all grew in frequency and severity for Ida. The president endured the pressure, even when it took him to the brink of a nervous breakdown (he once collapsed into tears after admitting to a friend that his wife's condition and the mounting pressure for war with Spain were more than he could handle). Ida, for better or worse, insisted on playing the role of first lady as often as possible. Though much of her time was taken up with crocheting, blackouts, and the ingestion of barbiturates, she openly spoke out against the president's critics, offered him plenty of advice on everything from the cabinet to the Philippines, and insisted on taking her place in receiving lines (even if that meant greeting guests with a blank stare from a stuffed chair). Stubborn as ever, she simply refused to let another female family member take over White House hostessing. Changes to protocol were made to accommodate her—for instance, the president insisted on having Ida sit next to him at dinner parties, whereas previous first ladies were expected to seat themselves opposite their husbands. It caused some trouble with pedants, but McKinley would not be moved on the subject.

Despite all the worries, the president did his job well enough to win reelection in the first year of the new century. Right on cue, Ida's health shaped the beginning of her husband's second term. While the first couple was making a cross-country trip in 1901, an infection in Ida's finger spread to the rest of her body. Soon, she was closer to death than she'd ever been, and William postponed a trip they were supposed to make to Buffalo. After she made a surprising recovery, the Buffalo excursion went ahead for September 5, scheduled to coincide with the city's Pan-American Exposition. There, on September 6, an anarchist named Leon Czolgosz shot McKinley, dealing him a wound that would take his life eight days later. The president, more than anyone, understood immediately what was at stake should he die. "My wife—be careful how you tell her," he gasped to a secretary while bleeding on the ground. "Oh, be careful!"

To everyone's astonishment, McKinley's concern seemed strangely unfounded. Ida sat by her dying husband during his final week, comforting him tenderly and suffering nary a breakdown throughout. His death deprived her of the living crutch that had supported her for nearly thirty years, producing in her an emptiness that fell away only with her death less than six years later in Ohio.

⌒ THE PUNISHER ⌒

Ida took the death of her sickly daughter in 1873 as a sign from God, a punitive act that was meant to remind her of her motherly faults. Thus stricken, she brooded over the welfare of her remaining daughter, Katie, with Old Testament dread. The impressionable little Katie took her mother's morbid protectiveness very seriously. Once, when asked if she wanted to go for a walk with her uncle, Katie responded with an excuse that would make any child psychologist wince: "No, I mustn't go out of the yard," she explained, "or God will punish Mama some more."

COVER-UP

William McKinley's devotion to his wife was remarkable in its constancy and sincerity. Ida, of course, knew it—she even had a painted portrait of him placed near her bed for her to gaze upon when he wasn't there to ease her suffering. Though she remained on a scary regimen of drugs throughout much of her life—including bromide-based sedatives and even lithium—they didn't always work, and Ida usually insisted on being where the action was, whatever her condition. William had no desire to hide her (a rather extraordinarily forward-thinking stance for the time), and got accustomed to bracing himself for the worst when in public. Should Ida suffer a severe fit, he instructed White House staffers to help him take her quietly away where she could be alone. For those spasms that didn't merit such drastic action, he had another solution: Listening for the sounds that warned of a minor epileptic seizure, McKinley would simply take his handkerchief and drape it over Ida's face to soothe her. Guests became used to it and were expected to carry on conversation with the first lady after her spasm passed as if nothing had happened.

MYSTERY WOMAN

Owing to her frail condition, Ida McKinley was usually out of sight during her husband's 1896 presidential campaign. As a result, rumors soon started circulating that Ida was a freak, a spy, a victim of spousal abuse, or worse. To thwart them, the Republicans produced a campaign biography of her to educate voters about her true nature. It was the first time such an act had been taken by a party on behalf of a candidate's wife.

SLIPPERY PASTIME

Ida McKinley wasn't always bedridden or drugged up during her stint as first lady. In addition to following her husband's policies and attempting to make an impact on them, she busied herself with a rather curious hobby: She is estimated to have crocheted some 3,500 pairs of house slippers, which she offered to be sold for charity. They were color-coded for the intended wearer—blue for those who'd sided with the North during the Civil War and gray for Southern sympathizers.

Strange Bird

Ida McKinley was one of the richest women ever to have been first lady, having inherited thousands from her father. And she was fond of showing it off—the press took to reporting every gorgeous gown she wore (and there were plenty). But at least one of her fashion choices didn't go over so well. Ida liked to wear an ornamental tuft of feathers called an "aigrette." Unfortunately, this fashion accessory was constructed with feathers from egrets—and it proved so popular, the poor bird became an endangered species. No wonder the Audubon Society issued a formal protest to the first lady.

THE HEALING POWER OF WIDOWHOOD

Though Ida McKinley seems to have been an epileptic, the truth is that we'll never really know for sure. What is certain is that her constant illnesses were accompanied by a need for affirmation, directed particularly at William. As uncomfortable as it is to believe, she displayed a consistent desire to take advantage of her condition to secure a unique and abiding place in her important husband's affairs. Nothing offers more evidence of this than the life she led immediately following the president's assassination. As far as historians can tell from people who knew Ida for the six years after William's death, she never once suffered another seizure.

Alice Lee Roosevelt

1861–1884

It's hard not to look at Alice Lee as a romantic intermezzo for Theodore Roosevelt, a rosy respite from his connection to Edith Kermit Carow. Edith had been a childhood friend of Roosevelt's who evolved over the years into something more. But by the time TR ended up going to Harvard, some nasty disagreement had ended their chances of marriage—at least for the moment. At Harvard, he met Alice, the daughter of a prominent Boston banker and, by all accounts, a stupendous catch. She was spirited, pretty, charming, intelligent. The young TR was smitten. (Edith *who?*) After waiting out her hesitance to marry, TR met Alice at the altar in October of 1880. Two years later, Roosevelt had joined the New York State legislature, beginning a career in politics that would take him to the White House. Alice became pregnant the following year, and it was decided that she should remain at TR's mother's house in New York City to deliver the child. In February of 1884, that's just what she did—and two days after giving birth, she died of Bright's disease. TR was crushed (his beloved mother died on the very same day from typhoid fever) and began a period of escapism that would one day inadvertently take him back to Edith Carow.

21

Edith Kermit
ROOSEVELT

August 6, 1861–

September 30, 1948

MARRIED:

December 2, 1886

PRESIDENTIAL HUSBAND:

Theodore Roosevelt

CHILDREN:

Theodore Jr., Kermit, Ethel Carow, Archibald Bulloch, and Quentin

FIRST LADY:

1901–1909

ASTROLOGICAL SIGN:

Leo

RELIGION:

Episcopalian

SOUND BITE:

"One hates to feel that all one's life is public property."

In 1894, Theodore Roosevelt tinkered with the idea of running for mayor of New York City. He'd run before and lost. Now, turning to his wife, Edith, for advice, he got precisely what he did not want to hear: Alarmed by the lack of

> First Lady Edith Roosevelt had no use for the Eighteenth Amendment, and gladly served cocktails to whomever wanted them.

financial security that came with elective office, she told him frankly that the mayoralty was a bad idea, and he should forget it. Roosevelt took her advice so badly that she promised herself never to voice her opinions on his career again. It was a promise she ended up breaking on more occasions than anyone could possibly count.

Edith learned to worry over money from a very early age. Though born into the privileged society of New York City, her father, Charles Carow, had two outstanding faults: When he wasn't blowing the family's wealth on bad business decisions, he was gulping it down at local taverns. With family life at the Carow residence in constant flux and tension, Edith—the elder of two Carow daughters—took to hanging out with her best friend and classmate Corinne Roosevelt.

She also became pals with Corinne's brother Theodore, developing a rela-

tionship that, as they grew older and maintained a constant and lively correspondence, became increasingly flirtatious. They were both highly educated, enjoyed literate conversation, and moved in the same circles of New York aristocracy. The two thought the world of each other, and there is some evidence that Roosevelt proposed on several occasions. But whether owing to an argument or some other parting of the ways, Theodore ended up proposing in 1880 to someone else—and got an answer in the affirmative. Her name was Alice Lee, and Roosevelt was utterly smitten with her. Cruelly, Edith was the first person outside of the Roosevelt family to hear the news of Theodore's engagement— from Theodore himself, no less—and was crushed.

She remained close to the Roosevelts nevertheless and got accustomed to the idea of having Theodore in her life as merely a dear friend. But everything changed in 1884 when her "dear friend" lost his wife to Bright's disease following childbirth. Theodore—whose mother also died on the very same day—was emotionally destroyed. He turned his new infant daughter, Alice, over to his sister for safekeeping, finished his stint in the New York legislature, and headed west to become a cowpoke. A staunch opponent of second marriages, he parried all inquiries from friends about romance. Significantly, he also avoided his old friend Edith Carow like the plague—terrified, perhaps, of what might transpire should they ever meet again. Despite all his efforts, they did just that—by accident, in September 1885 at the home of Theodore's sister Anna. To no one's surprise, Theodore abruptly ended his ban on courting. He proposed after two months, and they were married in London the following year.

"Edie," as her husband had always called her, now found herself married to one of the most outsized personalities in the country. Roosevelt was a scholar, an author, a politician, an athlete—in short, a man who devoured life's smorgasbord in giant gulps (sometimes literally, a fact to which his portly stomach could attest). Edie offered a counterweight to his beaming, let's-have-at-them buoyancy with patience, discipline, and reserve. Lots of reserve. Many contemporaries, including Theodore, thought her capable of imperiousness, even of withholding affection. Strict and practical, she was the ballast in the relationship— and both of them knew it.

The newlyweds quickly started a family (Edie was pregnant by the time they returned to New York from their European honeymoon). Though Edith ended up bearing five children of her own, she inherited a freebie—Alice—from Theodore's previous marriage. The result was a growing family into which Edie could pour her heart, intelligence, and knack for regimentation. In the meantime, Theodore wrote books and secured a series of respectable offices: Civil Service commissioner, New York City police commissioner, and assistant secretary of the navy. Having become accustomed to her husband's bellicosity and lust for action, she supported his decision to become a volunteer officer in the Spanish-American War, where he became a legend for storming up San Juan Hill.

Roosevelt's heroics bought him a ticket to the governor's mansion in Albany. Things went swimmingly there for Edie, who ran a household as warm and welcoming as it was well ordered and still found time to indulge her love of reading, travel with her husband, and spend plenty of time at Sagamore Hill, their treasured Long Island retreat. In fact, Edie was so pleased with their setup in Albany that she reacted with some alarm to the Republican Party's notion of making Theodore the vice presidential candidate on the McKinley ticket in 1900. After all, why rock the boat when he had a job that was going so well? And what was the big deal with being vice president anyway? Edith helped her husband write a statement that took him out of the race, but events proved much more difficult to manage. The party nominated Roosevelt anyway, and he soon became McKinley's veep.

It wasn't long, of course, before McKinley found himself at the business end of an anarchist's revolver. Upon McKinley's death, Theodore Roosevelt—at forty-two—became the youngest man ever to assume the office of president of the United States. He would dominate the office, and the country, with a wisdom and integrity that seemed well beyond his years. And Edith, true to form, would dominate the White House.

She had her work cut out for her. To begin with, there were the kids—all six of them, including Alice. They were a rambunctious lot, not least because of their father, whose love of frolicking fostered some impertinent stunts (e.g., smuggling a pony into the upper levels of the White House via the elevator). Then there were the finances. Because Theodore had no money sense, Edie had her fingers on the purse strings—she even gave the president an allowance ($20 a day). In addition, the mansion itself was finally getting renovated. Congress gave the administration half a million bucks to cover it, including a wing of offices on the west side. When the president got involved in the details, his wife fended him off, insisting that domestic matters—however large and expensive—were her bailiwick. He dutifully obeyed.

It all made for a lot of work, but Edie was up to it and more. She did all the housekeeping herself, managed an ambitious entertainment schedule, and actively participated in her husband's executive duties. Despite her promise to never involve herself in Theodore's career decisions, she combed the newspapers for him, offered frequent and intelligent advice, and influenced administration appointments by voicing her opinions on applicants. During the Russo-Japanese War, Edie even played a crucial role in bartering the peace that would earn Theodore a Nobel Prize by acting as the unofficial contact with the British diplomat on whom the administration relied for European intelligence. To ease the burden of her growing workload, she hired a secretary, Isabella Hagner, the first government-paid employee in American history to call the first lady "boss."

But if Edie was a commanding presence as first lady, she nevertheless abhorred the attention to her family that such notoriety invited. Nothing was as important to her as the big fat line she drew between her personal and professional lives. She never spoke to the press and went so far as to exercise draconian influence over photo ops—images of the president and his loved ones were carefully staged for newspapers.

Though Theodore eschewed a bid for reelection in 1908, it hardly marked the end of the family's political life. Roosevelt ran for president once more in 1912, and lost—confirming him, finally, as a full-time private citizen, much to Edie's delight. The couple continued to travel widely and, after 1914, crossed the country in public appearances meant to whip up support for getting America into the World War that was devouring Europe. Their wish finally came true in 1917, and both Edie and her husband swelled with pride as all four of their sons donned uniforms for the fight.

Of course, wars have a habit of getting people killed, and the Roosevelts' chest-beating came to an abrupt conclusion when their son Quentin died in the fighting. Edie was devastated, but Theodore was pretty much ruined. His health, already unsteady, became worse, and finally claimed him in January of 1919. His widow went to Europe after the funeral to visit the grave of her son Quentin, then came back to her beloved Sagamore Hill—where, years later, she would receive news of the death of two more sons, Kermit and Theodore, during World War II. It was a lot of death for one life to witness, and Edie began to lose much of the spirit that had made her such an impressive figure. After a prolonged illness, she finally passed away in 1948.

Edie Roosevelt often referred to her charismatic husband as "her fifth boy," and it is in this respect that she made her biggest impact on history. Theodore's vision, courage, boundless adventurism—all the things that made him a leading character in the nation's drama—were given shape and purpose by the wife who grounded him, humbled him, and often even mothered him. If only for this reason, we owe her a great debt of gratitude.

ON HER MAJESTY'S SECRET SERVICE

Edith Roosevelt had a strict moral compass that never varied—and that she was more than willing to apply to others. As first lady, she summoned weekly meetings with fellow women of influence—many of them cabinet wives—who were charged with keeping tabs on society folk who didn't share Edith's passion for proper behavior. From alleged adulteresses to husbands who visited the burlesque to notorious tipplers, Washingtonians with a lax moral code were watched, their scandalous behavior dutifully reported to the first lady—who would dish out the appropriate punishment: being taken off the guest list for White House events.

DRESSING DOWN

Though Edie Roosevelt wasn't the first first lady to chafe at the intrusiveness of the public's curiosity, she certainly was one of the most determined in fighting it. Even fashion was off limits. After having her gown made for Theodore's inaugural ball, she instructed its creator to destroy the garment's design and even the fabric from which it was made, making it impossible for copies to be sold to a public eager to emulate presidential styles.

NO ADMITTANCE

Seminal to the Progressive movement of the turn of the century, Theodore Roosevelt tended to have forward-looking beliefs about women's education and suffrage, as well as the equality of African Americans. He even invited Booker T. Washington to lunch at the White House. But Washington was one of the very few of his race to step into the executive mansion during the Roosevelt years. The first lady, her Progressive politics notwithstanding, took a rather different view toward blacks—and it wasn't all that favorable. In fact, she forbade any black women from coming to a single White House event.

Who Wants a Drink?

Nothing illustrates Edith Roosevelt's bullheadedness better than her stance on Prohibition. While she is known to have been suspicious of alcohol, owing to her father's bibulous behavior, she was the sort of Republican that viewed any government ruling on personal habits as a profoundly inappropriate intrusion on American liberties. Hence, though something of a teetotaler, she positively loathed the ban on alcohol that came with the Eighteenth Amendment. She immediately took to rebelling against it in her own way, throwing parties at Sagamore Hill in which she'd serve cocktails to whomever wanted them. She rarely partook of the stuff herself, but the act of getting other people drunk gave her a high all its own.

FAMILY VALUES

Edith Roosevelt was a lifelong Republican, and nothing—not even family—could dissuade her from her chosen political path. In 1932, her late husband's distant cousin Franklin Delano Roosevelt, a Democrat, ran for president. Many thought that, because he was an in-law, Edith would rally to his support. Nope. An enthusiastic hater of public statements, Edith nevertheless broke her ban on speaking before the press to issue spirited support of Franklin's opponent, Herbert Hoover. It was the first time she'd ever made a speech to the media, and it was made for the sole intention of defeating a member of her family. Edith received a great deal of criticism for her treachery, and was accordingly punished: FDR won the election.

22

Helen Herron
TAFT

June 2, 1861–May 22, 1943

MARRIED:

June 19, 1886

PRESIDENTIAL HUSBAND:

William Howard Taft

CHILDREN:

Robert Alphonso, Helen Herron, and Charles Phelps

FIRST LADY:

1909–1913

ASTROLOGICAL SIGN:

Gemini

RELIGION:

Episcopalian

SOUND BITE:

"Of my own experience I can testify that 'A Hot Time in the Old Town' makes a perfectly good funeral march when reduced to a measure sufficiently lugubrious."

When Helen Herron was seventeen years old, she visited the White House with her family and discovered her life's ambition: to return some day as first lady.

In fact, "Nellie" could've been president herself, had she not lived at a time when such a thing was a pipe dream. To put it simply, this woman was a hotshot. She was born into a huge family in Cincinnati, Ohio, the fourth child of prominent lawyer John Williamson Herron and his wife, Harriet Collins Herron. With money to burn and connections all over the place, the Herrons were in a position to educate their eleven children and set them up for big things. Nellie ended up attending Miami University, where she acquired an undying passion for knowledge and all the doors that it opened. What's more, she excelled at almost everything, a fact that became as much a curse as a virtue when she found herself utterly confused as to which path to follow in life. Should she become a writer? A musician? Activist? Businesswoman? She taught for awhile, worked in her father's law office, and hit the social scene of Cincinnati's aristocracy with a blend of titillation and bemused boredom. Though she got a kick out of raising eyebrows by smoking cigarettes and quaffing beer at local taverns, it seemed more a way of

dissipating boredom than anything else. She was passionate, observant, fiercely independent, and not a little frustrated at a woman's lot in the world.

The wavering evaporated when she met William Howard Taft. He was a large (eventually very large, at over 300 pounds), jolly fellow whose infectious smile and sincerity made everybody around him feel all warm and fuzzy. He was also a darn good lawyer. But to Nellie, Taft's most attractive quality was his devotion to her. Will saw his beloved Nellie for the rising star she was and showered her with syrupy compliments about her wit, intelligence, and wide-ranging abilities. She soon realized that he personified the answer to her ambitions: Rather than chart a course for her own career, she could imprint all her energy and brains onto her sycophant. White House, here we come.

But not so fast. Following their marriage in 1886, Nellie's husband displayed a galling capacity to follow his own ideas about what he should do for a living. If elective office and political power were the Holy Grail for Mrs. Taft, Will had his heart set on the bench. To his glee and her chagrin, he was appointed in 1887 to the superior court of Ohio. Three years later, President Benjamin Harrison made him solicitor general of the United States. Then it was back to Ohio in 1892, where Will hitched a ride on the federal circuit. The jolly jurist was living a

Surf's up! Helen Herron Taft was the first (and maybe only) first lady to ride the waves in Hawaii.

dream, but his wife just stewed, fretting over what she viewed as the "narrowing effects of the bench." To Nellie, the judge's robe looked more like a straitjacket, and she never missed an opportunity to nudge Will toward grander ambitions.

Something grander came—not from Will, of course, but from President William McKinley, who hit Taft in 1900 with a proposition that made Nellie's heart race with joy. Will was asked to lead a commission to the Philippines charged with establishing a new civilian government. For Mrs. Taft, adventure beckoned at long last, and the family (they had three children now) embarked upon an odyssey to the distant and exotic East.

Grand? Nothing could be grander. Now Nellie Taft was truly in her element, and she would shine. After stopping long enough in the Hawaiian Islands for

Nellie to give surfing a try, the Tafts arrived in the Philippines, where a military occupation by American forces since the conclusion of the Spanish-American War had created a cowed and suspicious native populace. The Tafts set about undoing the damage. While Will waded through the daunting business of creating civilian rule (a task he did ably enough to be made governor-general), his wife set about making herself into the great white Queen Mother of her new Filipino charges. She took Spanish lessons (Nellie was a natural at foreign languages), learned a few local dances, implemented health-care modernizations, threw lively entertainments, and journeyed into remote island regions like a conquistador of old. She wasn't just tireless and inquisitive—she was also entirely without racism (remarkable for the age), imaginative, and an invaluable aid to her husband, whose administration became enormously popular.

Taft took his Filipino mission seriously enough to turn down two offers of a seat on the Supreme Court back in the States. But in 1903 came an offer from Washington that neither he nor his wife could refuse: President Theodore Roosevelt wanted his buddy Will to be his secretary of war. Though it was hard for Nellie to give up her gilded existence in Manila's splendiferous Malacanang Palace, the cabinet appointment "was in line with the kind of work I wanted my husband to do," she later wrote, "the kind of career I wanted for him and expected him to have." Having cut her political teeth in the Philippines, Nellie was now the fully vested partner in Taft's future—a role she would play to the hilt from then on.

With her mission clearly laid out, Nellie infiltrated capital society to get her own take on its labyrinthine relationships, continued to browbeat Will into giving up his confounded preoccupation with the Supreme Court, and began pushing him for a presidential run in 1908. She'd come as far as the cabinet, dammit all, and she wasn't going to jettison that White House dream now for anything—not even her husband's dreams or his outspoken distaste for high-level politics. Taft became, in effect, the congenial front for his wife's ambition, and his reliance on her brains and skills occasioned the inevitable result: he surrendered. Besides, Nellie's co-conspirator in the effort to get her husband psyched about the White House was none other than the indefatigable Theodore Roosevelt. It was a tag team that Will was powerless to resist. To his surprise, he won comfortably against his presidential opponent William Jennings Bryan.

And so began the Taft administration—the Nellie Taft administration. Sure, Will was president. This was a guy with heavyweight credentials under his belt (no pun intended), a genuine darling of the Republican Party who'd gotten where he was through no small amount of cleverness and education. And, despite his hand-wringing over the dirty confrontations of the political arena, Taft had real leadership talent. But he continued to look over at the Supreme Court building with big puppy-dog eyes, his imagination conjuring images of black robes and weighty legal matters. What was he doing in the White House?

Oh yeah, his wife. It wasn't that Nellie Taft didn't believe in her husband's generosity, expansive mind, or executive ability. It's just that she had too much going on upstairs not to become a huge part of the excitement that was the presidency. That energetic intellectual who'd once dreamed of stepping into the White House as its occupant had arrived, and she felt the need to control, influence, shape. Congressmen coming to the White House soon discovered that it was impossible to speak with the president without his wife racing over to interject herself into the discussion. Nellie forcefully advised Will on treaty negotiations, cabinet appointments, tariff issues, and pretty much everything else that crossed his desk. Taft openly joked that he was only a co-president and, in truth, treasured his wife's inclusion in the decision-making process. Others, however, were less enamored of "Nervous Nellie's" meddling. The mansion's staff considered her a tyrant and began showing their displeasure with resignations. It didn't help that she replaced the White House steward with a housekeeper named Elizabeth Jaffray, a fellow pedant who drove the hired help like a chain gang. Then there were the liveried footmen, who drew criticism from people who smelled aristocratic excess. Washingtonians, whether they loved her or hated her, had to admit that the first lady was a doer.

Suddenly, tragically, it all came to an abrupt halt. Less than three months into the administration, Nellie suffered a stroke. The president, utterly disconsolate, took time away from his responsibilities to sit by Nellie's bedside and read to her, joke with her, coax that towering personality of hers back into the light. Though it took over a year, the first lady came back to herself. She retained a slight speech impediment that would cause her some embarrassment, but Nellie returned to the role she adored so passionately. Just in time to see it threatened by the resurgence of her husband's erstwhile friend.

Theodore Roosevelt was back—and determined to regain the office of the presidency. Though Will had soldiered through a successful four years, Roosevelt thought them a betrayal of the Progressive agenda. Their battle, which divided the Republicans, made it a cinch for Democratic candidate Woodrow Wilson to defeat them both. A sickened Nellie wrote TR off as a traitor and dismissed her husband as a bumbling jackass who hadn't seen it coming. (Harumph. Men!) She lingered overlong in the White House before departing amidst the hushed anticipation of hostile servants who kept glancing at clocks, a pained diva whose time in paradise had come to an end—and much too soon.

Nellie may have been bitter, but her husband was born anew. After teaching at Yale for a time, Will got his precious Supreme Court appointment in 1921. It was the zenith of his public career and allowed him to go with a smile when he finally passed in 1930. Nellie outlived him by thirteen years, the highlights of which were annual trips to Europe—the scholarly adventurer never left her. As for her years in the White House, she has few peers. Though a little power mad, this was a woman of unique influence and character. Frustrated with the female status quo, she made efforts to champion women's suffrage (though, interestingly, she didn't believe women fit for public office). A consummate student of the world, she never slackened in her devotion to reading everything from poetry to geology books. And her conspicuous lack of prejudice found expression on numerous occasions, from her work with prominent Jewish families to create the Cincinnati Symphony Orchestra to her efforts in the White House on behalf of impoverished immigrants at a time when Americans were clamoring for an end to the influx of "filthy undesirables." Heck, Nellie was even the first presidential wife to get her memoirs published (in 1914). Julia Tyler may have coined the phrase "Mrs. Presidentress." But Nellie Taft personified it.

SLEEPING BEAUTY

Nellie Taft advised her husband on all manner of things, playing an integral role in his success (or, for that matter, failure) as a public figure. But of all the services she provided for the advancement of William Taft's career, few were as important as her efforts to keep him awake. Whether because of his enormous girth or because he simply liked to doze, Will was constantly falling asleep—at meetings, funerals, public receptions, you name it. It may sound trivial, but this was no small feat on the part of Nellie. Consider what she was up against: One night, in the Philippines, Taft actually slept like a baby through the entire destructive duration of a Pacific typhoon.

Shotgun!

On March 4, 1909, outgoing president Theodore Roosevelt made an announcement: he was breaking tradition, deciding not to ride back to the White House with his successor Taft in the inaugural parade. True to form, Nellie Taft's mind was immediately one step ahead of everyone else's—the breach of protocol offered her a window, and she jumped right through it. No first lady had ever ridden in the procession with her newly inaugurated husband, but that didn't stop Nellie—indeed, it thrilled her. "Of course, there was objection," she wrote in her memoirs, "but I had my way."

DRIVING AMBITION

Upon becoming first lady, one of Nellie Taft's chief concerns was presidential transportation: Carriages simply would not do any longer. She petitioned Congress for an automobile appropriation, and their less-than-generous response led her to make a groundbreaking decision. Nellie approached the Pierce-Arrow company with a request to give the administration a discount on their cars—a request they gave in to with the proviso that they be allowed to advertise the fact that they were the official automobile of the White House. No first lady before Nellie would've dared go there, but Mrs. Taft wanted those beautiful rides. She gave in, affording Pierce-Arrow the right to ensnare buyers with copy that advertised their executive connections.

WHERE'S THE BEEF?

The first lady's stroke in 1909 posed a thorny problem for the Taft administration. How was such a public woman's sudden convalescence to be dealt with? The president had no intention of disclosing the truth to the public, both for the sake of his marriage's privacy and the sake of the American people, who might have been alarmed by such a development. The solution was terribly imperfect at best, but largely effective: Taft and his staff told the curious that Nellie was exhausted by all her efforts and was taking time to recuperate. But as the months dragged on, Nellie's situation became harder and harder to conceal, and her stroke became an open secret. Nevertheless, it remained a source of embarrassment both to her and to her husband, who took steps—many of which were a bit absurd—to remove her from the mainstream. Nothing illustrates this more clearly than the fact that, during much of her recovery, Nellie—who insisted on overseeing White House dinner parties herself, whatever her condition—took her meals near the mansion's pantry. There, behind a screen, she ate her dinner while listening to the conversation beyond, conveniently hidden from the other diners to ease their digestion.

EXECUTIVE BRANCHES

Nellie Taft's most enduring legacy is also her most beautiful. As first lady, Nellie was determined to remake Washington's Potomac Park. Cherry trees, whose splendid blossoms had so dazzled her in Asia, were brought from all over the capital area to the city for planting. There weren't enough, however, until an old acquaintance decided to help out. Yukio Ozaki, mayor of Tokyo, got word of Mrs. Taft's landscaping operation and offered some assistance in honor of the visit the Tafts had made to Japan during their travels. He arranged for a shipment of cherry saplings to be sent, nearly all of which died. Undeterred, he got another batch under way. They fared much better, as everyone who visits Washington today can see for themselves.

23

Ellen Axson

WILSON

May 15, 1860–August 6, 1914

MARRIED:

June 24, 1885

PRESIDENTIAL HUSBAND:

Woodrow Wilson

CHILDREN:

Margaret Woodrow, Jessie Woodrow, and Eleanor Randolph

FIRST LADY:

1913–1914

ASTROLOGICAL SIGN:

Taurus

RELIGION:

Presbyterian

SOUND BITE:

"Three daughters take more time than three canvases" (on her struggle to balance art with motherhood).

When newly elected President Woodrow Wilson gave his inaugural speech in 1913, there was one woman in the audience who wasn't satisfied with her seat. Shortly after Wilson began, she got up and stood right before the podium, intent on hearing every word. She was his wife, Ellen Wilson, and she had already heard every word several times (Woodrow had practiced the speech on her), but seeing him give it as chief executive was an opportunity she wasn't going to miss. And to everybody who saw her there beaming up at him, one thing was overwhelmingly clear: She loved the guy deeply.

Ellen first met Woodrow Wilson when she was just a little tyke growing up in Georgia, the eldest of four children born to Margaret Jane Hoyt Axson and her husband, the Reverend Samuel Edward Axson. But it wasn't until 1883 that the sparks began to fly. By then, Ellen had become a stunning and utterly brilliant young woman with a love of literature, foreign languages, and art, an accomplished intellectual with a fiercely independent streak. Woodrow, a lawyer and fellow Southerner who'd come to hear Ellen's father preach, was smitten by her immediately. The feeling soon became mutual, and they were engaged five months later.

Wilson performed no small feat in getting Ellen to accept his proposal, for

she had a reputation as an avowed cynic when it came to marriage. But there were greater challenges, as well: The Reverend Axson had become terribly sick, and Ellen felt duty-bound to look after him until his death in May of 1884. Then, with the money she inherited, Ellen decided to make a dream come true. She took off to New York City to study art and give flight to her bohemian urges. She painted, taught, mixed with the creative crowd, and began to develop real commercial talent as an artist. They were the last months of her life in which she lived completely for herself.

As profound as Ellen's love was for art, she had developed another love, one that would shape the remainder of her life. Woodrow Wilson had thrilled to his fiancée's experiences in New York and continued his studies as a graduate student at Johns Hopkins. After they married in the summer of 1885, it was off to

For many years, Ellen Axson Wilson slept with a revolver under her pillow.

Bryn Mawr, where Woodrow had been offered a teaching position. While there, they set about creating the pattern that would continue in their relationship for years. Mrs. Wilson put her enormous intellectual faculties at the service of her professor-husband, poring over texts on everything from German to political philosophy, turning herself into a kind of full-time teacher's aide for Woodrow. She began to raise their daughters, with the help of a nurse, and continued to devote time to her beloved painting. But it was as the scholarly counterpart to her husband that Ellen truly excelled. Together they made a brainy match. With his wife's support, Woodrow went on to secure another posting, at Wesleyan College in Connecticut, and, then in 1890, at Princeton.

New Jersey was the beginning of big things for the Wilson family. As her husband's exploding schedule of teaching and writing began to take its toll on his nerves, Ellen made things easier on him by becoming a model homemaker. She took care of their daughters, continued to offer her intellectual services to Woodrow, and entertained in a home that had a revolving door for friends and family. There seemed no end to Ellen Wilson's list of talents and interests—she even found time to act upon her progressive politics by volunteering for a women's employment agency. Things got more hectic for her when Woodrow became president of Princeton in 1902, forcing her into the limelight as never before—and forcing her to keep an ever-watchful eye on her husband's erratic health.

Wilson had a bad habit of working too hard. In the summer of 1910, after years of being a devoted scholar and academician, he decided to get into a line of work that wasn't nearly as strenuous: politics. He won the race that year for governor of New Jersey and found himself given a chance to act upon all his book learning, rather than just passing it on to the next generation. Ellen's profound influence on his ideas and lifestyle continued—in fact, she instigated the meeting that would change her husband's career forever. In 1911, Ellen arranged a dinner engagement with William Jennings Bryan, a prominent Democrat who was keeping an eye on Wilson's impressive legislative programs in the Garden State. He and Wilson got along famously, developing a relationship that would get Woodrow the Democratic nomination for president in 1912.

Wilson's frail constitution remained an issue, however, and Ellen couldn't help wondering if her husband was up to the job. But other instincts won out: He was the smartest man in the country, as far as she was concerned, and who was she to stand in the way of greatness? Besides, she adored him. And he wanted to be president.

When Wilson won the election, Ellen resolved to do her part to preserve his stamina and sanity. In addition to lending her considerable mind to the creation of his speeches and agendas, she made sure he got enough rest and relaxation—two words that often seemed absent from her husband's otherwise expansive vocabulary. She also entertained a great deal, with the eager help of her three daughters, earning a reputation as an elegant hostess. But it was in her efforts on behalf of the downtrodden that Ellen truly shined. In addition to bettering the lot of female employees of the government and getting involved with the fight against child labor, Mrs. Wilson became the first first lady to tour the slums of Washington. Appalled by what she saw there, Ellen played a leading role in drafting the Alley Dwelling Bill, which sought to better the conditions of "model houses" in which so many of the capital's black citizens suffered. It was soon dubbed "Mrs. Wilson's bill."

The year 1913 kept getting busier. After spending some happy months at an artists' colony in New Hampshire, Ellen arranged for the White House wedding of daughter Jessie in November and then exercised her artistic muscles by planning an overhaul of the mansion's gardens. It was a lot to handle for a woman who continued to keep an eye out on her overworked husband. In fact, Ellen had been paying so much attention to Woodrow's well-being that she'd overlooked her own. A nasty fall in March of 1914 put an end to that. Upon examining her injury and performing minor surgery, the doctors found more than they bargained for—namely, tuberculosis of the kidneys and Bright's disease.

Ellen lived long enough to see two final, important tasks through. Her daughter Eleanor was married in May, an event too dear to the first lady's heart not to plan, despite her plummeting health. But Ellen also urged the president to get Congress to pass the housing bill that had been named for her. They did it just in time for her to learn of it—a fitting send-off for such an extraordinarily public-minded woman.

Better Than a Security Blanket

One of Ellen Axson's favorite pastimes while growing up in Georgia was shooting. Apparently, she never gave up the fondness for firearms—years later, as an adult, she began keeping a revolver under her pillow at night while she slept.

SURROGATE ESCORT

By the time she met Woodrow Wilson, Ellen was an avowed free spirit who believed in the independence of women and who leaned toward a certain skepticism about marriage. Though utterly taken by the ardent Wilson and happy at her engagement to him, she was a little reluctant to kiss her single days goodbye. While studying art in New York City, Ellen was delighted to discover how perfectly normal it seemed for women to go out on the town unescorted—a concept that had yet to make it to her Southern home. To the enterprising men of Gotham, Ellen seemed eminently available—a notion she only fostered by wearing Woodrow's engagement ring on her forefinger. One of those men was Arthur Goodrich, an intelligent New England lad who accompanied Ellen to museums, the theater, and all the other places that made New York City so tantalizing. Unfortunately, he was soon tantalized by Ellen, who never bothered mentioning that she was already engaged. Interestingly, she mentioned Goodrich again and again in her correspondence to Woodrow, who finally put his foot down and told her to stop leading the guy on. So Ellen did—and after a few awkward confrontations, the whole matter was finally put to rest.

PECK-ADILLO

Woodrow Wilson had a legendary libido. Though his critics, particularly Republicans, dismissed him as a prim and proper bookworm, he had a passionate side that found expression in seeking the company of pretty, admiring women. He was also quite frank in his correspondence with Ellen about sex and his explosive anticipation of it. But in at least one instance, Wilson's ardor ended up exploding in a very different way. His close friendship with Bermuda socialite Mary Peck in the years leading up to 1910 became the subject of scandalous rumors. Historians remain divided over whether Woodrow and Mrs. Peck acted on their obvious attraction; but Wilson himself later admitted that his attentions to Mary had been "a passage of folly and gross impertinence." As for Ellen, she claimed that the Peck to-do had been the only time in their marriage when Woodrow made her unhappy. And, though she never admitted to any knowledge of sexual indiscretions between the two, she is known to have burned some correspondence from the period to avoid its being used by future scandalmongers.

24

Edith Bolling
WILSON

October 15, 1872–

December 28, 1961

MARRIED:

December 18, 1915

PRESIDENTIAL HUSBAND:

Woodrow Wilson

CHILDREN:

None

FIRST LADY:

1915–1921

ASTROLOGICAL SIGN:

Libra

RELIGION:

Episcopalian

SOUND BITE:

"I am not thinking of the country now, I am thinking of my husband."

In 1912, Edith Bolling Galt was so politically clueless that she was unaware of the names of the candidates vying for president that year. It wasn't long, however, before she learned a great deal about politics—and became the most powerful woman in the country.

Nothing about the girl's Virginia upbringing was auspicious. Edith found herself the seventh in a line of eleven children, and as likely to get a good education as she was a large bedroom to herself. She learned what she could in dribs and drabs, and pined for something greater. So, at nineteen, she moved to Washington, where she was to meet the man who bought her a ticket out of boredom and poverty.

His name was Norman Galt, and he fell under Edith's spell almost immediately. The magic wasn't exactly working for her, however, and she felt strained to summon any feelings about Norman that went beyond good friendship. Nevertheless, a marriage of convenience was better than no marriage at all (at least as far as Edith was concerned), and she consented to marry Norman after a four-year courtship. "Convenient" the marriage definitely was, for Norman soon became the sole owner of his family's Washington jewelry store, affording Edith the sort of lifestyle she'd always dreamt of. Tragedy struck when their only child died just days after a difficult birth that left Edith unable to bear

children the rest of her life. But aside from this, life as Mrs. Galt was a long party: dazzling jewelry, the latest fashions, trips to Europe.

Her sugar daddy gave up the ghost in 1908, but now all the candy belonged to Edith—and she proved herself a capable businesswoman by running the jewelry store at least as well as her late husband had. When management issues got sticky, she sold the jewelry shop to its employees and resumed her career as a

Edith Wilson brought a flock of sheep onto the White House lawns— and auctioned off their wool on behalf of the Red Cross.

full-time woman of leisure. Though liberated by wealth, Edith remained in the following years the retired widow of a tradesman, a life that—for all its theatergoing and socializing—put her in a markedly separate aristocracy from the political one that governed in Washington. It was a distinction that suited her just fine; for Edith seemed utterly devoid of causes, party loyalty, or any of the other claptrap that made those public service types such an infernal bore.

But fate intervened to change all that. Edith's good friend Alice Gertrude Gordon had fallen in love with none other than Admiral Cary Grayson, the naval doctor who now served as President Wilson's aide. Through Grayson, Edith got to know and befriend Helen Bones, who'd been acting as surrogate White House hostess since the tragic death of First Lady Ellen Wilson in 1914. In March of 1915, while visiting with Mrs. Bones for tea in the White House, of all places, Edith stepped out of the mansion's elevator and nearly ran into . . . the president of the United States. Wilson agreed to join their little tea party and proceeded to hit it off with Mrs. Galt. Indeed, the president laughed on several occasions, something that nobody had seen him do since the horror of Ellen's death. The chief executive seemed to come alive again.

Which was a good thing, as far as his closest intimates were concerned. Woodrow had been moping around the White House like a wet noodle on barbiturates since Ellen's funeral. Indeed, there were some who thought his very life depended on finding romance. Notoriously sexual, Woodrow Wilson without a female preoccupation was like a car running on fumes. Now, seemingly overnight, he had a new obsession.

And he acted quickly. Very quickly. He proposed to Edith within two months, for crying out loud. Edith tried to compensate for his outrageous lack of caution by putting him off, the sort of tactic that only made a dog like Wilson pant more lasciviously. Her hesitations were nothing if not solidly grounded. Sure, she was taken by this brilliant, powerful, eloquent, randy man. But she barely knew the guy, a fact she insisted on reminding him of. Besides, how would it look for the president of the United States to remarry so quickly after his beloved wife's death? Ellen's tombstone had yet to be erected! She ended up giving in anyway, of course, and they agreed to a secret engagement in June.

Secret, perhaps, but an open secret—especially to those who spent a lot of time with Wilson, like his advisers. The president's daughters may have been giddy at the color in his cheeks and the skip in his step, but his political circle started seeing red flags all over the place. An engagement this soon spelled political disaster. Knowing Woodrow's runaway carnal proclivities and the impossibility of derailing them, the cabinet—in league with prominent Democrats—hatched a scheme to break up the happy couple so as to avoid scandalizing the public before the 1916 election. The president was informed that his old flame Mrs. Peck had been making waves, threatening to publish incriminating correspondence if the president went ahead with his engagement to Edith. It was a reprehensible falsehood, but Wilson bought it. Ashamed and terrified, he exposed the whole Peck thing to his beloved and offered to cancel the engagement.

The plan backfired. Not only did Edith forgive her beloved and see through the ruse, she decided to move up the formal announcement of their engagement, much to Wilson's delight. In October of 1915, the American public was notified of its president's betrothal to Mrs. Galt. The couple sealed the deal the following December.

There were plenty of people who made the politicos' nightmare come true, ranting about the impropriety of the president's swift remarriage. But the first couple didn't seem to notice. Hopelessly in love with each other, they commenced with a White House relationship that was as close as any ever got. Edith did everything with her husband—ate, slept, motored about in the executive car, read, played golf, you name it. They were like honeymooners whose honeymoon never ended. Along the way, Edith received a top-notch, extensive education in statesmanship and the hurly-burly of politics. The president shared all of his responsibilities with her, from domestic legislation to dispatches from foreign dignitaries. Edith began acting upon her education, advising Woodrow on virtually every document that crossed his desk. She spoke out against the women suffragists who pestered her husband everywhere he went, dismissing them as "disgusting." And Woodrow, happy to have a bedmate once again, a voluptuous and intelligent woman with whom he could share his burdens and dreams, just encouraged her. Before long, she was actually decoding State Department messages for him from nations embroiled in the Great War—a war that, in April of 1917, finally ensnared the United States.

Edith responded to World War I with a patriot's heart. She clamped down on the family finances, oversaw a strict cutback in White House domestic expenditures, and even bought sheep for the mansion's lawn whose wool was auctioned on behalf of the Red Cross. She also made sure her husband (still the workaholic) got enough rest and relaxation (a billiard table was installed for his diversion). But the war was nothing for her and Woodrow compared to the fight that would come afterward.

In December of 1918, Mr. and Mrs. Wilson traveled to what remained of Europe to take part in the Versailles peace negotiations. The president was making a personal appearance to present his idea for a League of Nations, an organization for international cooperation that was designed to avoid the catastrophe that the world had just experienced. It was a quintessential Wilsonian vision, and Europe ate it up. His own country, however, started choking on it. To help America—and, in particular, a hostile Senate—wash it down, the president and his wife embarked upon an insanely ambitious tour of the country, making speeches at every stop in support of the treaty. Predictably, Wilson insisted on playing the tireless workaholic, committed to making his dream come true at any cost. That cost, to Edith's alarm, was his health, which had always been an issue and that now became acute.

He suffered a stroke. Then, after cutting the whistle-stop tour short and racing back to the White House, he suffered another. What happened next remains one of the most extraordinary developments in American history. While her husband convalesced in the old Lincoln bed, Edith Wilson forbade anyone from seeing him. Not even Vice President Thomas Marshall was admitted. Nobody involved in the business of government was allowed to see the president's real condition or to discuss vital matters with him. For all they knew, he was already dead. Edith, by sheer force of will, guarded his bedroom door like Cerberus and made herself the sole conduit between her ill husband and the officials who reported to him. She had always been a woman with a single cause, her husband, and she now threw herself into that cause with astonishing determination, relying on the crash course in politics that he had given her to decide, for herself, what was important for him to see and what was not. As the League treaty got stuck in the Senate, cabinet members and others in Congress appealed to Edith to get her husband to compromise on some of the treaty's issues in order to get it passed. But Wilson retained enough vigor to reject the idea outright, and Edith supported him.

With half of Washington decrying the first lady's stewardship as "petticoat government" and a "regency," and the president unable to act personally on behalf of his beloved League idea, the treaty was ultimately killed in the Senate. For the Wilsons, it was a disaster. Woodrow made a steady recovery and somehow started to flirt with the notion of a third term—an idea even Edith couldn't take seriously. The situation helped Republican Warren Harding capture the 1920 election.

The couple stayed on in Washington, and Edith got to enjoy her husband's company for a few more years. He died on February 3, 1924. Widowed for the second time, Edith went on to publish an autobiography in 1939, reigned as a very popular Queen Mother during Franklin Roosevelt's administration, and came close to getting married again—to Bernard Baruch, an old crony of Wilson's. But most of her remaining years were dedicated to helping others honor Woodrow's memory. The professor never stopped being her great cause.

THE PRINCESS

Edith Bolling Galt Wilson was a descendant of Pocahantas. It was an ancestry that Edith was proud of and wished to show off. During World War I, the navy asked her to provide names for many of the ships being launched for the war effort, a responsibility she took very seriously. She became the first first lady to

christen a ship bound for active duty—the Quistconck. Virtually every name she chose from then on was Native American in origin.

The Pocahantas connection became particularly handy in Europe. While visiting there with her husband for the Versailles treaty negotiations after the war, Edith was snubbed by a prominent French duchess who didn't think that an American first lady was worthy of being welcomed as fellow aristocracy. Upon hearing that Mrs. Wilson was a descendant of the great American princess Pocahantas, however, she did an about-face. Edith was cordially invited to the duchess's home and was received with all the etiquette appropriate to a royal visit.

Bitter Dregs

Edith's Native American ancestry was a well-known fact. But to one concerned citizen, it produced a rather thorny conundrum. The administration received a letter reminding them of the old law forbidding the possession of liquor by American Indians. The writer went on to insist that, as the first lady had been seen imbibing alcohol in public at social events, a warrant for her arrest be issued and acted upon forthwith.

For the record, the president did not act on the suggestion.

OVER THE TOP

As first lady during the First World War, Edith Wilson insisted on doing her part—and then some. While most Americans worried about whether their sons and husbands would come home in one piece, Mrs. Wilson took it upon herself to fret over the soldiers' chastity. She penned an open letter to the women of Europe, pleading with them to prevent American doughboys from giving in to the temptations that came with "the unnatural life of the camp." We can only assume the soldiers themselves wished that their first lady hadn't been so concerned.

ADDING INJURY TO INSULT

Edith Wilson was a rather provincial woman with almost no formal education to speak of—and, despite this, the only first lady in history to achieve something like executive power. Her "regency" during Woodrow's illness was unprecedented, and it scared the bejeebers out of plenty of people—for good reason. Though she had a quick mind and a great deal of character, her notions of government had come solely as the result of being Wilson's wife and confidante. These aren't exactly presidential credentials, and Edith's decision-making processes at times could be pretty screwed up.

Take the Craufurd-Stuart case, for instance. Charles Craufurd-Stuart was the attaché to British Ambassador Lord Grey and something of a wag. In the months following the formal announcement of President Wilson's engagement to Edith Galt, stories started circulating like wildfire about the couple's premarital sexual relations, a topic that had become popular ever since Woodrow and Edith were seen spending so much time together. "What did Mrs. Galt do when the president asked her to marry him?" went one joke. "Fall out of bed." This particular little crack was a favorite of Craufurd-Stuart's, who liked to tell it at dinner parties.

That the witty Brit's impertinence made it back to the White House is hardly surprising. But it did much more than merely irritate the first lady. It steered the course of government legislation. When Lord Grey offered his invaluable assistance in helping the Wilsons to get the League treaty passed by the Senate, Edith refused to let him see her husband. In fact, she—and, hence, the White House— refused even to acknowledge Grey, an ugly first in the course of British-American relations. And why? Because that irreverent little guttersnipe Craufurd-Stuart was Grey's attaché. Until Grey fired him, Edith insisted, the president would remain off-limits to the British ambassador. Grey, appalled at the pettiness of the situation, went so far as to demote Craufurd-Stuart, but it wasn't enough for the first lady, who seemed not to realize how her shallow instincts were killing the best chance for her husband's League idea to get by the Senate. Exasperated and incredulous, Lord Grey finally gave up and went home.

25

Florence Kling
HARDING

August 15, 1860–
November 21, 1924

MARRIED:

March 1880 (to Henry De Wolfe);
July 8, 1891 (to Warren Harding)

PRESIDENTIAL HUSBAND:

Warren G. Harding

CHILDREN:

Eugene Marshall De Wolfe

FIRST LADY:

1921–1923

ASTROLOGICAL SIGN:

Leo

RELIGION:

Methodist

SOUND BITE:

"Well, Warren Harding, I have got you the presidency. What are you going to do with it?"

It is ironic that the first presidential election in which women could vote in the United States sent a shameless adulterer to the White House. But perhaps the greatest irony of all is that Warren Harding couldn't possibly have become president without his incomparable wife, whose ambition, savvy, and outspokenness were proof positive that American women had truly come into their own.

Florence Kling was born in Marion, Ohio, the eldest of three children to Amos and Louisa Kling. Amos, one of the town's richest businessmen, was an insufferable disciplinarian who wasn't above whipping his children with a switch when they chafed against his authority—which is something that Florence did often. Much to her father's wrathful displeasure, she developed an independent streak early on in life, a personality trait that got only stronger after she went to study music at the Cincinnati Conservatory. Upon returning, she took to staying out late with the wrong crowd and getting locked out of the house by angry Amos.

It wasn't a touching father-daughter relationship, to be sure. But of all the things that got her father to foaming at the mouth, nothing was worse than Florence's habit of choosing the wrong man. In 1880, she foolishly eloped with a local inebriate named Henry De Wolfe—and, six months later, bore him a son.

Needless to say, Amos was furious about his daughter's irresponsibility, especially when she came back home with little Eugene Marshall in her arms after being abandoned by her husband. Amos flatly refused to admit them, and Florence was forced to support herself and her child by giving piano lessons. By 1885, she'd filed for separation from that dreamboat De Wolfe, and her father—convinced that Florence had learned her lesson—agreed to adopt her child as his own in exchange for washing his hands of Florence's financial security. Enticed by the prospect of freedom, she took her father's offer and brought the whole nasty chapter to an end in 1886 by finalizing a divorce.

Florence Harding was the first first lady to fly in an airplane—and she insisted on a female pilot.

It wasn't long, however, before Florence was again exhibiting her questionable taste in men. Warren Harding, publisher of the *Marion Star*, was easygoing and handsome. That was enough for Florence, who proceeded to chase after his affections with alarming determination. She was five years older than he and hardly as attractive as the usual sort of women with whom Harding typically socialized. Florence kept at him, however, and Warren (perhaps tempted by her father's wealth) eventually gave in. As Harding's own father once admitted, it was a good thing that Warren wasn't a girl: he'd always be pregnant because he could never say no.

The wedding in July 1891 was held sans the father of the bride, who, predictably, had formed a poor opinion of the weak-willed newspaperman his daughter insisted on marrying. Amos not only boycotted the ceremony, he threatened those who went with a severing of loans from his bank. The nuptials went ahead despite Mr. Kling's punitive measures, commencing what would become one of the strangest marriages in American political history.

Warren soon began doubting his choice to marry. Indomitable, suspicious, and manipulative, the new Mrs. Harding had been giving her father no end of trouble her entire life. Now she gave it to her husband. Between the responsibilities of running the *Star* and the ceaseless nagging by his bride, Warren—never the steadiest of men—suffered a nervous breakdown. While he recuperated at the Kellogg Sanitarium in Battle Creek, Michigan, Florence did what came naturally to her: she meddled. Specifically, in her husband's newspaper business. And the results were positively astonishing.

Few women of the age embraced the new feminism as sincerely as Florence did. She'd always been independent, but now, in her thirties, she drew on the tension that had shaped her youth to forge a personality based on a driving need to see things done her way. The *Marion Star* was soon done her way. Updated equipment was installed, lapsed accounts were pushed into the black, coverage was dramatically expanded, circulation skyrocketed. Florence even hired a woman reporter, something that was virtually unheard of at the time. The newspaper became a raging success, thanks to the tireless Mrs. Harding, who now became known as "the Duchess" to all, including Warren, who jumped when she said to. Now it was time to remake that husband of hers.

Warren had developed a habit of escaping his domineering wife by traveling to Republican events, and he soon got a reputation as a better-than-average speaker and loyal party member. By 1899 he had made enough chums to win a seat in the Ohio Senate. Three years later he became lieutenant governor. The shiftless newspaper publisher was going places, thanks to his campaign manager. The Duchess organized everything, from Warren's speeches to his photo ops. Florence's experience at the *Star* had made a peerless businesswoman out of her, and it was all to her husband's benefit.

He knew it, of course. Harding had a face and manner that put people at ease and drew them in, but he had no head whatsoever for the managerial side of things. That was the Duchess's province. But as Warren rose to the giddy heights of public affirmation, he responded to the influence accorded him by giving in to temptation. In 1905, Florence suffered the first in a series of kidney malfunctions that would dog her for the rest of her life. She spent months recovering from the surgery, during which time her husband expressed his sympathy by starting an affair with one of Florence's best friends, Carrie Phillips. The relationship would endure for years, much to Florence's ignorance. But in 1911, perhaps as a result of intercepting a love letter, the Duchess found out about Warren's infidelity. The resulting melee affirmed the parameters of what had already been something of a business relationship: Florence, after threatening divorce, realized how much she'd already invested in her boob of a husband, while

Warren couldn't imagine carrying on in any political capacity without her direction. They reached an understanding, though the Duchess—justifiably pained—forever remained on the lookout for Warren's playthings.

Harding had lost a bid for Ohio governor in 1910, but had gone on to win a seat in the United States Senate in 1914. In Washington, while he maintained a sleazy affair with Carrie Phillips even as he began a sleazier one with a woman named Nan Britton, the Duchess continued to shape her husband's policies and career as she took a shine to life in the capital. As a senator's wife, her ambitions had been realized, a pleasure made possible by her continuing ignorance of Warren's philandering. Indeed, she looked with some trepidation at the Republican Party's hope of replacing Woodrow Wilson with her husband in 1920. Anyone could see by looking at the bedraggled Wilson that the presidency was a death sentence. Besides, Warren had a bad heart. The office would surely kill him.

But Florence Harding couldn't say "no" to the White House. Encouraged by so many Republican strategists, the Duchess accompanied her famous husband to the party convention in Chicago and truly shined. No candidate's wife had ever played such a pivotal role in a campaign. Florence worked her cozy press connections to the hilt, holding forth with unprecedented candor about everything from her husband's views to her own suffragist beliefs. Gauche, dowdy, wearing a pince-nez, and given to an excess of makeup that made her look rather absurd at times, Florence hated being photographed. She posed for the cameras anyway and soon had the journalists eating out of her hand. She was earthy, folksy, a paragon of small-town America who shied from no question and offered herself as is. With her dashing husband's optimism about returning the country to "normalcy," it was irresistible. The Hardings beat the pants off of Democratic opponent James Cox.

With women being allowed to vote in 1920 for the first time, America was expecting an assertive first lady. They got her in spades. The Duchess took on the cause of war veterans, whom she endearingly referred to as "my boys." She visited them in hospitals, intervened on behalf of their benefits and treatment, and began holding annual White House garden parties at which they were the honored guests. And, above all, she became the government's most visible champion of women's causes. Florence held press conferences specifically for women reporters (with whom she felt a close bond), worked to improve the lot of working women, and even lent her public support to the National Women's Party, a controversial organization that pushed for an equal rights amendment. She became the first first lady to fly—which she insisted on doing with a female pilot. And she went so far as to organize a White House women's tennis championship. No doubt about it, this was one feminist who walked the walk.

And her husband? "Better ask the Duchess" became his mantra. And therein lies the problem. For all her chutzpah and shrewdness, Florence wasn't any better at choosing talent than her beleaguered husband. While Warren played poker, slept with his mistresses, and fretted over his profound lack of executive credentials, his wife peopled the administration with unscrupulous cronies who used their appointments to fill their pockets. Popularly known as the "Ohio Gang," they sank the Harding presidency into a slough of corruption.

The crisis came to an end for the Hardings tragically and abruptly. In the midst of a cross-country tour in 1923, the president suffered heart trouble in California and died. "No one can hurt you now" is what Florence was heard murmuring to his corpse as he lay in state at the White House. She was right. Harding died a popular man, untainted by the scandal and sublime carelessness that would define his presidency. As for the Duchess, the woman mostly responsible for it, she would also escape public outrage. She died the following year.

The final irony of Florence Harding is this: Having come after a long and distinguished line of extraordinary first ladies who loved to flirt with the emerging influence of women, she crossed the line into real equality, living and embodying what other women activists only dreamt of. She was difficult and abrasive, true, but a remarkable woman by any measure. Nevertheless, the principal object of her efforts—her hapless, unimaginative, fearful, and dishonest husband—must stand as an abject failure. Warren Harding was a disaster as president. At least in part, we have the Duchess to thank for that.

CLOCK WATCHER

Florence and Warren Harding's wedding began at 8:00 p.m. on July 8, 1891, and ended precisely a half-hour later. The final moments of the ceremony were hastened so as to conclude exactly at that time. Why? Florence had a superstition that no momentous event should end in the midst of the minute hand's journey from six to twelve.

MADAME MARCIA

"I do not intend to permit him to run." Such was Florence Harding's initial response to a reporter's query about her husband's presidential aspirations. The Duchess was worried about the health of Warren's heart, and she didn't think the White House was a good place to test its limits. Yet soon enough she would change her tune, and not just because there were plenty of persuasive people in the Republican Party who swayed her mind. Florence paid a visit in 1920 to Madame Marcia, the capital's most celebrated seeress (the same soothsayer, incidentally, who had predicted to Edith Wilson that she would become first lady). Marcia told Florence that her husband would become president. This, combined with the party's support for her husband, was enough to convince the Duchess that she had to allow Warren to go for it.

Carrie-ing On

Warren Harding's torrid affair with Carrie Phillips was an ongoing source of irritation to the Duchess. Though she was under no illusions about her husband's dalliances, she certainly had no desire to be reminded of them. Carrie in particular was persona non grata, especially during the 1920 presidential race. Her occasional appearances at the Hardings' home in Marion during Warren's front-porch campaign only fueled more rumors about the candidate's dissolute lifestyle, and Florence once actually hurled a piano stool at the woman to chase her out. The Republican Party was just as worried about Carrie—they ended up paying her enough money to take a nice, long vacation abroad, where she'd be out of reach for questioning by nosy Democrats. Problem solved.

WETTING THE WHITE HOUSE WHISTLE

Prohibition had gone into effect by the time the Harding administration began, meaning that all official entertainments at the mansion were dry. The unofficial ones, however, were quite another story. A passionate poker player, President Harding routinely organized games with the Ohio Gang on the second floor of the White House. The Duchess was usually present, and sometimes she'd play a hand or two. But her primary responsibility was serving drinks to the players. Playing poker without liquor simply wasn't an option, not even for the president. Florence's source for the alcohol was one Jess Smith, a friend of the Hardings who got around the Justice Department's ban on booze by acquiring a "B" license for its purchase, meaning it was for medical purposes. It wasn't known how Smith had finagled the license, and neither Warren nor the Duchess really wanted to find out. Unfortunately, Smith was eventually outed as one of the most notorious bootleggers in Washington, requiring the Hardings to distance themselves from him. He ended up committing suicide.

UP IN SMOKE

Neither the president nor his determined wife were properly minding the store during the Harding years, leaving plenty of dishonest folks—many of whom were part of the infamous Ohio Gang—to rob the country blind. Foremost among the scandals that tainted the administration was Teapot Dome, in which navy oil reserves in the west were taken over by the secretary of the interior to be leased out to private businesses for a fat profit. By 1923, Mr. and Mrs. Harding were becoming aware of the scale of their carelessness, a fact that only worsened their respective health issues. Once her husband was dead, Florence became obsessed with expunging the record for the sake of posterity. Before she died in 1924, the Duchess systematically burned every government receipt, document, memo, or letter that in any way could impugn Warren's leadership. It was entirely illegal and not entirely successful. Most of the dirty truths would end up getting exposed anyway, damning Warren Harding to the bottom of the presidential popularity list.

WASTING WARREN

That Harding escaped the full public revelation of his incompetence seemed a little *too* convenient to many at the time. Did the Duchess poison him in an effort to spare his reputation? Many have speculated on that, perhaps because she devoted so much time after his demise erasing as much evidence as she could. We shall probably never know—though she did forbid an autopsy of the corpse.

26

Grace COOLIDGE

January 3, 1879–July 8, 1957	
MARRIED:	
October 4, 1905	
PRESIDENTIAL HUSBAND:	
Calvin Coolidge	
CHILDREN:	
John and Calvin Jr.	
FIRST LADY:	
1923–1929	
ASTROLOGICAL SIGN:	
Capricorn	
RELIGION:	
Congregationalist	
SOUND BITE:	
"I am rather proud of the fact that after nearly a quarter of a century of marriage, my husband feels free to make his decisions and act upon them without consulting me or giving me advance information concerning them."	

alvin Coolidge's proposal to Grace Goodhue was nothing if not direct. "I'm going to be married to you" is all he said. It may not have been the most romantic way to begin a marriage. But it was classic Calvin: terse, emotionless, and commanding. It was also a moment that set the tone of their life together: Grace, one of the most personable and beloved of all first ladies, was a woman who got used to being told what to do by a husband who had none of her charisma, zest for life, or regard for people.

Grace first spied her future husband through the window of a house in Northampton, Massachusetts. He was shaving in his underwear with a hat perched upon his head to keep the hair out of his face, a sight that sent Grace into hysterics. Amused by her reaction, Calvin Coolidge decided to court her, and they fell in love almost immediately.

They were both native Vermonters. Aside from that, Grace and Calvin had nothing in common. She had grown up in Burlington, Vermont, the daughter of an engineer who inspected steamships on Lake Champlain. An only child raised with good old-fashioned Puritan values, Grace had pluck, and plenty of it. She attended the University of Vermont, became an immensely popular social but-

terfly, and even founded the school's chapter of the Pi Beta Phi sorority. She was beautiful, interesting, inquisitive, and sincere. She also had a desire to help people, a passion that drew her to Northampton after graduation. There, she enrolled in the Clarke School to become a teacher of the deaf, beginning a vocation for which she seemed ideally suited and that would last her entire life.

Calvin Coolidge, a lawyer, had also come to Massachusetts to start a career. A veritable caricature of the laconic New Englander, he had a gift for concise speech, when he bothered to speak at all. But beneath his painfully subdued exterior hummed a vigorous political ambition. He and Grace made an unlikely couple in the extreme, but seemed hopelessly hooked on each other, and married in the fall of 1905.

The first time Grace Goodhue laid eyes on Calvin Coolidge, it was through a bathroom window—and her future husband was naked except for his underwear and hat.

If Calvin believed that people were ready for his brand of understated leadership, he was right. Beginning with the Northampton City Council in 1898, he rapidly rose through politics. But it was his career and his alone. Grace had nothing to do with it. In his own quiet, imperturbable way, the stoic politician enforced upon the Coolidge family his brand of conservative regimentation. Women were for washing dishes and raising children, and that was that. While Calvin was off doing his government thing, Grace became reconciled to perpetual domesticity. She brought up their two sons, John and Calvin, virtually on her own. Calvin's parsimoniousness made socializing impossible. When she wasn't looking after the boys, she was making clothes for them or darning her husband's socks. Calvin shared nothing of his political world with her, nor did he ask her opinion on matters of government.

But Grace's world was about to blow wide open. Calvin had cut his teeth as mayor of Northampton, state senator, lieutenant governor, and, after 1918, governor. Though Grace had been made eastern regional president of her fellow Pi Phis in 1915, she was still a kept housewife with virtually no experience as hostess or political spouse. But in 1920, Calvin was elected vice president on the

Harding ticket—and even a legendary penny-pincher like Calvin could see the futility of keeping his family up in Northampton.

Not that his penny-pinching came to an end, of course. The Coolidges took a suite in Washington's Willard Hotel rather than rent a house. But there was no hiding Grace anymore—she was second lady now, and that meant that she had to become a hostess. With the help of Lois Marshall, wife of the outgoing vice president, Mrs. Coolidge boned up on all the entertaining and society details that she'd been kept from for years. And she was apparently a quick study, because she became an overnight sensation. Enthusiastic and genuine, the perfect foil to her dour husband, Grace made everyone want to know her and became a darling of the newspapers from the moment she appeared in a gorgeous red dress at the inaugural gala. Even press-savvy Florence Harding was jealous.

And none of it was lost on the vice president. Calvin may have been a repressed, unromantic stick-in-the-mud, but he had always relied on the love and support of his wife. Now he began to rely on her in other ways. Though he continued to play alpha male to the hilt, dictating what Grace could and could not do and say, Calvin cultivated her as the attractive half of their political coin. Or, more precisely, she cultivated herself, and Calvin let her. She was now appearing with him in public all the time, and for good reason: The people ate her up like candy. Proud of his wife's athletic physique, he made a conspicuous exception to his cheapskate spending habits by lavishing expensive gowns on her. Stylish, sexy, and gregarious, Grace attracted attention wherever she went.

Few vice presidents' wives have ever been as popular as Grace, and the country had already gotten to know her by the time Warren Harding's death sent her to the White House. As president, Calvin continued to exert an absurd degree of influence over her. He insisted on personally approving every menu and guest list, prowled the kitchen and pantry to make sure nothing was being wasted, and habitually scheduled events for her without even consulting her, forcing the first lady to have a hat and gloves ready at all times for unforeseen outings. But Mrs. Coolidge remained as buoyant as ever—indeed, the White House staff nicknamed her "Sunny." The entertainment schedule in the Coolidge White House was unprecedented in its scale—Grace and Calvin threw more teas, dinners, parties, and receptions than anybody before them.

But there were no interviews. Not a one. Though ubiquitous and adored, the first lady did not offer opinions on current issues. That had always been her husband's department, and nothing had changed. Her popularity, however, remained indispensable to the administration and played a profound role in getting Calvin elected to his first full term in 1924.

The victory was bittersweet. In July of that year, Calvin Jr. had died an agonizing and senseless death from a blister he'd contracted on the White House courts that developed into blood poisoning. Grace recovered and maintained her astounding public persona throughout the rest of her husband's passive presidency, but a sense of mortality hung over the Coolidges. Calvin, having developed heart trouble, announced in 1927 that he would not run again the following year.

The country was sorry to see Grace go and proceeded to make retirement back in Northampton a little uncomfortable by crowding outside the Coolidge house to ogle. Calvin, tired of having to look at tourists every time he went out on the porch to sit in his rocker, bought a larger place with plenty of lawn as buffer. He could afford it, too, with all the writing he was doing for magazines and newspapers. When he died in 1933, he left Grace a pretty enormous chunk of change—and her freedom. "Nobody is going to believe how I miss being told what to do," said the widow Coolidge. But she soon learned how to tell herself what to do. She went back to devoting her time to the deaf, and became president of the board of the Clarke School. Her leisure time was just as empowering. After a lifetime of being forbidden by her husband to dance, to ride in a car, to go horseback riding, or even to bob her hair, Grace started doing all the things she'd always wanted to do. Back when she was first lady, Charles Lindbergh invited her to go up in his plane. "I promised my husband I would never fly," she sheepishly replied. Years after Calvin's death, she decided to take a trip to Europe—by plane.

Calvin must've rolled over in his grave.

SLUGGER

Grace was athletic all her life. She took long, vigorous walks almost every day, had one hell of a throwing arm, and took to swimming and canoeing with ease.

While fishing in the Black Hills with Calvin, the first lady was reported by the press as having a better technique than her husband (she caught a trout on her first try). Chief among her sporting passions, however, was baseball. She taught her sons how to play when they were children and developed a lifelong love of the game. The Red Sox were her team, and sometimes they even let her sit in the dugout during games. Once, during the early fifties, Grace wasn't able to make her usual appearance at the World Series because of health problems. The president of the American League sent her flowers.

Baby? What Baby?

For reasons that must be apparent by now, President Coolidge was dubbed "Silent Cal" by the American public. Grace, for all her popularity, was just as tight-lipped, not only about her husband's opinions (as well as her own) but also about their private lives. The Coolidges' uncommunicativeness could sometimes have bizarre consequences. In 1925, rumors began circulating that the first lady was pregnant. Nothing could have been further from the truth. But while most first couples would have taken the time to issue press statements refuting the notion, Mr. and Mrs. Coolidge remained quiet. The gossip continued, and soon the White House was inundated with diapers and baby toys from an adoring (and mistaken) public. The packages kept arriving for roughly another nine months, by which time it was obvious that no presidential papoose was on the way.

CRYING FOWL

In her later years, Grace Coolidge was asked by a reporter about the nature of her early romance with Calvin. In a rare moment of candor, she blurted, "Have you ever met my husband?" Sullen and withholding, Calvin Coolidge may have been the last of the lukewarm lovers. But as biographer Carl Sferrazza Anthony reminds us, he had a sense of humor and wasn't above being teased about it. He and Grace once visited a chicken farm in Maryland, where the first lady witnessed a rooster copulating with a hen. Upon asking the farmer if the rooster did that often, Grace was informed that he did it several times a day. "Tell that to the president," she responded, and the farmer did just that. "To the same hen?" was Calvin's reply. "No, Mr. President," said the red-faced farmer. "Tell that to Mrs. Coolidge," said the president.

LONG LEGS AND BLACK HILLS

Grace's Secret Service escort during most of her term as first lady was a young and handsome (and married) fellow named Jim Haley. He followed her wherever she went, and it became a common sight to see the agent in Washington trying to keep up with the athletic first lady on her regular walks. When people began gossiping that the dashing Haley's connection to Grace was more than just professional, the president reacted with his usual irritation. But things came to a head in the summer of 1927 when the Coolidges and company repaired to the Black Hills of South Dakota for a presidential vacation. One morning, Grace told Calvin that she was heading out for a hike into the woods with her escort Haley that wouldn't take them more than an hour.

It took five hours. By the time the two breathless hikers returned, the president was fit to be tied, having spent all morning worrying about her safety. He gave Grace a stern talking-to in private, then decided to have Haley transferred from his post as guardian of the first lady. The incident had all the makings of a tabloid nightmare, and the press acted predictably, inferring that a jealous president had suspected the worst and gone after the young stud who'd spent way too much time in the wilds of South Dakota with his wife. Though Calvin's chief concern during Grace's absence had been that she was missing or wounded, his dismissal of Haley only fanned the flames of public speculation. We'll certainly never know for sure what happened out there in the Black Hills. But Grace, for one, thought that Haley's transfer was unjust.

PIONEER

Grace Coolidge racked up a few intriguing firsts as a first lady. She was the first to bring a radio into the White House (which she listened to constantly), the first to receive an honorary doctorate (from Boston University), and the first to appear in a "talkie"—after leaving the White House, she appeared in a film intended to drum up contributions to the Christmas Seals for victims of tuberculosis. Interestingly, she was also the first first lady to give cigarette smoking a try, though she only indulged in private.

27

Lou Henry
HOOVER

March 29, 1874–January 7, 1944

MARRIED:

February 10, 1899

PRESIDENTIAL HUSBAND:

Herbert Hoover

CHILDREN:

Herbert Clark Jr. and Allan Henry

FIRST LADY:

1929–1933

ASTROLOGICAL SIGN:

Aries

RELIGION:

Episcopalian, then Quaker

SOUND BITE:

"I enjoy campaigning because my husband makes all the speeches and I receive the roses."

Without a doubt, Lou Hoover was the worldliest first lady in American history. A globetrotting scholar who loved roughing it in the outdoors almost as much as she loved bettering the lot of her fellow human beings, she

> During the Boxer Rebellion, Lou Hoover transported supplies to the front lines via bicycle. The work was so dangerous, her obituary once appeared in a Peking newspaper.

was a paragon of empowered womanhood. Every voter had just cause to expect great things of her and her equally gifted husband, Herbert Hoover. And great things would doubtless have happened, had the Hoovers been fortunate enough to be in power at an ordinary time in the nation's history. Instead, they found themselves confronting the gravest American crisis since the Civil War—a crisis too daunting and pervasive for even a remarkable woman like Lou Hoover to overcome.

Lou Henry was a native Iowan whose family moved to California when she was eleven years old. Her wealthy father, Charles Delano Henry, was an avid outdoorsman who passed his love of camping, riding, and fishing on to his two daughters. After graduating from high school, Lou studied to be a teacher. But

observing the natural world remained her greatest passion, and she went to Stanford to study geology.

Women simply didn't go into rocks back then, and Lou found herself the only woman in her classes. But of all the men who surrounded her, one stood out. Fellow geology student Herbert Hoover had also come to California from Iowa and shared Lou's love of the wilderness. "Bert" couldn't believe his luck: Who'd have thought he would find a tall, beautiful, intellectually dynamic woman who loved fingering shale and wielding a pickax as much as he did? After agreeing to an informal engagement, Bert took off to pursue his mining career in Australia while Lou finished up her studies at Stanford.

While in Australia, Bert was hired by the Chinese Engineering and Mining Company. It was the opportunity of a lifetime, and he excitedly wired Lou in Stanford to officially become his bride and accompany him to the Celestial Empire. He then returned to California, where the two were married by a Spanish priest (they couldn't find a Quaker to do the job), and Mr. and Mrs. Hoover sailed for Asia.

Once in Tientsin, the Hoovers were in their element. It wasn't just that they were prospecting and mining, doing the sort of thing that fascinated them (for lots of money). They were also ensconced in a deliciously exotic culture, something that set both of their studious minds on fire. Lou in particular drank it all in. She'd always had a knack for languages and had begun to learn Chinese on the long journey by boat from California. Now she began to take lessons as often as possible, developing a fluency in the tongue that was extremely rare among Westerners. She accompanied her husband on long journeys into the surrounding hills, often by mule, braving bandits and extreme weather, and helped Bert gather and translate Chinese mining laws for codification. The challenges were many—physical, intellectual, cultural—and Lou savored every minute of it.

Unfortunately, their Asian adventure was dramatically cut short by the Boxer Rebellion, in which throngs of antiforeign Chinese took up arms against Western settlements like the one in Tientsin. The Hoovers were lucky to escape with their lives, but the taste for travel remained. From their new home in London, they continued to rack up the miles in business jaunts that took them around the world: Japan, Burma, Australia, Ceylon, Russia. The birth of sons in

1903 and 1907 hardly slowed them down (indeed, Herbert Jr. circumnavigated the globe an astounding two times before he was a year old). The Hoovers acclimated themselves to the native situation wherever they went and earned a reputation for mining developments that were as conscious of workers' needs as they were efficient and lucrative. They even found time to translate an obscure text from the 1500s, Agricola's *De re Metallica*, an arduous chore of translation and lab work that took five years.

World War I changed everything in 1914. Having amassed an enormous fortune, Bert started spending much of it to help beleaguered Americans get the heck out of a Europe that was blowing itself to bits. He continued his Herculean and selfless task in Belgium, where he devoted himself to helping countless war refugees. Lou, who had been her husband's full partner in their extensive business ventures, now played just as large a role in his relief efforts. She worked in London on behalf of British women workers and went back to the States to whip up American dollars for war relief. When the United States entered the conflict in 1917, the Hoovers just kept going. Bert was made the nation's food administrator, charged with organizing conservation for the war effort, while Lou became his poster girl, imploring her fellow women to run a lean household and to plant "war gardens" to grow their own produce.

The Hoovers had become the dynamic duo of public activism, a tireless couple of civic-minded eggheads who seemed to scream "Engage! Get involved!" wherever they went. And they had gotten too good at their vocation to let the conclusion of the war bring it to an end. Bert went back across the ocean with President Wilson to help patch up Europe, and Lou—while overseeing the construction of their Stanford dream house in California—also helped her husband's continuing relief efforts. By 1921, Bert's extraordinary organizational skills had endeared him to virtually everyone in power, and President Warren Harding made him commerce secretary.

Now Lou was a cabinet wife, and she was determined not to squander the opportunity. She was a liberated woman with one hell of a head on her shoulders, a wife who'd known nothing but equity and partnership in her marriage and who envisioned a nation of women who . . . well, were like her. During the war, she had volunteered as the leader of a Girl Scout troop, beginning a connection to the Girl

Scouts that would endure until her death. The organization was seen by Lou as the ideal training camp for young women who could become fully vested, informed members of a voting populace. The Girl Scouts, however, were only the beginning. Lou acted on her love of physical activity by becoming the only woman officer of the National Amateur Athletic Federation and, in 1923, sponsoring the creation of its women's division. She spoke at every opportunity of the need for women to become more involved in politics and in the workplace. Dynamic, confident, composed, and eloquent, she became an inspiration to her gender.

So who wouldn't want to send these folks to the White House? The Hoovers had gotten rich through hard work and sheer brainpower, had spent a lot of their earnings on unimpeachable causes, and were as interesting and educated as they were admirable. Bert's presidential victory in 1928 seemed like the beginning of big things—not least because this brilliant and benevolent man was bringing a truly admirable woman with him into the administration. Lou immediately began putting her own indelible stamp on the office of first lady, doing away with a longtime custom she considered superfluous: calling on the long list of other political households to leave a card in person or to visit briefly. Entertaining, on the other hand, became a Hoover hallmark, and absolutely nothing was considered too extravagant. Lou insisted on the finest food for her guests, of which there were plenty—the president and his wife almost never dined alone, keeping the White House servants and kitchen staff on their toes every day. The Hoovers had class, to be sure, and the first lady played the part, dressing in expensive gowns that were tastefully understated and refurbishing parts of the White House with the artifacts acquired during a life of travel.

But class didn't count for much after the stock market crash of October 1929. The nation soon found itself sunk in a Great Depression, with unemployment rising at a dizzying rate and communities of indigents gathering on the outskirts of every city. Lou was devastated by the calamity and drew on her old sense of responsibility to do things. She issued a constant stream of radio messages and press releases imploring Americans to help each other and to not lose confidence or hope. She began complementing her chic wardrobe with dresses made from homegrown cotton to promote American agriculture and industry. And, most remarkably, she answered nearly every piece of mail that was sent to her by ordinary people across the country who were in need of help, writing checks both large and small to individuals for whom she thought it was possible to make a difference. The president knew virtually nothing about his wife's extraordinarily ambitious charity campaign, and little wonder—he had his own problems. The man who'd been able to make such a huge impact on countless people's lives now found himself helpless to stem the tide of national disintegration. His obsession and frustration over the issue drove Lou to create a refuge for them in the Blue Ridge Mountains of Virginia, an idyllic collection of cabins dubbed Camp Rapidan. There the president and first lady were able to commune with the natural world they continued to adore while the rest of the country slid slowly down the drain.

Few Americans knew about the Hoovers' extensive charitable efforts during the Depression because they insisted on making them a private affair. And while Bert and Lou scored an "A" in the individual-good-works department, they flunked the official course altogether, failing to come up with a style of leadership or legislative agenda that was equal to the enormous task before them. The result was sad and predictable: America got sick to death of the Hoovers. In 1932 they lost the White House to a couple of radicals named Roosevelt whose ambitious ideas, so Bert and Lou believed, would ruin the country. Events would prove the Hoovers wrong.

Nevertheless, they were now free to do the things at which they actually excelled. Lou threw herself into campus life at Stanford, holding court with her husband at their beautifully modern new spread in Palo Alto. In 1935, Lou was rewarded for her continuing efforts on behalf of the Girl Scouts by being elected president of their national council. When World War II broke out in Europe, Bert stood up once again on behalf of the victimized by setting up shop in New York to organize relief for refugees. Lou accompanied him and, true to form, rose to the occasion in her own way, leading an effort on behalf of the Salvation Army to provide clothes for a million European refugees. Ultimately, demands like this one made her a casualty of war. In January of 1944, she died from a heart attack in New York, her reputation still tainted somewhat by her husband's disastrously ineffective term in office. But to many American women, the cosmopolitan Lou Hoover would be missed—some 200 Girl Scouts attended her funeral.

CLOSE TO THE ACTION

During the Boxer Rebellion in 1900, Lou Hoover gave a marvelous display of her bravery and defiant spirit. As hostile Chinese forces surrounded the foreign settlement in Tientsin, Bert insisted that his wife get to safety and stay there. Not likely. She learned how to handle a revolver, helped organize defenses right along with the men, and brought tea and other supplies to the front lines by bicycle. One trip almost cost her her life when the tire was flattened by a stray bullet. Even their house was a dangerous place. Lou was playing solitaire one day when a shell burst through a window in the adjoining room and nearly blew the staircase apart. When a group of witnesses rushed in to check on her safety, they saw her calmly sitting at the table with her cards. She then asked them to join her for tea.

It is hardly surprising, considering the circumstances, that Lou's obituary appeared in a Peking newspaper. Upon reading it, she was thrilled to discover that the editors had devoted three columns to her. "I was never so proud in my life," she quipped.

Staff Infection

Toward the end of her stint as first lady, Lou Hoover gave her replacement, Eleanor Roosevelt, a tour of the White House. But when Mrs. Roosevelt asked for a look at the kitchens, Lou insisted that the housekeeper would be better suited to give that part of the tour. "I never go into the kitchens," said she to Eleanor.

Bert and Lou may have been publicly minded, but they were also class conscious. Nobody knew this better than the White House staff, who quickly found themselves having to cope with the peculiarities of Hoover hauteur. The president insisted on distancing himself from hired help and actually required that they "disappear" upon hearing his approach in the mansion. Lou was hardly more proletarian. By the time their four years were up, the Hoovers had dined alone on only a handful of occasions. The first lady was constantly inviting guests to her soirees at the last minute, requiring the frustrated and exhausted staff to magically produce more food in record time—and, of course, only the finest comestibles would do. Butlers were reminded to blend into the background and were reprimanded if they so much as made a noise while clearing dishes after a course. Obsessed with efficiency and intent on interacting with the servants as little as possible, Lou went so far as to devise a series of hand signals for giving instructions (for instance, touching her glasses meant that it was time to clear the table).

COLOR BARRIER

The Hoover presidency was nothing if not unpopular. But the greatest scandal to break out during those four years had nothing to do with the Great Depression. On June 12, 1929, the first lady invited a select group of political wives to a tea—"select" because they had to be rather open-minded. For joining them that afternoon was a congressman's wife whose very presence in the White House could cause irreparable harm. She was Mrs. DePriest, wife of Illinois Republican Oscar DePriest. And she was black. Having been screened by Lou beforehand for their lack of racism, none of the white women present on June 12 cared very much about Mrs. DePriest's color. It was a White House tea like any other, and the African American in their presence was just another guest like the rest of them. Other parties, however, weren't nearly as unfazed. Newspapers throughout the South lambasted the first lady, accusing her of stupidly hurting her husband's political reputation by crossing the color line. But Bert couldn't care less—the following week, he lunched in the White House with a black scholar from Tuskegee College.

28

Eleanor

ROOSEVELT

October 11, 1884–
November 7, 1962

MARRIED:

March 17, 1905

PRESIDENTIAL HUSBAND:

Franklin Delano Roosevelt

CHILDREN:

Anna Eleanor, James, Franklin Jr., Elliott, Franklin Delano Jr., and John Aspinwall

FIRST LADY:

1933–1945

ASTROLOGICAL SIGN:

Libra

RELIGION:

Episcopalian

SOUND BITE:

"If I feel depressed, I go to work."

In 1940, Franklin Delano Roosevelt was nominated by his fellow Democrats for an unprecedented third term as president. But the convention in Chicago had descended into chaos. Though the party was united behind the idea of keeping

> **Eleanor Roosevelt wasn't interested in elaborate menus or fancy foods. While first lady, she once served hot dogs to the King and Queen of England.**

FDR in the White House, they weren't nearly as enthusiastic about his insistence on having Henry Wallace as his running mate. To them, the president had gotten a little too high on his horse and was treating the Democratic Party like a big rubber stamp to approve his edicts. FDR refused to budge on the Wallace issue, however. And to win the battle of wills with the conventioneers in Chicago, he pulled out his biggest gun: his wife, Eleanor.

The first lady flew to New York City, picked up her son Franklin Jr., flew on to Chicago, gave a heroic speech to the Democratic Party that convinced them to rally around the president's decision, and flew back to her Val-Kill cottage in New York State. Mission accomplished. It had taken less than a day. On the trip to Chicago, she even took over the controls of the plane for a while, just for the thrill of it.

The adventure was pure Eleanor Roosevelt and an indication of the

astounding prominence to which she'd risen. And yet, this was the woman who, just eight years before, had dreaded the prospect of being first lady. When she heard that Franklin won the presidential election in 1932, she quietly wept in private, mortified that she was about to lose her identity.

She need never have worried. If there was one thing that Eleanor Roosevelt always had in abundance, it was identity.

Her mother would've disagreed. Anna Hall Roosevelt was one of the beautiful people of New York aristocracy who did little besides look pretty at society events and shower attention on her two sons. She nicknamed Eleanor "Granny," convinced that her frumpy daughter with the odd teeth would never amount to much. Eleanor's father, Elliott, adored his only daughter, whom he affectionately dubbed his "own little Nell." But he adored liquor as much as he did his little Nell, eventually driving his famous brother Theodore to consign him to a sanitarium. By the time Eleanor was ten, both her parents and one brother, Ellie, were dead, leaving her and her remaining brother Hall in the care of an imperious grandmother.

At fifteen, Eleanor was a depressed and insecure girl who had known almost nothing beyond tragedy and disapproval. That would change with the help of an extraordinary woman named Marie Souvestre, in whose English boarding school Eleanor was enrolled in 1899. Suddenly, the ugly duckling was everybody's favorite student. She excelled at her studies, became a star at field hockey, and learned to see things in a whole new light with the encouragement of Mademoiselle Souvestre, a brilliant and caring feminist who drove her girls to seize the day and do some good in the world.

But what would that "good" entail? After returning to the United States and making her 1902 debut in New York society, Eleanor was expected by her family and class to become a wife and mother. Her nascent sense of mission inspired her to take classes and do volunteer work, but eligible bachelors were knocking at her door, none more loudly than distant cousin Franklin Delano Roosevelt. Like Eleanor, FDR was a well-bred New Yorker with a sense of public duty, and the two began to hit it off. In 1903 she accepted his proposal of marriage, and they made it official in 1905 at a ceremony in which Theodore Roosevelt himself gave away the bride.

In 1910, FDR won a seat in the state senate. Eleanor always had a genuine love of people, and she now relied on it to make connections, both social and political, and to become an accomplished hostess. Her public persona continued to blossom after 1913, when Franklin was made President Wilson's assistant secretary of the navy. Washington was a thrill a minute for her—she called on other political wives every day, continued to educate herself on political subjects, and spent nearly every evening socializing with fellow pols and intellectuals. The more she did, the more energy she seemed to have. After America entered World War I, she entertained troops, volunteered for the Red Cross, and still managed to devote plenty of time to her five children. Her schedule was crazy with obligations—and she had never been happier in her life.

Franklin was pretty busy himself—with Eleanor's social secretary, Lucy Mercer. In 1918, Eleanor came across one of their love letters, adding herself to the droves of Washingtonians who already knew about the affair. Hurt and humiliated, she confronted her husband with divorce. Franklin didn't like the idea for two reasons: one, it would seriously jeopardize the political career he was building; and two, his mother would cut him off without a penny if he so much as thought about it. With divorce out of the question, he promised never to see Lucy again. But the Roosevelt marriage had turned a corner, and any romantic connection they shared seemed to dissolve.

In many ways, it was the rebirth of Eleanor Roosevelt. From then on, her life would take an increasingly independent course. The Roosevelts remained devoted to each other and continued to lend support to each other's causes. But it was understood now that Eleanor's life was truly her own, a fact that allowed her to become one of the most powerful—and controversial—women of the century.

The decade that witnessed Eleanor's transformation into an independent political heavyweight began, ironically, with a tragedy that brought her closer to her husband. In 1921, Franklin contracted the polio that would rob him of the full use of his legs. Though encouraged by his mother to give up public life and become a full-time fop at the family's Hyde Park estate, FDR decided to recover, make the best of things, and plan on a return to politics. In the meantime, Eleanor would be his surrogate. She had already acquired a reputation as an intelligent and devoted pol, throwing her energies into such organizations as the League of Women Voters and the Foreign Policy Association. Her friends included feminist educator Marion Dickerman, suffragist Carrie Chapman Catt, reformer Esther Lape, and other prominent female activists. And she had gotten a crash course in national campaigning during Franklin's unsuccessful bid for vice president in 1920. Now, with the encouragement of Franklin and his adviser Louis Howe, she would keep the Roosevelt name alive by fighting for the issues that they—and she—believed in: labor concerns, public housing, relief for the unemployed, education, and protection of women's rights.

An indefatigable campaigner, Eleanor edited newspapers and newsletters, took a teaching job in New York City, raised funds, and hired a coach to improve her public speaking. It wasn't long before she became prominent in the Women's Division of the New York State Democratic Committee. Sure, it was all on behalf of her husband—but Eleanor was having a blast. And it all worked. By 1928, her efforts had made her a national figure. Franklin reaped the benefits by becoming governor of New York in 1929.

As New York State's first lady, Eleanor found a serene sense of fulfillment. She had achieved her lifelong goal of making a difference, Franklin was back in action, and their partnership was becoming a force to be reckoned with. From his wheelchair in the governor's mansion, FDR completed his wife's political education by making her his eyes and ears. She toured the state on inspections for him, becoming adept at spying trouble spots and earning the respect of people who knew a formidable activist when they saw one. Eleanor combined her savvy and determination with a gift for really communicating with everyone, high and low, powerful and powerless. Her confidence and ability increasing with every day, she earned hordes of admirers—and just as many angry detractors, shocked at her radical liberalism and independence of action. FDR just shrugged them off, visibly taking pride in the invaluable compatriot he came to refer to as "my missus." The Franklin-Eleanor modus operandi had fully taken shape.

And it would take them far. Granted, going for the White House was Franklin's idea. For Eleanor, becoming first lady meant drowning in a flood of tea parties and losing her ability to freely act on behalf of her beloved causes. But she had helped her husband build a momentum that wasn't easy to stop, and the presidency was the obvious terminal. Besides, she had no one to blame but herself—Eleanor's popularity and connections were instrumental in FDR's victory over Herbert Hoover in 1932.

The new first lady quickly got over her anxieties, realizing that she was now in a position to do more than ever. Eleanor continued to champion women's issues, writing a manifesto entitled *It's Up to the Women!* In newspaper and radio interviews, she preached the gospel of New Deal legislation and pressured her husband to adopt her daring solutions to labor disputes. She boldly fought against racism with the National Association for the Advancement of Colored People, answered piles of mail from concerned citizens across the country, oversaw the creation of a National Youth Administration to help young people find work, and, most of all, traveled. From the dingiest transient community to the remotest soup kitchen, the first lady met with average Americans, shook hands, made contacts, and reported it all back to the president. No first lady had ever possessed such an aversion to staying put, and Americans from coast to coast got used to the idea of seeing the ubiquitous Eleanor popping up out of nowhere to check out the local scene.

The big scene, however, was turning ugly. With war raging in Europe and Asia, FDR created the Office of Civilian Defense in the fall of 1941 as a precautionary measure. Eleanor was asked to direct many of its programs, but her insistence on using the department to advance her welfare agendas got her in hot water with Congress, and she had to quit. It was a sign of things to come—World War II was consuming FDR's time and energies at the expense of the New Deal, and Eleanor was increasingly finding herself at a loss for direction. Things just got worse after the Japanese bombed Pearl Harbor in December, forcing America into a war that, as Eleanor saw it, might jeopardize all the social programs that she and Franklin had sponsored since coming to the White House in 1933. The president excluded her from his top secret war councils, but Eleanor was far from being excluded from the war effort. In 1942 she made an incredibly popular tour of England, dropping in at army bases and airplane factories. She made a repeat performance in 1943 in the Pacific, going into harm's way and cheering the wounded wherever she showed up.

It all came to an abrupt halt in April of 1945 when, in the company of Lucy Mercer, Franklin died in Warm Springs, Georgia. Eleanor did her best to advise incoming president Harry Truman and declared "The story is over." Not likely.

Truman sent her to the new United Nations as America's delegate, where she played a crucial role in getting that body to adopt a Universal Declaration of Human Rights. In addition to publishing her memoirs, she never stopped working for the causes that were dear to her, from advising the Peace Corps for President John Kennedy to working with the United Jewish Appeal. By the time she died from tuberculosis in 1962, she had become one of the most recognized women on the planet. Both the liberals who idolized her and the conservatives who derided her were agreed on one thing: No first lady had ever used the role so aggressively. Eleanor remains in a class by herself.

Fast Food

With all her ambitious projects as first lady, Eleanor ended up neglecting something that most of her predecessors considered fundamental to the role: basic housekeeping. It wasn't long after the Roosevelts moved into the White House before tourists began noticing how shabby the place looked. Nor was Eleanor very interested in creating elaborate menus. Back during the First World War, the Roosevelts threw regular soirees with fellow Washingtonians known as "the Club" to talk shop and, virtually every time, eat the same meal—scrambled eggs and salad. Years later, while first lady, Eleanor served hot dogs to the visiting king and queen of England at Hyde Park. To compensate for her lack of interest in the kitchen, the first lady hired a housekeeper named Henrietta Nesbitt—who, unfortunately, wasn't much better at whipping up tasty fare than Eleanor was. Mrs. Nesbitt's notoriously bland, basic dishes became the butt of FDR's jokes throughout the administration. It's a good thing the Roosevelts were such lively conversationalists, because it was the only thing that guests had to look forward to on visits to the White House.

THE SHOOTIST

Eleanor was never big on bodyguards. They merely got in the way, especially when she was trying to look like one of the people. She loved meeting with crowds, a fact that worried her husband sometimes and drove the Secret Service nuts. At the insistence of those who were concerned about her safety, Eleanor learned how to handle a pistol. Sort of. After seeing her in action at the FBI firing range, J. Edgar Hoover told the president that Eleanor couldn't hit a barn door and probably shouldn't be walking around with a weapon. Eleanor's only bodyguard, a former New York State trooper named Earl Miller, took the time to coach the first lady in firearm use, but she seems never to have taken it seriously. She ended up keeping the gun in the glove compartment of her car—unloaded.

HANKY PANKY

FDR wasn't exactly the most faithful husband a woman could have. In addition to Lucy Mercer (whom he began seeing again in 1944 after promising his wife not to years earlier), he had a White House fling with his assistant Missy LeHand. But what about his wife? Did Eleanor have any affairs? Consider the case of Lorena Hickok, an Associated Press reporter who began covering the Roosevelts during the 1932 presidential campaign. "Hick" and Eleanor became fast friends. In fact, Hick became so enamored of Mrs. Roosevelt that she no longer felt capable of reporting objectively, and she quit her job as a journalist to take a post in the administration. The two women developed a deeply close relationship, and some historians are convinced that they shared a physical relationship—especially during the years that Hick spent living in the White House, in a room right across from Eleanor's. One thing is certain: the first lady's outrageous schedule made it impossible for her to devote as much time to the relationship as Hick would've liked, and the former journalist eventually became involved with other women.

THE LINCOLN MEMORIAL WILL DO NICELY

Eleanor's most famous stance against racism occurred in 1939, when the Daughters of the American Revolution refused to allow black singer Marian Anderson to perform in the organization's Constitution Hall. The first lady resigned from the DAR almost immediately, but didn't leave it at that. With Eleanor's sponsorship, Anderson went on to give a concert anyway—on the steps of the Lincoln Memorial before a huge crowd.

29

Bess
TRUMAN

February 13, 1885–
October 18, 1982

MARRIED:
June 28, 1919

PRESIDENTIAL HUSBAND:
Harry S Truman

CHILDREN:
Mary Margaret

FIRST LADY:
1945–1953

ASTROLOGICAL SIGN:
Aquarius

RELIGION:
Episcopalian

SOUND BITE:
"A woman's place in public is to sit beside her husband, be silent, and be sure her hat is on straight."

Bess Truman had the exact same reaction as her predecessor to becoming first lady: she wept. But if Eleanor Roosevelt was worried that she was destined to become a mere extension of her important husband, Mrs. Truman's

> **The White House wouldn't have survived without the spectacular renovation efforts of Bess Truman. Congress wanted to raze the building and start over, but Bess fought to keep the landmark preserved.**

reservations about the White House were over something closer to home. To Bess, being a president's spouse meant surrendering her family's privacy and exposing to a greedy public the painful event that she had striven so mightily to forget.

That event was her father's suicide. By 1903, David Wallace's drinking and debt had overwhelmed him, and he checked out with a pistol. His wife, Madge, the daughter of a wealthy flour miller, had enough money to support herself and her four children in their large home in Independence, Missouri. But she never got over David's tragic death and surrendered to her eldest child Bess the role of running the family. With her mother and three younger brothers relying on her, Bess developed an attachment to hearth and home that only became stronger

with time. She was a tomboy who could hit a baseball out of the sandlot and ride horses with ease; at finishing school in Kansas City, she even won the shot put.

She also won the heart of Harry Truman—though for years she didn't even know it. According to Harry, he fell head over heels for her when he was only six and they were in Sunday school together. But Bess was as close to aristocracy as you could find in Independence, and Harry was at the other end of the social spectrum. His chances with Bess became even slimmer when he left town to work on his family's farm after high school. Then, in 1910, he returned to Independence to visit his aunt—and was given a golden opportunity by a cake pan. His aunt had borrowed it from Mrs. Wallace, and when Harry heard that she was about to go over and return it, he snatched it and ran over to the Wallace residence himself. Bess invited him in and saw something in the grown-up dirt farmer that she hadn't before. She agreed to see him again. Harry was elated.

Their courtship was a long one. Madge wasn't crazy about her daughter's attachment to a guy with soil under his fingernails and kept hoping that their relationship was merely a phase. Besides, America's entry into World War I meant postponing their wedding further while Harry went off to fight as an artillery officer. When he returned in 1919, Truman opened up a men's clothing store with a war buddy and finally married the love of his life.

The newlyweds couldn't afford a place of their own, so they moved in with Madge, whose reservations about her son-in-law's prospects soon seemed justified. The haberdashery went belly-up in 1922. Harry refused to file for bankruptcy, spent years paying off his creditors, and—with a postwar recession raging—decided to give politics a try. He'd made contacts with the local Democratic machine through fellow veterans, who convinced him to run for a minor administrative judgeship. The shady pols who pursued Harry gave Bess the willies, but her husband had made up his mind, and he won the election.

The new job wasn't much, but it paid some bills—which continued to mount after the birth of daughter Mary Margaret in 1924. The Trumans continued to live at the Wallace homestead, where Bess looked after her mother, raised her daughter, acted as matriarch to her brothers, and watched her husband's political career blossom. By 1934 he had become big enough in Missouri to make a run for the Senate. Bess was mortified by the prospect of leaving the only community she'd ever loved, but she supported Harry anyway. And soon they were off to Washington.

Something about her father's suicide had always left a bad taste in Bess's mouth, a feeling that her parents had not been present fully enough in each other's lives. She resolved that her own marriage would be different—and, though hesitant about the idea of leaving Independence for the national capital, Bess was determined to be as involved as possible in Harry's career, to understand and support the cares that confronted him. She read the Congressional Record cover to cover, followed debates in the Senate, and ran Harry's office when he wasn't there.

Truman eventually made quite a name for himself in the Senate, especially for his investigations into defense contracts during World War II, an ambitious task that saved the government scads of dollars. His reward came right from the top: President Franklin Roosevelt wanted Harry as his running mate in 1944. Bess hated the idea for several reasons: first, there was the matter of her father's suicide, whose exposure would go hard on her and even harder on Madge; second, there was Margaret to think of, a girl who deserved better than to read about her own evolution into womanhood in the newspapers; and third, there was FDR—anyone could see that he had one foot and perhaps an arm in the grave already and was unlikely in the extreme to last another four years in office. Was Harry, at the age of sixty, up to being leader of the free world in wartime? Even Harry himself had doubts about the offer. But his sense of duty to the Democrats and to the country eventually swayed his opinion. Bess, who could've put her foot down and nipped the whole thing in the bud (Harry had been calling her "The Boss" for years), swallowed her dread and bowed to fate. It wasn't easy. After watching Harry secure the vice presidential spot at the convention before cheering crowds, she asked him in a fit of pique, "Are we going to have to go through this for the rest of our lives?"

It wasn't long before Bess's worst fear came to pass. FDR died in April 1945, and Mrs. Truman could've kicked herself for letting her husband accept the vice presidential post. The situation was dire: Though Germany and Japan faced imminent defeat, the war was not yet over. And coming on the heels of Franklin and Eleanor Roosevelt, two of the most sensational and hyperactive leaders in American history, were two small-town Missourians without so much as a single college credit between them. Even those who had hated the Roosevelts were holding their breath, wondering what in God's name a failed haberdasher and his brusque wife could possibly bring to the highest office in the world.

The question weighed most heavily on the Trumans themselves. Harry felt overwhelmed by his new gig, and he needed his wife more than ever. Ironically, he was in no position to act upon that need, finding himself—for the first time in his political career—unable to inform Bess about all that he needed to deal with. Military secrets were just that, and nobody—not even a first lady—was privy to them. As Harry shared less and less with Bess, she became more and more frustrated, and their marriage entered a crisis—one that didn't end when the war did. The president finally came around after a few tense moments and even tenser arguments, and the first couple resumed their working relationship.

And it was a close one, to be sure. They had always been loving and respectful partners, two people with enormous esteem for each other who knew the other's strengths and weaknesses. Those qualities were now harnessed to forge leadership in a country that had assumed a unique place in the world. Every evening, Bess disappeared with her husband into his study, where she edited his speeches, gave her opinion on policy decisions, and offered an objectivity to criticism that Harry was notoriously incapable of realizing himself. No one was as influential to the president as the first lady was, and Harry acted upon every one of her suggestions. She directly affected his cabinet appointments, styled his responses to queries and attacks, calmed his legendary fits of temper, and helped him see to completion such vital legislative agendas as the Marshall Plan to relieve war-torn European populations.

But nobody knew that. Family was still the most important thing to Mrs. Truman, and she guarded its privacy with ceaseless, stoic silence, preferring a role in the background that adopted no causes, made no stir. Her husband was the elected one, not she, a fact that the frustrated press corps learned early on. Of all Bess's challenges as first lady, none was as daunting as the fact that she wasn't Eleanor Roosevelt. She was no co-president, and anyone who had a problem with that could stuff it. Her influence on Harry was as secret as it was profound, and the first lady's two favorite words became "no comment," thrown indignantly at reporters who wanted to dig deeper than she was willing to go. She took pride in overseeing two responsibilities that Eleanor had neglected—keeping the White House clean (the mansion was a disaster area when the Trumans moved in) and restoring the sort of elegant entertaining that hadn't been seen since before the Great Depression.

The fact that nobody thought Harry had a chance of reelection in 1948 came mostly as good news to Bess, who couldn't wait to retire back in Independence. But when he secured a surprise victory, it allowed her to undertake one of her most important projects. The White House's problems went far beyond peeling paint and rats—it was literally falling apart, proof of which came when daughter Margaret's piano nearly fell through the floor. That we have to this day the same executive mansion in which Abigail Adams hung her laundry is due mostly to Bess Truman, who insisted that the government pay for a very expensive renovation rather than razing the old structure and erecting a new one. The first lady broke out of her preferred anonymity to lobby congressmen like crazy, eventually convincing them to preserve the White House as is with steel reinforcement to prevent its collapse.

Harry's reluctance to run for a third term came as great news to Bess. They went back to the old Wallace homestead in Independence, where the former president wrote his memoirs and remained a feisty source of opinions, political or otherwise, until his death in 1972. His wife kept up the tradition, offering spirited support to Democratic candidates but keeping her lips as tight as ever during interviews. Besides marking the end of an extraordinary life, her death in 1982 is significant for two reasons: She remains the longest-lived first lady of them all at 97. And she was the first to have her role inscribed on her gravestone: "First Lady, 1945–1953."

LITTLE WHAT'S-HER-NAME

Bess Truman suffered through two miscarriages before she delivered a daughter, Mary Margaret Truman, on February 17, 1924. But excitement over the successful birth quickly gave way to confusion over what to call the child. While Harry wanted to call her Mary (after a Truman), Bess insisted on her mother's name, Margaret. Four years passed before the parents could agree on a name. Bess won out—Margaret it was.

HARRY PLAYS THE BLUES

During a National Press Club meeting that Harry attended while vice president, he decided to entertain his fellow partygoers by showing off his talent at the piano. But upon playing, he was joined by a fellow entertainer named Lauren Bacall, who proceeded to draw herself up into a sexy pose on top of the instrument. Harry did his best to look uninterested, but the paparazzi caught the whole scene anyway. Upon seeing the picture in the newspapers, Bess remarked that it was time her husband quit the piano.

Crash

Bess Truman wasn't big on public appearances, and her first one as first lady gave her plenty of reason not to be. When called upon to dedicate a naval airplane, Mrs. Truman gave a very brief message into the microphone, then proceeded with the launching ceremony by smashing a champagne bottle against the machine's hull. The bottle, however, had not been properly prepared and remained as heavy and unyielding as a club. To her sublime embarrassment, the first lady swung away several times without any result—until a dockworker agreed to smash the thing with a wrench.

LAUNDRY ON THE HILL

Bess Truman's attachment to Independence, Missouri, was always a strong one. She even preferred the laundromats back home. Upon moving to Washington after Harry's election to the United States Senate, she was so unimpressed with capital cleaning establishments that she insisted on having her laundry delivered by long-distance mail to Kansas City for washing.

KEEP OFF THE GRASS

President John F. Kennedy's assassination in 1963 inspired the federal government to provide Secret Service protection for all previous presidents and their families. But Bess Truman wasn't thrilled at all when her agents showed up in Independence, convinced that they'd be another threat to her treasured privacy. She didn't even allow them onto the property.

30

Mamie Doud EISENHOWER

November 14, 1896–
November 1, 1979

MARRIED:
July 1, 1916

PRESIDENTIAL HUSBAND:
Dwight D. Eisenhower

CHILDREN:
Doud Dwight and John

FIRST LADY:
1953–1961

ASTROLOGICAL SIGN:
Scorpio

RELIGION:
Episcopalian

SOUND BITE:
"Every woman over fifty should stay in bed until noon."

For Mamie Eisenhower, moving into the White House came naturally. It was government housing, after all, something she was long familiar with as a former army bride. Becoming chief hostess of the country (and a pretty popular one at that) was the crowning moment of a military odyssey that saw no small amount of hardship and adversity and that nearly claimed her marriage—and her life.

Interestingly, hardship and adversity were two things that were conspicuously absent from Mamie's childhood. Her father, John Sheldon Doud, made so much money with his Iowa meatpacking business that he retired in his thirties and moved with his wife and four daughters to Denver, Colorado. There, Mamie attended Miss Wolcott's finishing school for "ladies of refinement," perfecting her dance steps and posture. She made her debut at the Douds' winter home in San Antonio, Texas, in 1915, and blossomed into a lively and very popular society girl with no shortage of interested males in tow.

At nineteen, Mamie was a pretty, pampered princess with a world of options. But while wealthy beaux crowded about her, the only fellow she seems to have taken seriously was hardly upper-crust material. Dwight David Eisenhower, known as Ike, was a newly minted second lieutenant out of West Point who was stationed at Fort Sam Houston in San Antonio. He was handsome,

devoted to his duties, and anything but rich—something that alarmed Mamie's father at first, until he got to know the affable young officer. The issue of living on an army salary, however, was a sobering one. And though the Douds gave their blessing to the lovebirds at their 1916 wedding, Mamie's father had seen fit to warn his coddled daughter about what she was in for.

The warning went unheeded, and the new Mrs. Eisenhower soon found herself immersed in a nightmare for which she was consummately unprepared. The society belle who had been schooled in piano and voice instruction was now required to cook and clean without servants, to make do in army base housing that was grimy and often without electricity, and—worst of all—to confront the fact that she would never be as important to Ike as his country. Money was almost as scarce as Ike, who was often called away on military business for long stretches, and Mamie . . . well, she was lonely and miserable.

It was Ike's turn to be miserable when the United States entered World War I in 1917. Denied the overseas posting that was the Holy Grail for all sanguine

Mamie Eisenhower never missed an episode of *As the World Turns*. Her staff scheduled appointments before and after (but never during) the program.

soldiers, he resigned himself to his stateside training duties—a job that nevertheless took him away from Mamie yet again. The birth of their first child, Doud (nicknamed "Icky"), merely exacerbated her loneliness with exhaustion. After sinking into a coma, she was warned by doctors not to strain her heart, which had suffered a blow from rheumatic fever years before.

And so it went. From posting to posting, Mamie did her best to raise Icky, endure the separations from Ike, and acquire vital hostessing duties in filthy hovels that the military had the nerve to call "housing." Though popular with other army couples for their dinner parties and card games, the Eisenhowers found their marriage deteriorating from stress. In 1921, things went from bad to worse. Icky died from a bout of scarlet fever, mixing grief and guilt into the frustration and estrangement that were already threatening their relationship. The army seemed not to notice and made things harder on the Eisenhowers by packing them off to the fetid wilds of Panama.

Mamie had become accustomed to low expectations, but what she found in Panama took the cake. Consigned to a moldering pile that was literally infested by a menagerie of uninvited guests, she spent her hours swatting at clouds of mosquitoes, dodging lizards and cockroaches, and watching Ike chase bats around the bedroom with his sword. After traveling to the States to deliver a second son, John, she took her time returning to Panama—and then, in 1923, left again, her health a shambles. By the time she mustered the strength to go back, she had turned a corner, resolving to make the marriage work at any cost.

The improvement in the Eisenhower relationship coincided with Ike's rise to prominence in the army. After attending the Command and General Staff School at Fort Leavenworth, Ike took his family to Paris to write a book on World War I battlefields. Then it was back to Washington, where Ike became Douglas MacArthur's chief of staff and Mamie earned her stripes as a celebrated hostess of capital caliber. They followed MacArthur to the Phillippines (where, despite a car accident that sent her into a coma, Mamie continued to entertain her husband's fellow officers with panache), then came back to the United States for a series of postings that stretched from Washington State to Virginia. Through it all, Mamie evolved into the ideal army wife, a devoted and charming homemaker whose parties at "Club Eisenhower" became legendary.

World War II posed the final and perhaps greatest challenge to the Eisenhower marriage. After Ike was sent to England as European theater commander in 1942, Mamie remained in Washington, DC, where she socialized with fellow war wives and volunteered for the Red Cross and the Women's Volunteer Services. But coping with the separation from her now-famous husband was only part of the challenge. The other part had a name: Kay Summersby. She was one of Ike's drivers and—if rumors coming back from Europe were to be believed—one who shared more than just a Jeep with the general. Ike bent over backwards in his touching correspondence with Mamie to deny the affair, and she seems to have believed him from the outset. But it did nothing for Mamie's peace of mind, especially as her legendary husband's exploits launched her into a fame with which she was uncomfortable at first. Though convinced of Ike's fidelity, Mamie found herself wrestling with public opinion for the first time as Summersby's name made the gossip circuit.

Something else was making the gossip circuit as well: Ike for president. In true apolitical military fashion, Eisenhower denied the notion flat out. As for Mamie, she found herself torn between the tantalizing possibilities and the horrifying responsibilities. The idea simmered after the war while Ike became president of Columbia University and then, in 1951, spent a year commanding NATO troops in Europe. As if bowing to his fate, Ike came around to the presidential idea in 1952, winning the Republican candidacy.

Dwight Eisenhower was a demigod who had liberated Europe from fascism, a Kansas-raised roughneck whose intelligence, political savvy, and profound sense of duty had allowed him to become the engineer of one of the greatest victories in human history. And yet in the 1952 presidential campaign, his greatest asset was . . . Mamie. "Where's Mamie?" cried the throngs that gathered around his campaign train during the whistle-stop tour. "I Like Ike," proclaimed the campaign buttons, "But I LOVE MAMIE." This embattled army spouse with a bad heart and claustrophobia had become an overnight sensation, and she loved every minute of it. Mamie gave interviews with enthusiasm, shook hands, preened before the crowds, and welcomed the sight of cameras. A *New York Times* columnist equated her with fifty electoral votes, and Ike never ended an appearance without asking her to come out and appease her cheering fans.

The Eisenhower juggernaut was irresistible. But for all her energy and presence during the campaign, Mamie—whose fans expected huge things from her—stayed in the background during her husband's two terms. Like Bess Truman before her, the new first lady insisted that her husband was the elected official and that she was his wife. No more, no less. "Ike runs the country," she quipped, "and I turn the lamb chops." She set up her headquarters in bed, out of which she would not emerge until afternoon. Her press appearances were few and then only to offer information of a consistently non-political nature. As hostess, however, she was outstanding, making regular appearances with her husband and throwing events in which she'd shake thousands of hands in a single day. With all their connections to influential military and political figures, the Eisenhowers threw important entertainments a-plenty, all of which were run with an eye to detail and spit-and-polish formality—in fact, the first lady made some enemies on the

White House staff for her insistence on regimentation and hierarchy. Nicknames were forbidden, as were rides in the mansion elevator. It was all the result of Mamie's experience with entertaining in military circles. The domestic side of things was her bailiwick, as it had always been, and Ike complied. But just as intense as Mamie's devotion to social affairs was her absence from political ones.

Not that she didn't have causes. In addition to replying to nearly every letter that was sent to her by average Americans, she lent her voice to the fight against racism in her own cunning fashion: Marion Anderson was asked to sing at Ike's swearing-in ceremony, Mahalia Jackson crooned at Mamie's birthday party, and even the White House Easter egg roll—revived for the first time since 1940—was fully integrated in a capital city that still held on to segregation.

Health had always been an issue with the Eisenhowers. If Mamie was a collection of frailties that ran from her gallbladder to her inner ears, Ike was no tower of constitution either—he suffered a heart attack and a stroke during the presidential years. For this reason, more than any other, they looked forward to retirement in their house outside Gettysburg, Pennsylvania—the first home they had ever owned in their lives. After Ike died in 1969, Mamie—who had always considered him her chief hobby—made the sanctity of his memory her primary concern. She lived long enough to see the 1979 miniseries on network television about her husband's alleged affair with Kay Summersby, which she still considered a bunch of claptrap.

BETTING ON THE COCKS

Mamie's years in Panama were hellish. But on at least one occasion, she eased the pain of confronting insects and reptiles by betting on fowl. Cockfights were a diversion and not only because she usually collected on her bets—the spectators who accompanied her were "so fascinating I couldn't pay much attention to the cocks."

EARACHE

Mamie Eisenhower began to drink a bit more than she used to during the Second World War while her husband was away. And who could blame her? Ike was

across the ocean in harm's way, and that's what a lot of army wives did while their husbands fought overseas. Unfortunately, Mamie wasn't just any army wife—and rumors began circulating about Mamie's "alcoholism." She eventually got things under control, however, and began limiting herself to one a day. But the rumors persisted, fueled by those who had seen "Mrs. Ike" stagger at some party or other event. In fact, the weaving had nothing to do with liquor. It was the result of Ménière's syndrome, an affliction of the inner ear that affects balance.

In the Pink

At President Eisenhower's first inaugural ball, his wife sparkled—literally. Woven into her dress were thousands of pink rhinestones, complemented by a pink purse encrusted with pink pearls. She rounded out the look with gloves and shoes that were . . . well, you know. It was a sign of things to come. Mamie redid her White House bedroom in pink, from the wastebasket to the sheets and curtains, and woke up every morning with a pink bow in her hair. Even the Eisenhower's private house at the Augusta, Georgia, golf course (called "Mamie's Cabin") sported a pink interior. It wasn't long before the first lady's favorite color became the official pigment of the fifties. Manufacturers began churning out household products in "Mamie Pink," from linoleum flooring to plastic containers.

AFTERNOON DELIGHT

Mamie Eisenhower was a big fan of *I Love Lucy*, and even entertained the cast at the White House (a bold move, as Lucille Ball had recently been labeled a "communist" in Senator Joseph McCarthy's witch hunts). But her favorite television show was the daytime soap opera *As the World Turns*, and she never missed an episode. Those on the first lady's staff quickly learned not to schedule anything at all that might conflict with it.

ALL HEART

Mamie Eisenhower was a smoker. Ironically, one of the very few causes she adopted as her own was the American Heart Association—for which she became an extremely successful fund-raiser.

31

Jacqueline Bouvier KENNEDY

July 28, 1929–May 19, 1994	
MARRIED:	
September 12, 1953	
PRESIDENTIAL HUSBAND:	
John Fitzgerald Kennedy	
CHILDREN:	
Caroline Bouvier, John Fitzgerald Jr., and Patrick Bouvier	
FIRST LADY:	
1961–1963	
ASTROLOGICAL SIGN:	
Leo	
RELIGION:	
Roman Catholic	
SOUND BITE:	
"I don't think there are any men who are faithful to their wives. Men are such a combination of good and evil."	

In 1941, an eleven-year-old Jacqueline Bouvier visited the White House as a member of a tourist group. "It seemed rather bleak," she later recorded. "There was nothing in the way of a booklet to take away, nothing to teach one more about that great house and the presi-

> Jacqueline Kennedy had to confront her husband's infidelity on numerous occasions—like the time she discovered another woman's underwear in their bed.

dents who had lived there." Little did she know that one day she would correct that situation—as one of the most boffo first ladies in American history.

Jackie's childhood was at once privileged and troubled. Her mother, Janet Lee Bouvier, was a beautiful New York City society woman who tried for as long as possible to deal with the alcoholism and philandering of her husband, a bigoted and irresponsible stockbroker named John Bouvier. She severed the relationship in 1936, and, six years later, married Hugh Auchincloss, who was wealthier and more stable than John Bouvier. Jacqueline and her younger sister Lee did their utmost to play father against stepfather in an emotionally charged family chess match in which they as daughters reaped all the benefits. Jacque-

line went to the finest private schools in New York and Connecticut, enjoyed weekends in the Hamptons, and became an extraordinary equestrienne.

Jackie was intense and somewhat aloof. But beneath the shell that she showed the world worked an indefatigable mind. She was an artist and litterateur right from the get-go, an insatiably curious girl who loved to draw, read the classics, and write poetry. She entered Vassar in 1947, studied at the Sorbonne in Paris during her junior year, and graduated in 1951 from George Washington University. When *Vogue* sponsored a "Prix de Paris" contest for aspiring young journalists, Jackie went after it with all she had, producing a series of spreads for the magazine that blew its editors away. The prize was an internship at the magazine's Paris office, but Jackie turned it down (her parents convinced her that if she went to France, she'd never return). Her hard work in the contest ended up paying off anyway when, with the help of her stepfather, she became the "Inquiring Camera Girl" for the *Washington Times-Herald*.

Soon she was engaged to a New York stockbroker named John G. W. Husted—and going on dates with a Massachusetts congressman named John Fitzgerald Kennedy. Though somewhat apolitical, Jackie was drawn to the handsome and engaging JFK, who loved to read as much as she did and whose wealthy family offered the sort of tantalizing security that she had learned to appreciate from her childhood. Kennedy was utterly taken by this beautiful intellectual who could translate French texts for him and look stunning at political dinners. "Jack," as he was usually called, became a senator in 1953, and the couple announced their engagement that summer.

Their huge and very ritzy wedding in Newport, Rhode Island, was a fitting encapsulation of Jackie's past and future. A gala society affair, chockablock with the nation's elite, it dramatically demonstrated the power and influence that a Kennedy-Bouvier/Auchincloss match could mean. But old wounds reopened when Jackie's father ended up getting too drunk to walk her down the isle, requiring her stepfather, "Uncle Hugh," to do it for him. And the bride was intimidated and exhausted by the throngs of ogling guests, giving her a very real lesson in the struggle for privacy that would come to define her life.

Jackie set about making herself into the thing she now wanted more than anything to become: an ideal senator's wife, a "distraction" for Jack from his demanding responsibilities. She became an expert in all the required fields: wine, entertaining, golf, bridge. She threw classy parties, delighted Jack's colleagues with her incomparable wit and learning, and even overcame her political ambivalence by following the debates that consumed her husband in the Senate. When he underwent serious spinal surgery, she buoyed his spirits with frequent visits to the hospital. When he decided to write *Profiles in Courage*, she did much of the research for him. And when he lost a bid in 1956 for vice president, she wept for him. It all took a lot out of her—by the time she gave birth to Caroline in 1957, she had already suffered a miscarriage and a stillbirth.

But she was becoming a major asset to her husband's career. During Jack's 1958 reelection campaign for the Senate, Jackie spoke to Latino Americans in their own tongue and proved herself a savvy and tireless promoter. She still retained a residual boredom with politics and politicians, but you wouldn't have known it to see her in action. It was more of the same during JFK's presidential run in 1960—interviews, public messages in foreign languages, personal appearances with her husband, and more. She had to turn it down a notch after getting pregnant but continued to reach out to voters through "Campaign Wife," a column in which she would write about life on the campaign trail.

Jack beat Richard Nixon by the slimmest of margins but ended up beginning his administration with a bang anyway: Less than three weeks after winning the election, his wife gave birth to a son they named John Kennedy Jr. The event served to emphasize the youth and exuberance of the new presidential couple, convincing many Americans that a new age had been born in that hospital room right along with John Jr. In many ways, perhaps, they were right. But this gorgeous and lively first lady—the first to be born in the twentieth century—would begin her term in anything but a spirit of youthful vigor. Still recovering from the birth (it had been a cesarean), Jackie became so exhausted during the inaugural festivities that her husband had to attend many of the events that night alone.

She had also been given the traditional tour of the White House by outgoing first lady Mamie Eisenhower, throughout which Jackie winced in pain—and not only because of her surgical scars. "Mamie Pink" was just one of many dubious decor choices that assaulted Mrs. Kennedy's eyes that day. To her, this majestic and storied building, the national treasure that had been home to Abigail

Adams and Abraham Lincoln, had become an offensively drab reservoir of gaucheries. Fixing it became her obsession, an ambitious project ideally suited to her sense of taste and appreciation for history. She scoured the mansion's property in search of forgotten antiques, successfully lobbied her husband and Congress to grant museum status to the building and provide a full-time curator, and hunted down collectors across the country who had historical treasures to donate. She even oversaw the creation of a guidebook to the mansion (which is updated regularly and used to this day) and, in 1962, gave a televised tour of the restored White House that seemingly everyone in the country watched. It was just the beginning—Jackie made similar efforts on behalf of the decaying buildings around Lafayette Square, intervening to spare them from destruction and actively championing their restoration. The result was a rejuvenated neighborhood, much of which was funded by donations from ordinary Americans who were inspired by the first lady's extraordinary work and devotion.

Jackie's historical preservation projects were merely part of a program to make the White House into a center of culture as well as government. She was fiercely independent and often infuriated her husband by not taking some of her traditional first lady responsibilities seriously (she once blew off a lunch in her honor given by congressional wives, requiring Jack to go in her stead). But the White House had never had such a sophisticated guest list—artists, musicians, dancers, writers, poets, all made merry in presidential events that often ended with a concert or dramatic performance. Jackie directed the design and construction of Washington's first cultural center (later named the Kennedy Center), arranged for many of the country's foreign students to visit the White House to cultivate international understanding, and got France to lend the Mona Lisa for a while to give Americans a close look at her.

She was beautiful, dedicated, elegant, and glamorous. If Americans became fascinated by Jackie, the rest of the world went fairly berserk over her. In Venezuela, communist protestors held up a sign reading, "Kennedy No, Jacqueline Yes." In France, the president introduced himself as "the man who accompanied Jacqueline Kennedy to Paris." Women adopted her bouffant hairdo and bought cheap copies of her hats. She charmed the pants off of Soviet Premier Nikita Khrushchev and became the first incumbent first lady to have an audience with the pope. Even the communist bloc ate her up: Of the 100 or so countries that aired her televised tour of the White House, several were behind the Iron Curtain.

And then came 1963. In August, Jackie gave birth to a son named Patrick who died within two days. The national outpouring of sympathy had barely subsided when, on November 22, in Dallas, the first lady had to endure the horror of witnessing her husband's assassination. In an instant, the Kennedy dream was over.

Jackie fever, however, wasn't. And she knew it. After using her organizational skills to arrange for a dramatic funeral worthy of the nation's grief, she became dedicated to the well-being of her two fatherless children—children who had already experienced more national attention and tragedy than anyone should have to. She hoped to find peace and at least a measure of privacy in New York City, but her efforts to shape her late husband's mythic reputation brought her unwanted attention when she authorized a book by William Manchester entitled *The Death of the President*. Disagreement over some of the book's less flattering passages led to a lawsuit that was eventually solved by some editorial changes, but it was a sign of things to come. Try as she might, Jackie would never be able to control the public's impression of JFK or her relationship with him, both of which were coming under increasing scrutiny as the years passed.

It was the sort of thing that drove her further into the international circles she already knew, seeking escape in foreigners who weren't so close to America's ongoing Kennedy tragedy. Bobby Kennedy's assassination in 1968 was the last straw. "I hate this country," she fumed. "I despise America and I don't want my children to live here anymore."

All of which goes a long way toward explaining her strange decision to marry Greek shipping magnate Aristotle Onassis. Twenty-three years her senior, "Ari" offered tremendous wealth and intelligent companionship. But all the rest of the world saw was a shady Mediterranean gangster who would drag their beloved princess down into a world that hardly suited her. Jackie was willingly dragged, and the world mourned her besmirching. In 1975 Ari died, leaving his widow and daughter to fight it out over his millions. Jackie walked away with enough to put her in the black for the rest of her life.

Rich and twice widowed, Jackie returned to New York City, where she utilized her smarts and connections to become a book editor. Her ongoing patronage of the arts and devotion to career and family made her an icon of the women's movement during the 1970s. But an insatiable public still hounded her (one magazine even printed a map of where tourists could spot her making her daily rounds), and the protection of her privacy remained a priority. In time she began a romance with influential diamond merchant Maurice Tempelsman; it would prove to be her last. By 1994 she had contracted non-Hodgkin's lymphoma, which no amount of treatment seemed capable of stopping. Jackie checked herself out of the hospital and died—in private, on her own terms—in May of that year. To many Americans, it felt as if they'd lost a queen.

GRACE UNDER PRESSURE

When JFK entered a New York City hospital in 1954 for spinal surgery, Jackie did everything she could to provide distractions and lift his spirits. On one occasion, she got Grace Kelly to waltz into his room dressed in hospital whites and proclaim herself the new night nurse. But an exhausted Kennedy failed to recognize her. "I must be losing it," said the actress.

ATTENTION ALL SHOPPERS

Jackie had a famously sultry voice and didn't hesitate to use it on behalf of her husband. While campaigning for him in Wisconsin during the 1960 run for president, she went into a supermarket, co-opted the intercom, and proceeded to regale shoppers with reasons why they should vote for JFK. "Just keep on with your shopping," she said into the microphone, "while I tell you about my husband, John F. Kennedy."

BEWARE OF DOG

It wasn't long after becoming first lady before Jackie began to chafe under all the press scrutiny. Worried over her family's privacy, the constant intrusion by journalists became a source of irritation (she had a particular dislike of newspaperwomen, whom she often referred to as "harpies"). Once, when asked by a member of the press corps what her dog liked to eat, the first lady replied, "reporters."

⌒ ONE OF MANY ⌒

Jack Kennedy was a notorious philanderer, a fact that (needless to say) often put his wife in an awkward position. While giving a tour of the White House to a photojournalist, Jackie opened the office door of a female staffer and proclaimed, "This is a young lady who is supposed to be sleeping with my husband." On another occasion, she confronted Jack with a pair of panties she'd found in their bed, threw them at him, and, after asking if he could find whom they belonged to, declared, "They're not my size."

Bathing in Hot Water

In 1962, Jackie took a vacation to Italy—without her husband, but with her two children. While enjoying herself on the beach, she became the first first lady to be photographed in a bathing suit. Given her international renown, it wasn't long before the photos hit front pages all over the world. But whether or not Jackie happened to be the first presidential spouse who looked good in a bathing suit was hardly the issue to conservative groups back in the States. To them, she had finally broken through the thin ice on which she'd been treading for months and was sending entirely the wrong message to average American homes. When she returned to the United States, she was confronted by picketers at the airport who thought her beach antics were undignified.

No wonder the woman had a preoccupation with privacy.

32

Lady Bird
JOHNSON

December 22, 1912–

MARRIED:
November 17, 1934

PRESIDENTIAL HUSBAND:
Lyndon Baines Johnson

CHILDREN:
Lynda Bird and Luci Baines

FIRST LADY:
1963–1969

ASTROLOGICAL SIGN:
Capricorn

RELIGION:
Episcopalian

SOUND BITE:
"Flowers in a city are like lipstick on a woman—it just makes you look better to have a little color."

The year was 1934, a just-married Claudia "Lady Bird" Johnson was visiting friends en route to her honeymoon, and her new husband had noticed a run in her stockings. "You've got to change them, Bird," he said in front of everybody. Lady Bird, somewhat startled, hes-

> **Lady Bird Johnson never let anything— not even an accident where her car rolled twice—interfere with vigorous political campaigning.**

itated until he repeated the command.

Then she went and changed her stockings.

It was the second time that she'd encountered Lyndon Johnson's dictatorial side. The first was when he proposed. Following a furious and very brief courtship, Lyndon asked for her hand in marriage with something like an ultimatum: "We either get married now or we never will," he said, adding that a negative response meant "that you just don't love me enough to dare to." Mrs. Johnson would soon get used to being told what to do.

It wasn't an easy transition, particularly for a woman who'd had such an independent youth. Nicknamed at birth by a nurse who thought she was "purdy as a lady bird," she was driving to school by the age of fourteen. Lady Bird's mother died when she was five, leaving her father to raise her and her two older brothers on his own in Texas. Summers were spent with Aunt Effie in Alabama.

She was a shy kid and an outstanding student, graduating third in her high school class and making the honor roll at the University of Texas at Austin. She stuck around long enough to take graduate courses in journalism and soon became a reporter for the *Daily Texan*.

Intelligent, compassionate, and detail-oriented, Lady Bird had a love of self-improvement that would endure throughout her life but felt ill-prepared by her upbringing to be the sort of well-groomed lady that attracted men. Her widower father, a wealthy storeowner in Karnack, Texas, gave her charge accounts and plenty of love, but none of the dance lessons and makeup instruction that were usually a mother's province. Despite her misgivings, the boyfriends came one after another—including a tall, handsome, energetic, and intensely intelligent congressional aide named Lyndon Johnson. He poured out his soul to her on their very first date and proposed on the second. She turned him down at first but gave in just weeks later after Johnson's furious and insistent courtship tactics. His romantic blitzkrieg may have caught Lady Bird by surprise, but it impressed the dickens out of her father, who gave his blessing to the match.

The newlyweds lived in Washington initially, where Lyndon worked for Congressman Richard Kleberg, but returned to Austin in the summer of 1935 after Johnson was made director of the Texas National Youth Administration, one of the Roosevelts' New Deal programs. He made enough of a reputation for himself to try a run for Congress in 1937, a race that marked the beginning of big things for him—and that would require a tremendous amount of effort from his wife.

She would deliver and then some. But if a successful Lyndon had cause to celebrate, his wife had plenty of reasons to gripe during the first few years of their marriage. Right from the beginning, Lady Bird had been forced to confront the autocratic side of her husband. He may have been an ardent suitor when they met, smothering her with candid expressions of affection and pleading to become her spouse. But Lyndon's darker side sprang up, seemingly from nowhere, once the deal was sealed. Lady Bird was directed to shine his shoes, to bring him breakfast in bed, to make sure his cigarette lighter was filled, and a host of other things. She was no homemaker and had to learn overnight how to make the most basic meals. He also insisted that she learn as much as possible about his job, bringing home names, addresses, and other details that she was instructed to memorize. And as if all that weren't challenging enough, she had to deal with the rumors about her husband's extramarital affairs, especially the one with socialite Alice Glass.

So what did Lady Bird do? She coped. She hired a cleaning lady, did what her husband asked of her (and got really good at it, particularly the political part), and swallowed the anger about his infidelities, another skill at which she would learn to excel. But then she went the extra mile and a half by asking her father for a $10,000 advance on her mother's estate to fund Lyndon's 1937 congressional race. He couldn't have won the seat without it. Now that's devotion.

No, it wasn't the ideal marriage. But Lady Bird loved and respected her hard-driving legislator/husband, a man who consistently did something that she could appreciate—drive her to be and do more. And Lyndon came to rely on her more and more, especially after America's entry into World War II. While he took an officer's commission in the navy, Lady Bird ran his congressional office, saw to the needs of his constituents, and laid the groundwork for his reelection. In 1942, she bought a rundown Austin radio station with her family's money (LBJ would always rely on his wife's money), turned its flagging business around, and made it into a cash cow that would end up funding much of her husband's future political races. By 1947 she had added the raising of two daughters to her busy schedule of business owner/political surrogate, completing her transformation into a powerhouse manager who could juggle ridiculous schedules and process an overload of details while maintaining what virtually everybody who knew her called a calm, sunny disposition.

Such skills proved invaluable in securing Johnson a seat in the Senate in 1948, beginning what Lady Bird would always cherish as one of the marriage's greatest periods. While Lyndon scored legislative successes with his legendary blend of smooth-talking hucksterism and flagrant bullying, his wife sank her teeth into all the exciting opportunities of Senate wifedom. When she wasn't showing up at his office with Texas-shaped sugar cookies or schmoozing with other political wives, she was studying her husband's legislative agenda and helping him swing Senate votes. They had become a potent team, and both of them knew it. The White House beckoned.

It also beckoned for John Kennedy, who beat out Johnson for the Democratic nomination in 1960. Lady Bird urged her husband not to take the vice presidential post offered him, but like so many who confronted LBJ's persuasiveness, she couldn't say no when he chose to accept. Instead, she became a mighty asset to the Kennedy-Johnson ticket by campaigning like a maniac—she traveled over 30,000 miles, made scores of personal appearances, and charmed the pants off of countless voters. It was an impressive indication of how far the insecure little girl from Karnack had come. Robert Kennedy even credited her with getting the Texas vote.

Lady Bird was a second lady who got plenty of practice being first lady. Because Jackie Kennedy often refused to attend events herself, Mrs. Johnson became a frequent stand-in—at over fifty functions in the first year of the Kennedy administration alone. But her opportunity to put all that priming to use came at the grisliest price when JFK was assassinated in November of 1963. "You know we never even wanted to be vice president," she said to a grief-stricken Jackie, "and now, dear God, it's come to this."

Lady Bird made the best of a bad situation. "Can Do" read the sign she placed on her desk, setting the pace for a first ladyship that was shaped by an abundance of activity. She insisted on becoming very nearly as busy as her proactive husband, making plenty of speaking engagements and almost immediately becoming the most valuable member of LBJ's circle of advisers. She was honest, often brutally so, and never failed to offer criticism of her husband's agenda or performance. He would come to rely on those qualities.

And he came to rely on her to get him reelected in 1964. With the administration's civil rights agenda raising holy hell in the South, LBJ sent his diehard Southerner of a wife to patch things up (read "get some votes"). After calling governors and congressmen in Southern states ahead of time to enlist their support, Lady Bird boarded a train called the Lady Bird Special with her staff and made a series of appearances from South Carolina to Louisiana. The first lady did her best to pour on the Dixie charm, packing her speeches with colloquialisms like "He's noisier than a mule in a tin barn" and handing out her recipe for pecan pie, all while fending off racists and shouting through catcalls. But she reached hundreds of thousands and succeeded in getting her husband's message through in her own eloquent, patient way (much of which was the direct result of public speaking lessons she'd been taking for years). It worked. And at LBJ's inaugural ceremony in 1965, Lady Bird made another breakthrough by being the first wife to hold the Bible on which her presidential husband took the oath of office.

Soon Lady Bird was being compared to a woman she admired: Eleanor Roosevelt. LBJ undertook a legislative agenda that was nothing if not ambitious. Some of it worked, some of it didn't. But his wife found herself in the position of becoming a symbol for all that was noble about that agenda. Like Eleanor, she became her husband's scout in the field by traveling extensively and reporting back to him on the "War on Poverty," especially as leader of the Head Start program to get aid to underprivileged children.

But her most cherished project—and the one for which she would earn true immortality—was "beautification," a (rather inadequate) term that embraced everything from public conservation and road management to environmentalism and urban renewal. Lady Bird established the Committee for a More Beautiful Capital, which made epic strides to turn Washington into the sort of place that tourists wanted to visit. Millions of flowers were planted, parks were built, neighborhoods were cleaned up. She directed an effort to do the same to the rest of America, too (and got Congress to pass "Lady Bird's Bill," which limited the proliferation of billboards on national highways). As highway medians were refoliated and trash dumps disappeared, the first lady became an environmental celebrity. *National Wildlife* magazine dubbed her the "secretary of the exterior," and for good reason—Lady Bird traveled clear across America, becoming a promoter of the great outdoors and its preservation and, much to her husband's delight, getting average Americans to spend their holiday dollars visiting the Catskills or the Grand Canyon rather than Bermuda or Acapulco.

Unfortunately, plenty of Americans were visiting another place and not altogether willingly: Vietnam. Moreover, plenty of them weren't coming back alive. Antiwar protesters became increasingly vehement as the Johnson years dragged on, and Lady Bird became the object of much of them. At the first "Women Do-er" luncheon held by the first lady in 1968 was an actress named Eartha Kitt ("Catwoman" on the campy old *Batman* TV series), who proceeded to disrupt the tea-and-cookies ambiance by peppering Lady Bird to her face with a blistering verbal volley about the war and its heinous effect on America's youth.

The widely reported incident inspired as much sympathy for Kitt and her argument as it did for Lady Bird, who reportedly handled the tirade with stoic calm. But it was merely a sensational example of the sort of thing that was ripping the country apart. The Johnsons were getting bombed almost as much as the North Vietnamese. LBJ may have started out with a "Great Society," but he had ended up with a war-torn populace, and—with Lady Bird's insistence—he decided not to run again in 1968.

The end of LBJ's administration—and the end of his life—were stormy and difficult. He came back to the smoking that had once been forbidden by his doctors, his mood swings became untenable, and his fondness for other women continued to corrode his relationship with the wife he had always held as equal partner and adored mate. His death in 1973 came as no surprise to Lady Bird, who had been obsessing over his health since the first heart attack he suffered back in his congressional days. Her own life, however, continued to be as active as ever. Lady Bird remained a committed and esteemed player in the environmental movement and even joined the National Geographic Society and the National Park Service, in addition to accepting a position on the University of Texas Board of Regents. She didn't let up until 1982 when, at the age of seventy, she finally decided to take an overdue—and well-deserved—retirement.

Lord of the Ring

The Johnson wedding in 1934 was a hastily arranged affair with little preparation. In fact, Lyndon had forgotten even to get a ring to put on his bride's finger. After realizing this in the church, he sent a friend out to get one. The man returned with a collection of cheap jewelry from Sears, from which Lady Bird picked out a real beaut—worth $2.50.

⌒ STICKY RICE ⌒

Lady Bird had never learned how to cook before getting married, and it would be a while before she became any good at it. One of the Johnsons' first dinner guests, the wife of Congressman Maury Maverick, was stunned to discover a cookbook in Lady Bird's kitchen opened to a recipe for boiled rice. Lady Bird

apparently couldn't even get that right, however—the woman later claimed that, after that evening, she always connected boiled rice with "library paste."

NO TIME FOR INJURIES

Lyndon owed a lot to Lady Bird for his 1948 Senate victory. She had become an extremely engaged and energetic campaigner, a woman who went right to the people, shook hands, worked the phones, and more. Nothing exemplifies her sense of purpose more dramatically than the car accident she suffered on her way to make an appearance in San Antonio. After pulling herself out of the wreck (the vehicle had rolled twice), she hitched a ride, changed into a dress borrowed from one of the women at the rally, and proceeded to give her first statewide broadcast on behalf of Lyndon. Only after all that was accomplished did she find it prudent to make a trip to the hospital for X-rays. Fortunately, she suffered little more than scratches.

CRESTFALLEN

Lady Bird's favorite television show was *Gunsmoke*, and she almost never missed an episode—even after learning to her horror that James Arness, the program's star, was a Republican.

THE MINK COAT MOB

One of the most sensational events of Johnson's 1960 vice presidential campaign was also one of its ugliest. Lyndon and Lady Bird were in Dallas just days before the election when they found themselves confronted by a crowd of wealthy local women who were very well dressed, very conservative, and very angry with Johnson's liberal agenda. By the time the Johnsons and their companions had gotten through the mob, Lady Bird had been spat upon and smacked on the head with a sign reading "Let's Ground Lady Bird." Mrs. Johnson, shocked at the rage and disgusting behavior, began to shout back at them until her husband clamped his hand over her mouth. The incident inspired sympathy and admiration for the Johnsons in the newspapers, but running that gauntlet was one of the most trying moments of Lady Bird's life.

33

Pat NIXON

March 16, 1912–June 22, 1993

MARRIED:

June 21, 1940

PRESIDENTIAL HUSBAND:

Richard Milhous Nixon

CHILDREN:

Patricia and Julie

FIRST LADY:

1969–1974

ASTROLOGICAL SIGN:

Pisces

RELIGION:

Catholic, then Quaker

SOUND BITE:

"Oh, but you just don't realize how much fun he is! He's just so much fun!" (on her husband, in a television interview).

When Richard Nixon announced his loss in the 1960 presidential campaign to John Kennedy, cameras caught the tears in the eyes of his wife, Pat. She had plenty to cry about. The race had been incredibly close—so close, in fact, that Pat Nixon unsuccessfully tried to

Pat Nixon visited twenty-nine nations during her tenure as first lady—and often made headlines by immersing herself in local customs.

convince her husband to fight for a recount. But more importantly, she had to face the ugly fact that all the exhausting campaign work she'd done during the past year had been for naught—a frustrating revelation indeed, for it was the sort of work she abhorred.

Thelma Catherine "Pat" Ryan was no stranger to hard work. She and her two older brothers were born in Nevada, but grew up in California after their father, William Ryan, gave up life as a miner to run a farm outside of Los Angeles. Pat had little time for play—she spent much of her childhood picking vegetables to help keep the family in the black. Life wasn't much easier back at the house, where William tended to get drunk and pick fights with his wife, Kate. After Mrs. Ryan died from cancer, Pat—thirteen years old—began running the household in her stead and still managed to devote enough time to her school work to earn high

grades. Mr. Ryan died when Pat was seventeen, leaving his daughter to pay her own way through Fullerton Junior College by working as a cleaning lady at a bank.

Eager for travel and adventure, Pat interrupted her college education to travel to New York City. She'd convinced an elderly couple to let her drive them east in their equally aged Packard, for which she was paid enough money to get back to California by bus. She ended up staying in New York for two years, however, during which she dated often, studied radiology at Columbia, and got a job as an X-ray technician. Though Gotham was a blast, she went back west in 1933 to complete her education at the University of Southern California, paying her way as usual through odd jobs: dental assistant, telephone operator, store clerk. After graduating with honors and a teaching certificate, she moved to Whittier, California, to teach typing in the local high school.

Pat had model good looks and impressed a few movie directors with her acting ability in bit roles. Though a career in film didn't interest her, it was her fondness for occasional acting that ended up changing her life forever. While auditioning for a role in one of Whittier's local acting troupes, she met a fellow amateur player named Richard Milhous Nixon. Enchanted by the tall redhead, Nixon asked her out almost as soon as he saw her, but Pat gave him the brush-off with the timeless "I'm busy" line. "You shouldn't say that," he retorted, "because someday I'm going to marry you."

Pat thought he was some kind of nut job and put the awkward incident behind her. But Dick, while very probably a nut job, was entirely serious about pursuing Pat—which he proceeded to do with impressive tenacity for the next two and a half years. He waited for her while she went on other dates, endured her ambivalence toward him, and kept at her until she came around. After they got married in 1940 in a Quaker ceremony (she was Catholic, but embraced Dick's faith), Pat continued to teach while her husband got his law practice under way. Money was tight—with America's entry into World War II, they both went to work for the Office of Price Administration in Washington, D.C. After Dick joined the navy, Pat traveled with him from base to base and continued her work for the OPA after he went overseas. With a lifetime of experience working hard and managing her time, Pat handled her busy schedule of homemaking and bread-winning easily.

What she didn't handle so easily was Dick's decision to enter politics. In 1945, California Republicans approached him with the idea of running for the United States House of Representatives. Pat went along on the strict condition that she never be required to make political speeches and that their family's privacy never be intruded upon. Dick agreed.

Pat should've asked for this agreement in writing. If she was wary of the political world in 1946, she would in time come to hate it with a visceral passion. Dick's tactics only made it worse. His congressional campaigns—in 1946, 1948, and the 1950 run for the Senate—were full of mudslinging and unsavory accusations that soon earned him the epithet "Tricky Dick." Nixon had always been an extremely self-confident and ambitious man who believed he was destined for the White House, one of the qualities that endeared him to Pat in the first place. But his drive for results at any price, especially his work chasing communists for the House Un-American Activities Committee, attracted the sort of controversy and attention that Pat wanted most to avoid.

And yet he couldn't have done any of it without her. Right from the beginning in 1946, she was his most valuable worker—she ran his campaign offices, researched opponents' strengths and weaknesses, typed up pamphlets and mailed them out, and donated what little savings she had to his elections. And that was just the half of it—by 1948, she had two daughters to raise. Pat struggled to run their household on a small budget, did all the cooking and cleaning herself, and even made all the curtains and slipcovers for their home in Washington. It was a lot of work, to say the least—and Pat did it all without complaining.

After years of tolerating the hurly-burly and wearing forced smiles at public appearances, Pat finally broke her silence in 1952, when Nixon was made the vice presidential candidate on the Eisenhower ticket. Enough was enough— besides, she'd already exacted a promise from her husband to leave politics after the termination of his Senate term in 1956. But as she would do again and again, Pat gave in to her husband's ambition and then set about performing the tasks she loathed with extraordinary effectiveness. In fact, the only thing stronger than her detestation of politics was her support for Dick. When he was accused of taking personal advantage of inappropriate contributions, Eisenhower insisted he make a national television appearance to diffuse the situation. Dick would've preferred to just bow out, but Pat insisted that he go through with it. If he didn't, she warned, his career would be over. The TV spot worked, and Nixon became vice president.

For all her negative opinions about being a political wife, Pat was damn good at it—indeed, she may well have been the most extraordinary second lady in American history. President Eisenhower, who never liked Nixon very much, decided to get him out of Washington by sending him on a tour of the world as America's goodwill ambassador. His peregrinations were a major triumph—mostly because Pat came along. From Asia to South America to Russia, Mrs. Nixon was a paragon of graciousness, composure, and elegance. She made a habit of traveling to locations barred to local women, subtly but effectively spreading the message of feminism. She even held the first press conference ever arranged for women reporters in Japan. Pat had a gift that her husband utterly lacked: the ability to reach people, to look them in the eye, remember their names, put them at ease, and connect with them. President Eisenhower praised her, the press adored her, and Dick . . . well, he pushed her.

Right into a run for the presidency itself in 1960. (Heavy sigh.) Without a doubt, Pat's popularity was a major asset to Nixon, who had racked up plenty of enemies and who struck even some of his supporters as aloof and abrasive. The Republicans exploited her image to the hilt, but to no avail—Nixon lost to Kennedy in one of the closest races in history. To Pat, it was a traumatic and very emotional moment. She was exhausted by the campaigning, pained by America's rejection of her dear husband, and bitterly sick and tired of all the political nonsense that had put their family through so much.

The long-desired return to private life came as a tremendous relief. Dick took up with a Los Angeles law firm and, unbeknownst to his wife, began planning a political comeback. In 1962, when Pat heard from him over dinner with friends that he planned to run for governor of California, she left the table in tears. They moved to New York City after he lost, finally convincing Pat that her husband's political delusions were at an end. She is reported as saying by this time that if he ever ran for office again, she would kill herself.

Heedless as ever of his wife's deepest desires, Dick Nixon ran for president again in 1968. There are a couple of reasons why Pat didn't choke down a bottle of sleeping pills: first, despite her husband's self-absorption, she loved him; and second, she felt—as Dick did—that a certain amount of vengeance was in order. The 1960 fiasco was a close-run thing, leaving the Nixons with a bad taste in their mouths that they now saw an opportunity to wash away with sweet victory. Besides, Pat knew that no amount of pleading would dissuade her husband from going for it. And so, once again, the tough Irish lass who'd known years of emotional repression and self-sacrifice would go the distance one more time. And this time around, it would prove to be more than even she could take.

Nixon's very comfortable 1968 electoral victory began a one-and-a-half-term presidency that began gloriously and ended disastrously. It wasn't until around his 1972 reelection (another huge electoral victory that offers testament to his impressive first term) that the Watergate scandal and the seemingly interminable prolongation of the Vietnam War conspired to blow his administration to pieces. But if Pat Nixon eventually caught heat by association from her husband's explosive problems, her first ladyship stands in stark contrast to Nixon's presidency. Pat showed more of the grace and sheer pluck that distinguished her years as vice presidential spouse. In her first year alone as first lady, she shook the hands of something like a quarter of a million Americans, logging hundreds of miles as an emissary of the president and promoting her pet project, "volunteerism." She answered heaps of mail from ordinary citizens and used her influence to get action on their requests. No first lady had ever traveled so much—Pat visited twenty-nine nations, covering nearly 125,000 miles. In Vietnam she risked her life on the front line to visit wounded troops. In Africa she was welcomed like royalty and made headlines by donning local dress. And for her husband's history-making trip to China, she read Chairman Mao's "Little Red Book" from cover to cover to familiarize herself with the country's political atmosphere. She even struck out on her own turf by publicly advocating a woman for the Supreme Court, endorsing the Equal Rights Amendment for women, and wearing trousers for a magazine photo shoot (Nixon hated trousers on women). Unlike her husband, Pat was popular with virtually everyone, and for good reason. She was as gregarious, hardworking, and engaging as ever. It wasn't long before one Nixon adviser asked a colleague, "If we can't improve the President's public image . . . what do you say we drop him and run Mrs. Nixon?"

If only that had been possible. After a connection was made between the administration and a bunch of amateur cloak-and-dagger bozos who broke into the Democratic National Committee's Headquarters in the Watergate building, things started going downhill for Nixon. His wife remained as popular as ever with the press, but she increasingly found herself pressured to make statements about Watergate. She refused, and there was fallout. Denied access to the details by her husband (who had never really shared much with her when it came to political business) and compelled to put on a good face despite all the pressure, the first lady soldiered on with the forced smiles that had become her specialty and was soon being called "Plastic Pat." All her worst fears about Dick's political career were coming true—their privacy was invaded, his integrity was questioned, and their daughters were forced to deal with it all. The growing tangle of investigations infuriated and exhausted her, leading her to believe that a conspiracy was afoot. Nixon eventually decided to resign. The decision hit Pat like a freight train.

During the final months of Dick's administration, Pat had become a recluse, driven from the limelight by her confusion, grief, and anger. She had wanted to get out of politics, but not like this. Watergate continued to hound them even in retirement, and Pat responded by drawing herself further into seclusion in their San Clemente, California home. She suffered a stroke in 1976, from which she managed to gain control of her health once again through sheer hard work and exercise. After moving to New York City and then to New Jersey, Pat continued to experience health problems. They finally claimed her in 1993.

If only because we know that Dick shared so little of his official life with her, it is virtually assured that Pat Nixon knew nothing of the details of the Watergate break-in. She, along with every other American, shared the sense of national shame that defined that troubled era. But for her the shame was exacerbated by the fact that she had placed her own desires behind his for so long—an epic sacrifice that was rewarded by scandal and humiliation.

WHAT'S IN A NAME?

In 1952, when Richard Nixon came under suspicion of receiving secret contributions from business interests, he made a television appearance to the country in which he detailed his expenses. Called the "Checkers Speech," because of his reference to a dog named Checkers who'd been given to the Nixons by supporters, it served to put voters at ease. Throughout Dick's appearance, Pat sat beside him as a symbol of familial solidarity. Nixon referred to her in the speech, playing up her Irish background and her unwillingness to quit—and going so far as to tell viewers that she was born on St. Patrick's Day.

In fact, Pat was born the day before St. Patrick's Day. Her father, an Irish-American, had taken the proximity of her birth to the saint's day as a good omen and always referred to her as "Pat," though everyone else called her by her given name, Thelma. But when her father died, Thelma decided to honor his memory by referring to herself by the name he preferred. From then on, she called herself Patricia, or Pat.

BEYOND THE CALL

Not all of Pat Nixon's sojourns overseas resulted in feelings of goodwill. In 1958, she and her vice presidential husband embarked upon a trip to South America in which they encountered anti-American protests of unique ferocity. In the streets of Caracas, they cowered in their limousines as crowds of protesters shouted invectives and assaulted the vehicles with bats. Pat remained remarkably calm throughout the incident, but really showed her stuff later at the airport. There, with her husband, Pat listened to the Venezuelan national anthem while hostile hordes in the balconies above showered her with spit. As her face and red suit became streaked with saliva, the second lady maintained an uncanny level of concentration and decorum that inspired the rest of the embattled Americans. "That lady showed no fear," remarked a journalist. "She didn't panic, not even remotely." It was an exquisite example not only of her ability to bear up in a crisis, but also of how good she had become at finding a place within her to contain anger.

STEALTH

During the years of the Watergate crisis, Pat Nixon became good at maintaining her anonymity while roaming the streets of the capital in search of leisure and bargains. Once, while strolling the streets of Washington just a few blocks from the White House, a person recognized the first lady despite her scarf and sunglasses. "Shhhh," she said conspiratorially as he approached. "Just out for a little window-shopping."

Surprise!

Pat Nixon had an eye for antiques and is credited with continuing the White House restoration efforts of Jackie Kennedy and Lady Bird Johnson by dramatically increasing the number of treasures in the mansion. At one auction, she ended up getting into a bidding war over a particularly beautiful China tureen. Though Pat won the contest, the other bidder proved tenacious, and the first lady ended up paying much more for it than she had hoped. Not long afterward, she learned that her opponent had in fact been a friend who knew that Pat Nixon would love the tureen and had decided to get it for her. As if that weren't bad enough, Pat discovered upon returning home that the tureen was not a tureen at all. In fact, it was an elaborately decorated chamber pot.

34 Betty FORD

April 8, 1918–

MARRIED:

October 15, 1948

PRESIDENTIAL HUSBAND:

Gerald R. Ford

CHILDREN:

Michael Gerald, John Gardner, Steven Meigs, and Susan Elizabeth

FIRST LADY:

1974–1977

ASTROLOGICAL SIGN:

Aries

RELIGION:

Episcopalian

SOUND BITE:

"I don't like to dodge a question, and I guess I'm not astute enough to walk around it."

In the late 1980s, ABC aired a television movie about former first lady Betty Ford. When a reporter asked former President Gerald Ford why a film had been made about his wife and not him, he simply replied, "My wife is much more interesting!"

Betty Ford is an interesting woman indeed. She was born in Chicago, but moved with her parents and brothers to Grand Rapids, Michigan, when she was three. William Stephenson Bloomer, her father, passed away when Betty was only sixteen but made enough money selling industrial supplies to leave his family in relative comfort. His daughter's chief love was dancing—she showed an amazing natural talent and even taught modern dance in her adolescence. In 1938, after spending a couple of summers studying at the Bennington College School of Dance in Vermont, she convinced her mother to let her further her career in New York City at the famous school run by Martha Graham. She ended up performing and supplementing her income in the big city with modeling for the prestigious John Robert Powers agency.

Betty was having the time of her life—so much so, in fact, that her mother, Hortense, worried that she might never come back to Michigan. But New York's siren song didn't prove strong enough, and when Betty returned to Grand Rapids

for what was intended to be a visit, she ended up staying. She went back to teaching modern dance, choreographed her own dance troupe, and got a job as assistant fashion coordinator at a local department store.

Betty was a free spirit who had experienced more than most young women, but the pressures to settle down and make a family proved irresistible. In 1942 she married a furniture dealer named William Warren, whose erratic working habits and inability to stay in one place dragged his young wife through a series of temporary homes in places like Toledo and Syracuse. After suffering through jobs she didn't like very much to help support their foundering marriage (e.g., handling shrimp on a conveyor belt in a frozen-food factory), she ended up caring for Warren for two years while he knocked at death's door from diabetes. As

As a young woman, Betty Ford choreographed her own dance troupe—and even studied with legendary instructor Martha Graham.

soon as he was better, she filed for divorce and chalked the whole thing up to a learning experience.

By now she was back in Grand Rapids, working as the fashion coordinator of her old department store and determined not to enter into another serious relationship—not even with the handsome lawyer and former Michigan football star Gerald Ford. Having just come out of a stormy long-term relationship himself, Ford acted just as casually as Betty did. But despite their best efforts, things got more and more serious and the two soon found themselves in love. They married in the fall of 1948.

For the former Mrs. Warren, that autumn wasn't only the beginning of her second marriage; it was also the start of the political chaos that would shape the rest of her life. When Jerry proposed to her the previous February, he insisted—without explanation—that they couldn't get married until the following October. She soon discovered why: Ford planned on running for Congress and had decided to keep it a secret, even from his fiancée, until he committed. "Jerry's work will be the other woman," said Ford's sister-in-law to Betty, and it wasn't long before it became clear what that meant. Jerry had to leave the wedding rehearsal early to give a speech, showed up late to the ceremony itself because he'd been at a political meeting, and actually interrupted their honeymoon to attend rallies. Fortunately, it paid off. Ford won his seat in the House of Representatives and took his bride to Washington.

Betty didn't know diddly about politics, but she soon learned. In addition to helping out in her husband's office and devoting attention to his constituents, she became a popular figure in the Congressional Wives Club and spent as much time as possible giving herself an education in government by attending debates and reading up on congressional issues. She also acquired a gift for juggling the myriad duties of housewifery: by 1957 she had four children to look after, and when she wasn't helping out with homework or taking them to football games, she was overseeing Cub Scouts as a den mother and working with the PTA.

And her husband? Jerry's star continued to rise. After getting reelected again and again to his congressional seat, he became House minority leader in 1965. But his responsibilities took him away from home far too often, leaving Betty to raise the children alone and to wonder what she'd gotten herself into. Adding to the pain of loneliness was pain of a physical nature—including pancreatitis, arthritis, and a pinched nerve that sent her to the hospital. While Ford was enjoying the power and celebrity of his House minority leadership, his wife was falling apart and sinking into a morass of depression and anxiety. She avoided a complete breakdown only after seeking therapy and taking lots of painkillers.

The therapy restored her self-confidence and the painkillers worked—a bit too well. In fact, Betty began a close relationship with them that would ultimately end rather sensationally. But in the meantime, nobody seemed to notice. She remained the dutiful mother and congressional wife, admired by the likes of Lady Bird Johnson and Pat Nixon, and cherished by her terribly busy husband—whose career turned a sharp corner in 1973 when President Nixon asked him to take the place of Vice President Spiro Agnew, forced to resign amidst a financial scandal. Betty, who had been trying to live a life around her husband's career, was looking forward to his retirement from the House. But now, as second lady, she found a sense of purpose that she had lacked since attaching herself to Jerry. It was exhilarating, full of possibilities, a little scary—and short-lived.

Once again, Ford's career was reshaped by other people's screwups. Dick

Nixon, pummeled by Watergate, threw in the towel just eight months after his new vice president was sworn in. A breathless Betty now found herself first lady of the land, a position for which she was quite unprepared. Then, quite suddenly, a tragic turn of events offered an unlikely solution. Confronted by her doctors with the revelation of breast cancer, the new first lady underwent a mastectomy. Though risky and terrifying, the operation changed Betty Ford—and changed the nation. As she struggled through her recovery, women across America were talking openly about breast cancer for the first time. They went to get examinations in droves, resulting in countless diagnoses and saved lives. Betty spoke openly about her ordeal and fueled the revolution. Letters poured in thanking her for her candor and influence.

It was a revelation. Betty now understood the impact she was capable of exerting, an impact that—for the first time in her life—had little to do with her husband. The White House was offering her the ultimate cure to the confusion over her identity that had sent her to therapy and to bottles of pills. She began in earnest to make the most of it and not only by becoming a spokeswoman for the fight against cancer. She drew on her love of dance to become a champion of the National Endowment for the Arts, raised funds for handicapped children, and aggressively promoted better care for the elderly. Most of all, she adopted the women's movement as her own, becoming the most assertive and eloquent lobbyist on behalf of her gender in the history of the first ladyship. Betty evolved into an exquisite public speaker, a skill she relied on to fight for passage of the Equal Rights Amendment. She got her husband to appoint more women to government positions, publicly came out in favor of legalized abortion, successfully urged the president to mark 1975 as "International Women's Year," and urged her fellow Americans to embrace the feminism that was sweeping the country.

Just as important, she helped Jerry restore a sense of openness and joy to a White House that had been tainted by the previous administration. She once admitted, "Jerry and I are ordinary people who enjoy life and aren't overly impressed with ourselves." It showed—guests were soon leaving presidential events with smiles on their faces. State dinners featured plenty of dancing (of course), gaiety, and open conversation. Even the White House guards, instructed by Nixon to never address the president or his family, were given the freedom to respond when greeted.

Not that the Fords didn't have their detractors. Plenty of Americans, both men and women, were vehemently opposed to the ERA's passage and thought Betty's assertiveness and outspoken opinions were utterly inappropriate. And the president's controversial pardoning of Nixon brewed up quite a storm. But Betty was convinced that she and her husband had done well by the country and had gone a long way toward restoring faith in the White House. It's hardly surprising then that she felt personally betrayed when Ford lost to Jimmy Carter in the 1976 election. Jerry was terribly disappointed, but his wife was crushed, convinced that voters had forgotten all the years of public service that Ford had offered—and left wondering what she herself would do with her life now that the role that had given her such immense purpose was taken from her.

The answer to that question came in two forms: drugs and alcohol. After she and Jerry moved to California, Betty began complementing her exotic regimen of painkillers with a steady stream of cocktails. After a couple of years of watching her stumble about in a consistent and impenetrable fugue, her family decided to do something. There were two interventions. Betty was offended and indignant but eventually came around and agreed to enter a program at Long Beach Naval Hospital. The experience of sharing episodes over coffee and cigarettes with fellow addicts initiated the second transformation of Betty Ford. It didn't just get her to admit her affliction and clean up her life—it got her to act on her ingrained proclivity for service. In 1982 she founded the now-famous Betty Ford Center for drug and alcohol rehabilitation in Rancho Mirage, California, which she continues to chair.

First ladies aren't elected. But Betty Ford had even less of a mandate from the people than the other members of her sorority: Her husband remains the only American vice president and president who was elected to neither position. That she made the most of the situation and acted so ambitiously on projects dear to her is impressive enough. That she then went on to overcome her addictions, share them with the world, and draw upon her personal experience to help others in the same predicament—well, that's simply heroic.

⌒ LITTLE EATING MACHINE ⌒

To look at her when she was a child, no one would have believed that Betty would grow up to be a lithe dancer. She tended to run more than a little on the chubby side, a condition at least partially fueled by her habit of visiting local restaurants to ask for food from diners. The situation got bad enough that Betty's mother took to hanging a sign on her daughter's back that read, "Please do not feed this child."

The Truth in 60 Minutes

"I take a Valium every day," admitted Betty to the press when she was second lady. Mrs. Ford's candor soon became her hallmark. She later said, "I don't believe being first lady should prevent me from expressing my ideas." And express them she did, for better or worse. In August of 1975 she agreed to an interview with *60 Minutes*—the segment ended up becoming the most sensational example of Betty's openness. In it she admitted that she may very well have tried marijuana if she were a member of the younger generation; that the Supreme Court's ruling on making abortion legal was a "great decision"; and that she "wouldn't be surprised" if her daughter were engaging in a sexual affair. Fallout from the interview was pretty severe. One New Hampshire newspaper called it "a disgusting spectacle . . . [that] disgraces the nation itself." But many Americans were impressed by Betty's forthrightness and her willingness to express herself freely as an individual who wasn't concerned with affecting her husband's career. For his part, Ford—who often disagreed with his wife's viewpoints—took pride in her independence, even when it hurt. He believed the *60 Minutes* incident cost him 20 million votes, though his reaction was hardly explosive: While watching the interview with Betty, he picked up a pillow and threw it at her.

FLYING THE FLAG

Betty Ford's commitment to the Equal Rights Amendment was well known, but she never missed an opportunity to remind people of it. She even had a flag made to fly from her car that featured bloomers (in honor of her maiden name); red, white, and blue stars; and the letters "ERA" underneath the old Revolutionary slogan "Don't Tread on Me."

"BREAKER, ONE-NINE . . ."

President Ford's loss in the 1976 campaign hit Betty quite hard, not least because she had gone through such extraordinary efforts on his behalf herself. In Wisconsin, for instance, she spread her husband's message to workers and truckers on a CB radio. Her handle: "First Mama."

MAKING AN ASH OF HERSELF

While Betty Ford was first lady, one of her daily routines involved a gold statue of a woman whose grasp once held a document that had been lost. Believing that the figure should have something to hold onto, she took to placing one of her cigarettes in the statue's hand—and insisted on surreptitiously replacing it whenever the servants had it removed.

FIRST DANCER OF THE LAND

Though her arthritis and pinched nerve restricted some of the flexibility she enjoyed when she was younger, Betty Ford remained a lover of dance her entire life. As first lady she became famous for cutting the rug with everyone from Tony Orlando and comedian Marty Allen to Art Buchwald and the president of Finland. In the East Wing of the White House, she once placed a photo of herself dancing with Cary Grant—it was signed, "Eat your heart out, gals."

In the Bedroom

The Fords were the first presidential couple since the Coolidges to share a single bedroom in which they both slept every night. (Though other couples often slept together in the White House, they usually maintained two bedrooms for appearances.) Though Betty received quite a bit of mail castigating her and Jerry for what many considered inappropriate sleeping arrangements, the first lady was unfazed—and as blunt as ever. "I guess if you're president," she remarked, "you're supposed to be a eunuch."

35

Rosalynn CARTER

August 18, 1927–

MARRIED:

July 7, 1946

PRESIDENTIAL HUSBAND:

Jimmy Carter

CHILDREN:

John William, James Earl, Donnel Jeffrey, and Amy Lynn

FIRST LADY:

1977–1981

ASTROLOGICAL SIGN:

Leo

RELIGION:

Methodist, then Baptist

SOUND BITE:

"If I had, I wouldn't tell you!" (in response to a reporter's question as to whether she had ever committed adultery).

In the fall of 1953, Rosalynn Carter moved with her husband, Jimmy, to Plains, Georgia, to run his father's peanut farming business. And she was miserable about it. Having spent the previous seven years as a happy navy wife, Rosalynn looked at the move as a big step backward into the rural life she had chosen to leave behind. But it wasn't long before she changed her tune, throwing herself into the business that had brought them back to Plains and discovering that she had a knack for numbers and organization. It was the beginning of her growth as a professional woman— and the beginning of a Carter partnership that would take both Rosalynn and Jimmy to the White House.

In fact, Plains was Rosalynn's hometown. She lived an idyllic childhood with her parents and three siblings, a simple life centered on family, farming, and church. Her father, Edgar, who drove a bus and worked as a mechanic when he wasn't tilling the fields, died when Rosalynn was only thirteen, leaving her to help her mother, Frances Allethea ("Allie"), to run the household. Though money was an issue (Allie took a series of odd jobs after her husband's death to pay the bills), Rosalynn was a happy kid who studied hard, graduated valedictorian of her high school class, and then commuted to Georgia Southwestern College in nearby Americus.

Rosalynn had known fellow Plains native Jimmy Carter for years, mostly as the big brother of her best friend, Ruth Carter. But her platonic feelings toward him changed during her sophomore year in college when she saw a particularly flattering photograph of Carter in his Annapolis uniform. She was smitten almost immediately, a feeling that only grew when she saw him again while he was home on leave in 1945. They began courting and, though she turned down his initial proposal, it didn't take her long to reconsider. By July of 1946, they were married.

Plenty of military spouses have been driven crazy by the constant moving and unpredictable demands placed on them, but Rosalynn Carter positively ate it up. She loved the travel, from Norfolk to Honolulu, San Diego to New London,

> As first lady, Rosalynn Carter once posed for a snapshot with a Democratic party organizer named John Wayne Gacy. (Yes, the same John Wayne Gacy who murdered young men while dressed in a clown suit.)

Connecticut, and took pleasure in the satisfaction of running an efficient household during her husband's postings overseas. By 1952 they had three sons, and the joys of family life more than compensated for her growing responsibilities and Jimmy's occasional absences. Life was good.

Until Jimmy's father blew a hole in the boat by dying in 1953. The Carters' peanut warehouse business in Plains was now up for grabs, and Jimmy insisted that he resign from the navy to take it over. His horrified wife ranted and raved, but to no avail. Carter could not be moved on the subject. It was the first serious disagreement in their marriage, and Jimmy won. After moving back to Plains, Rosalynn moped for months, pining for the romantic navy days of yore. Then one day, Jimmy asked her to help out in the office while he went to visit some clients. She agreed—and stayed. Since the move back to Georgia, Rosalynn had spent her time cleaning, cooking, and teaching Sunday school. But balancing the books grabbed her like nothing else had. She started spending more and more time in the office, until she was practically running it, whether her husband was away or not. The Carters soon expanded their warehousing facilities to take advantage of good peanut crops, the business boomed, and Rosalynn started taking a shine to their new life after all.

Things may have been going well for the Carters, but they still had a bee in their bonnet—mostly over the contentious social issues that were racking the South. Amidst a community full of outspoken advocates of segregation, the integrationist Carters stood out like a couple of very sore thumbs. Jimmy's concerns over issues of race finally drove him to run for the state senate in 1962. In addition to running the family business while he campaigned, Rosalynn went door to door and did some pretty effective stumping herself. His victory in that year encouraged him to make a run for the governor's mansion in 1966. He lost to a staunch conservative and ardent segregationist. Four years later, however, the Carters came back with a vengeance. In her husband's 1970 gubernatorial campaign, Rosalynn did much more than just see to the peanuts. She became, in effect, a co-candidate. She overcame her sickening aversion to public speaking to make numerous appearances and ended up shaking nearly as many hands as he did. By dividing the effort between the two of them the Carters covered twice as much territory.

It worked. Now a mother with four children to look after, Rosalynn still found the time to champion her causes as governor's wife. The Carters had developed a close partnership based on mutual respect and equality, and their activities in the sphere of politics reflected that. Mrs. Carter had become her husband's closest adviser—he listened attentively to his wife's opinions, even when they conflicted with his own, and if her argument turned out to be the stronger, then he'd adopt it. The effectiveness of their seamless partnership became obvious during Carter's race for the presidency in 1976. Utilizing the tactics that had worked so well in the past, both Carters stumped on behalf of the candidate, but separately so as to reach more voters. Rosalynn knew his message at least as well as he did, and proved extremely adept at giving interviews, working the telephones, tapping the influence of powerful supporters, and turning on the charm. Soon this intrepid Southern belle with a seemingly endless reservoir of energy was being called the "steel magnolia" by the press.

The Carters celebrated their presidential victory by partying through all seven inaugural events and then sitting down to business. Jimmy Carter had been elected as a Washington outsider, and he was determined to run the executive branch as an outsider, damn the consequences. It wasn't long before he gave the nation a clear idea of how dismissive he was of convention. In 1977, just months into the administration, the president sent his wife to Central and South America—not as a "goodwill ambassador" but as his official representative on a state department mission. It was unprecedented. Not only was the first lady an unelected person engaging in vital government business; she was a woman charged with discussing substantive state matters with powerful men in a foreign culture dominated by machismo. After polishing her Spanish and absorbing all the relevant state department minutiae, Rosalynn took off on what many in Congress considered a fool's errand. It proved to be a major success. Welcomed by heads of state as a capable confidante of the American president, she strengthened ties in the countries she visited and brought back invaluable information to her husband.

Her influence hardly stopped there. She formed a task force to assess and improve federal programs for the elderly, helped organize a national child immunization campaign, and pushed the president to appoint more women to government posts than any of his predecessors. Her most cherished cause was mental health, and her efforts on behalf of this daunting issue were extraordinary. After Carter made her honorary chairperson of the President's Commission on Mental Health, she spearheaded an ambitious investigation into existing legislation and programs, and oversaw an immense effort to improve upon them nationwide. She was dedicated, tireless, and everywhere—including the president's cabinet meetings. It was Eleanor Roosevelt all over again: impressive and inspiring to many Americans, inappropriate and intrusive to just as many others. Rosalynn soldiered on in the face of criticism, relying on her religious faith, sense of mission, and . . . long underwear (the daily wearing of which became necessary after the president's decision to turn down the White House thermostat during the oil crisis).

In 1979 the first lady journeyed to Thailand to reconnoiter the otherworldly suffering of starving Cambodian refugees, a horrific sight that inspired her to drive the United Nations to greater relief efforts. But while she was away, a horror of a very different sort was occurring back in Washington: specifically, her husband's presidency. Despite some successes—including the momentous pact between Menachem Begin of Israel and Anwar Sadat of Egypt—Carter's administration succumbed to entrenched economic ills. Then, Iranian militants—enraged at the Carter administration's refusal to turn over the exiled Shah of Iran—took the American embassy staff hostage, creating a crisis that proved too much for the president to handle. Not that he didn't try, of course. In fact, his wife conducted most of his 1980 reelection campaign for him while he sweated away in the White House searching for a way to release the captured Americans. Rosalynn performed as remarkably as always, but it wasn't enough. Carter got slaughtered at the polls by Ronald Reagan.

Like Betty Ford before her, Rosalynn was indignant at the loss. She would later claim that her fellow Americans made a mistake by not voting for her husband in 1980. When someone noticed how well President Carter was taking the loss on election night, the first lady quipped, "I'm bitter enough for both of us." Indeed, she had more than Reagan's landslide victory to be bitter about: The Carters were walking out of the White House and straight into some serious debt, not least because of the neglect suffered by the peanut business in Plains during their presidency. Best-selling writing projects by both Jimmy and Rosalynn would help alleviate that situation in time, and they eventually found the security and money to build the Carter Center, a sort of souped-up presidential library that has continued to serve as a base for the Carters' ongoing efforts at international peace and humanitarian aid. She and her husband have even dedicated a great deal of time and effort to such projects as Habitat for Humanity, a program dedicated to building homes for the needy. As always, the partnership continues—with one notable exception. During the writing of their only joint book, entitled *Everything to Gain: Making the Most of the Rest of Your Life*, the Carters consistently differed over writing styles. In fact, the nasty disagreements got so bad that they ended up barely communicating for weeks at a stretch. Hey, every marriage has its limits—even the Carters'.

CUMBERSOME COMMODE

During her stint as first lady of Georgia, Rosalynn was accustomed to giving speeches at high schools. But one such sojourn proved challenging, to say the least. Upon being greeted at her arrival, she excused herself to go to the ladies' room. But the door of the stall she entered must've been a Republican—it simply wouldn't open, no matter how hard she jiggled the latch. Worried that she wouldn't be able to make her appearance in time, she did the only thing she could do. She pulled herself up and over the door. Fortunately, nobody entered to discover the governor's wife in what must have been one of the most compromising positions of all time. After completing her awkward extrication, she composed herself, exited the bathroom, and proceeded to deliver her speech without anyone realizing that she had just managed a narrow escape from a defunct toilet stall.

CLOWNING AROUND

As a first lady concerned with reaching as many people as possible, Rosalynn Carter allowed her photograph to be taken with countless average Americans. Unfortunately, one of them was an unassuming building contractor and Democratic party organizer named John Wayne Gacy—whose penchant for killing young men (even while he was making them smile in his clown outfit) was as unknown at the time to the first lady as it was to the Chicago community that would ultimately convict him of murder. Oops.

Visionary

Rosalynn Carter had two pairs of contact lenses, one for distance and one for reading. Interestingly, she often wore one from each pair while giving speeches so that she could read her notes with one eye and look at the audience with the other.

TOO MUCH DETAIL?

Jimmy Carter once gave an interview to *Playboy* magazine in which he admitted to having "lusted in [his] heart"—i.e., he felt attracted to women he'd seen from time to time, which, for him, was as bad as cheating on his wife. Rosalynn's reaction to the remark deftly made the most of a silly situation. "Jimmy talks too much," she offered, "but at least people know he's honest and doesn't mind answering questions." Now *that's* spin.

Jane Wyman
1914–

Born Sarah Jane Mayfield in St. Joseph, Missouri, actress Jane Wyman's eight-year marriage to Ronald Reagan seems almost a footnote in what must be considered a very storied and impressive Hollywood career. After attending the University of Missouri in the 1930s, she performed as a singer on radio using the name Jane Durrell and soon after signed a contract with Warner Brothers for work in films. She has since performed in numerous pictures with such stars as Ray Milland, Bing Crosby, and that other guy, Ronald Reagan; won a Best Actress Oscar for her portrayal of a deaf-mute in *Johnny Belinda* (1948); and, while her ex-husband was running the country, starred in television's *Falcon Crest*. After her marriage to Myron Futterman and before the two to Fred Karger, Wyman was hitched to fellow actor Reagan between 1940 and 1948. Apparently, one of the things that drove her to sever the relationship on the grounds of "extreme mental cruelty" was Reagan's habit of talking endlessly on matters she considered rather tedious, both political and otherwise. "If you ask Ronnie what time it is," she once said, "he'll tell you how to make the watch."

36

Nancy REAGAN

July 6, 1921–

MARRIED:

March 4, 1952

PRESIDENTIAL HUSBAND:

Ronald Reagan

CHILDREN:

Patricia Ann and Ronald Prescott

FIRST LADY:

1981–1989

ASTROLOGICAL SIGN:

Cancer

RELIGION:

Disciples of Christ

SOUND BITE:

"A woman is like a teabag—you don't know her strength until she's in hot water."

During one of the first interviews Nancy Reagan gave after her husband's election to the presidency in 1980, she was asked what her special project as first lady would be. She responded that she didn't have one—"My husband is most important." But if Mrs. Reagan didn't have a project in mind, she had plenty of something else—style. And after years of penny-pinching by Betty Ford and Rosalynn Carter, Nancy Reagan restored a sense of glamour to the White House that was dazzling, exorbitant, and extremely controversial.

She had acquired a lot of practice in the glitz department. Her mother, Edith Luckett Robbins (who nicknamed her daughter "Nancy" when she was a child), was a New York City actress whose friends included ZaSu Pitts, Lillian Gish, and Spencer Tracy. Nancy barely knew her biological father, a car salesman named Kenneth Robbins, who separated from her mother very soon after Nancy was born. After spending five years with her aunt and uncle in their tiny Maryland home, Nancy went to Chicago to rejoin her mother, who had remarried to an eminent and extremely wealthy neurosurgeon named Loyal Davis. Nancy became accustomed to the good life—the finest clothes, the finest restaurants, the finest company. She also adored her stepfather, who formally adopted Nancy when she was fourteen.

Though her mother had retired from the acting life by now, Nancy wanted

more than anything to follow in her footsteps and to become a part of the glamorous theater world. She focused on drama at Smith College in Massachusetts and then got her first break via family friend ZaSu Pitts, who offered Nancy a bit role in a production of *Ramshackle Inn*. It wasn't much, but Ms. Davis was on her way. As Spencer Tracy looked after her in the big city, she acquired further roles on Broadway, made several television appearances, did some modeling, and even dated Clark Gable. With the influence of Tracy, she was able to secure a screen test in Hollywood with MGM in 1949 and impressed the studio enough to get a seven-year contract.

Nancy was a capable actress who made a happy career by working in a dozen or so films but whose qualities never translated into superstardom. Nevertheless, the move to California changed her life. In 1949 she met the president of the Screen Actors Guild, a strapping film star named Ronald Reagan. Both of them had rather tragic romantic pasts—while Reagan was still getting over his

To fight the war on drugs, Nancy Reagan appeared as herself on the hit sitcom *Diff'rent Strokes*, urging Arnold Jackson (Gary Coleman) to "just say no."

divorce from starlet Jane Wyman, Nancy had to cope with the loss of a fiancé who got atomized by a locomotive while crossing a railroad track. Their courtship lasted some two years, during which Nancy became pregnant with their first child. Friends William and Ardis Holden were the only guests at their 1952 wedding in Los Angeles.

Nancy Reagan wanted nothing more than to become a full-time wife and mother. But with her husband's career in decline, she agreed to appear in a few more films (including *Hellcats of the Navy*, in which she played the romantic interest of the film's hero, played by Reagan). When "Ronnie" secured a contract with General Electric to be the host of its sponsored television show, things changed—and not just financially. The job allowed Ronnie to earn enough money for Nancy to put her film career behind her, but it also marked his gradual transformation politically. Up to this time he'd been a dyed-in-the-wool New Deal Democrat. But his responsibilities on behalf of General Electric included more than merely being its TV spokesman. He also spoke at conventions for the corporation, got to know the employees and management, and eventually became convinced of the evils of government intervention in business. Before long he changed his party affiliation and galvanized his Republican reputation by making appearances for Barry Goldwater's presidential campaign in 1964. He was good at it—so good, in fact, that fellow party members convinced him to make a run for the California governorship in 1966.

His victory sent the Reagans to a governor's mansion that doubled as a giant pile of kindling. Nancy arranged for them to move out of the firetrap, established their new home in the suburbs of Sacramento, and convinced the legislature to start building a new mansion. Nancy devoted efforts to the Foster Grandparent Program, in which the elderly were conscripted to work with special needs children, and spent a great deal of time on behalf of Vietnam veterans. Her primary project, however, had become her husband. Nancy's devotion to Ronnie was absolute. When he made an unsuccessful bid for the Republican presidential nomination in 1976, she let Reagan's staff handle strategy while she handled him—making sure he wasn't overworked, seeing to his schedule, and becoming the guardian of his health. When he ran against Jimmy Carter in 1980, Mrs. Reagan expanded her role somewhat into strategy sessions, personnel decisions, and public appearances that the candidate himself couldn't make; but she remained first and foremost his steadfast protector. The result was a huge Reagan victory.

The new first lady thought it crucial to imbue her husband's presidency with an air of pomp and glitter. Reagan's inaugural was nothing if not extravagant, a regal bash that included eight inaugural balls at $250 a ticket. Nancy lit up the night's events wearing a $10,000 trousseau and a mink coat of equal worth, as well as rhinestone-studded shoes and matching handbag. She was a vision whose slight model's frame offered the ideal opportunity for showing off the best of designers like James Galanos and Bill Blass. But if many thought that Nancy's fashion sense brought a long-overdue restoration of executive sparkle, plenty of others thought it the quintessence of bad taste at a time of economic hardship for average Americans. The press immediately began pinning unflattering nicknames on her (e.g., the "Evita of Santa Barbara") and wisecracking about her apparent taste for excess. Few first ladies had been off to such a bad start.

It got worse. Though funded entirely with private money, the first lady's decision to redecorate the private quarters of the White House and to acquire a huge china set priced at more than $200,000 convinced an already hostile press that Nancy was profoundly out of touch. Moreover, while newspaper columnists were barraging her with bad press, someone else decided to barrage her husband—with bullets. The 1981 assassination attempt on the president showed the Reagans at their best: Ronnie made a remarkable recovery while cracking jokes and Nancy stood by his side, demanded a constant flow of information from his doctors, and impressed the country with her courage and devotion. Though the event inspired an outpouring of sympathy for the presidential couple, there were plenty of White House advisers who remained terribly concerned about Nancy's reputation as a heartless would-be monarch.

The result of their efforts to change her image can be summed up in three words: "Just say no." Drug abuse had been a concern of Nancy's for years, and it was now upgraded to a full-fledged first lady's project toward which Mrs. Reagan would devote an amazing amount of effort throughout her husband's two terms. She made countless speeches and television appearances, inspiring America's youth to think more critically of drug use and getting all aspects of society to begin treating the subject with the severity it deserved. She even made a cameo appearance on the hit comedy *Diff'rent Strokes* and a triumphant speech before the United Nations. Critics questioned the efficacy of her endeavors in the face of her husband's cutbacks on drug programs, but Nancy's steady, consistent effort raised awareness of drug abuse to a new high. And just as importantly, it improved her public image—even those who questioned her sincerity toward the drug issue were willing to admit that "Queen Nancy" was a fading memory.

That Reagan won a second term by a landslide was proof that he'd never faced the severe character issues that dogged his wife. But the Reagans' second four years in the White House proved even more challenging than the first four. Sure, Nancy had evolved from administration liability into one of the most popular first ladies in recent years. Nevertheless, circumstances warranted her involvement in her husband's presidency to a level that assumed contentious proportions. Despite Ronnie's characteristic optimism, he was getting old, and fast—he underwent two operations during his second term, one for skin cancer and one on his prostate (Nancy herself had undergone a mastectomy). The first lady responded to these chilling developments by exerting even greater control over the president's schedule and workload, insisting that nothing was as important as his health and need for recovery. When the Iran-Contra scandal broke, she merely tightened the leash—and pushed herself further into the decision-making process, particularly in areas that she thought threatened Ronnie's reputation.

She had never wanted to find herself in this position. Indeed, Nancy had been so apolitical in her youth that she remained strangely ignorant of Eleanor Roosevelt's highly publicized visits to her campus at Smith College. But now many accused her of being the irresponsible power behind the throne. It was perhaps the inevitable result of her unflagging devotion to Ronnie, who seemed to age visibly with every week—Nancy's habit of feeding words to the increasingly foggy-minded president had become legion.

Fittingly, her beloved Ronnie remained her most important project for the rest of their lives together. Though Nancy wrote her memoirs and continued her campaign against drug abuse with the Nancy Reagan Foundation, her husband's struggle with Alzheimer's disease defined her post-White House years until his death in 2004. Like her husband, Nancy Reagan remains a controversial figure. But of one thing there can be no question: Nancy always placed her husband's welfare and reputation above all things. In that capacity she performed marvelously.

DEAD RECKONING

In the midst of the Second World War in 1943, Nancy worked as a nurse's aide in the Cook County Hospital. She exhibited a remarkable ability to work diligently and sensitively with wounded men, but her initiation into the ugly world of war injuries was traumatic, to say the least. On her first day, she gave a bath to a severely wounded veteran—who, by the end of the process, proved to be dead.

Bathtub Banter

After her husband entered the world of politics by fighting for the California governorship in 1966, Nancy Reagan developed an unusual method of letting off steam. While taking a bath, she would imagine herself arguing with her husband's critics and developing arguments that would put them in their place. As she debated with herself in the relative comfort of her bathroom, all opposition was emasculated and her husband always emerged victorious.

GENERATION SLAP

Nancy's relationship with her children became closer as Ronnie's Alzheimer's got worse. But it had often been a rocky road with them before then. Their daughter Patti once expressed her individuality by openly admitting during the 1980 campaign that, if she wanted to, she would live with a boyfriend and smoke marijuana even if her father became president. But Nancy's ties to her stepchildren were particularly strained. Ronnie had two children with first wife Jane Wyman—Maureen, born in 1941; and Michael, adopted in 1946. Neither of them took easily to Nancy after her marriage to Reagan in 1952, believing that their stepmother was determined to put a wedge between them and their father. That the two children dubbed Nancy "the Dragon Lady" is harsh enough—but Michael once admitted that, when his stepmother's car rolled off a hill and was totaled, he wished that she'd been in it.

CHIEF OF ASTROLOGY

President Reagan's signing of the historic Intermediate-Range Nuclear Forces (INF) treaty in 1987 was originally slated to be aired on television during prime time. The first lady, however, insisted on making a scheduling change—the signing would happen in the afternoon, not the evening. The reason was simple: Nancy's astrologer Joan Quigley had informed her that the afternoon slot was a better one, according to the star charts. It wasn't the first time that Mrs. Reagan had relied on Quigley's advice to alter the president's agenda. In fact, the astrologer had long since become a fixture in the administration. The relationship began in 1981 after the assassination attempt on Reagan (an event that Nancy forever after referred to only as "March 30"). Terrified that such a thing might easily happen again, the first lady enlisted Quigley, a San Francisco–based astrologer, to provide whatever "advice" she could about Reagan's schedule—the result was a color-coded calendar that warned of upcoming "good" and "bad" days, hours, etcetera. Mrs. Reagan took pains to conceal Quigley's influence. When calling the White House switchboard, for example, the astrologer was instructed to refer to herself as "Joan Frisc." The whole thing became an embarrassment when it came to light late in the administration, but hey—the Quigley connection served its original purpose: Reagan was never assassinated.

Sixth Sense

First Lady Nancy Reagan was once having lunch with Barbara Bush when she suddenly stood up in a state of panic and announced she had to leave. It was March 30, 1981, and her husband had just been shot across town. It's moments like this, perhaps, that explain why Mrs. Reagan was so superstitious. Her respect for unseen forces went way beyond the token "knocking on wood." She insisted on keeping a large talisman at their California ranch to ward off evil spirits, refused to store her shoes above the level of her head, and forbade herself from changing if she accidentally put on an article of clothing inside out.

SEVEN-YEAR STITCH

First Lady Nancy Reagan's extraordinary wardrobe ended up getting her into plenty of hot water with the press, who thought her extravagance was a bad idea while unemployment remained high. During the first few months of the administration her press secretary got into the habit of deflecting criticism by insisting that Nancy had received her Galanos and Adolfo gowns before she became first lady—specifically, seven years before. It wasn't long before one reporter remarked that Mrs. Reagan must've done a lot of shopping seven years ago. The issue was a serious one. Because the first lady rarely returned the articles of clothing lent to her by designers, she was violating a law against the acceptance of expensive gifts. That she failed to mention all of them on her tax forms didn't help the situation. In 1982 Nancy announced that she would stop the practice of accepting loans from designers; in fact, she kept doing so and admitted as much toward the end of her first ladyship. No legal action was ever taken against her, but the IRS eventually socked her with a million-dollar bill for unpaid taxes.

37

Barbara
BUSH

June 8, 1925–

MARRIED:

January 6, 1945

PRESIDENTIAL HUSBAND:

George Herbert Walker Bush

CHILDREN:

George Walker, Pauline Robinson, John Ellis (Jeb), Neil Mallon, Marvin Pierce, and Dorothy

FIRST LADY:

1989–1993

ASTROLOGICAL SIGN:

Gemini

RELIGION:

Presbyterian

SOUND BITE:

"How could George Bush have an affair? He can't stay up past ten o'clock."

In 1984, George Herbert Walker Bush campaigned for reelection as Ronald Reagan's vice president. His opponent was Geraldine Ferraro, the first woman of either party to run for national executive office in American history. To Bush's wife, Barbara, an outspoken ERA proponent, the fact that a woman was running for vice president was cause for celebration. But the fact that the woman in question was running against George Bush, her husband—well, that was another matter entirely. Barbara ended up referring to Ferraro as "that four-million-dollar . . . I can't say it, but it rhymes with 'rich.'" It was the sort of remark that reminded Americans of two things: first, that Barbara Bush was outspoken (to say the least); and second, that her husband was so dear to her that his opponents, whoever they may be, simply made her bristle with rage.

Family was always first on Barbara's list of priorities. Indeed, she ended up dropping out of college to start one with George Bush. By the time she met him during World War II, she had lived what many would consider a privileged life. Her father, Marvin Pierce, made a name for himself in the New York publishing world and eventually became president of the McCall Corporation, which published the famous women's magazine of the same name. Pauline, her mother,

was a beautiful and cultured society woman whose gift for horticulture earned her a leadership role in the Garden Clubs of America. Inculcated with a love of books from a young age, Barbara became a bright young woman who attended Ashley Hall in South Carolina, a posh private school that churned out polite young ladies. She ended up enrolling at Smith College in Massachusetts, but completed only a year of study.

The reason for that, of course, was a tall, good-looking Andover student named George Bush. Barbara had met him when she was only sixteen, before beginning classes at Smith. When he asked her in 1942 to be his date at his senior prom, it marked the beginning of a love affair. George ended up proposing to her, and Barbara left college for good to prepare for the wedding while George went off to become a torpedo plane pilot. He put his fiancée through hell by getting shot down while fighting Japanese in the Pacific (his plane, incidentally, was

Barbara Bush thrived during her three years in China—but succumbed to depression upon returning to the United States.

christened "Barbara"), but survived and married her upon his return in 1945.

Having done his time in spades, George was shunted around the country from base to base until the end of the war. Upon being discharged from the navy, he took advantage of the GI Bill by entering Yale, and Barbara began her long career as a homemaker. It wasn't long before their first child, future president George Jr., was born, and Barbara—having been brought up around servants—gradually learned to clean house, prepare meals, and become a devoted mother. Indeed, mothering was something that Barbara Bush excelled at—and a good thing, too, because the babes just kept a-comin'. George decided to go into the oil industry after his graduation from Yale and took the family to Texas in 1948. He became rich, and Barbara became busy as all get out with their burgeoning brood—by 1959 they had five children. Her life became a three-ring circus of Little League games and runny noses, a noisy world over which she presided with skill and patience (and plenty of exasperation).

From 1962 on, Bush proved as adept at making his way in politics as he had been at finding Texas tea. After chairing the Harris County Republican Party, he won a seat in the United States House of Representatives in 1966, to which he was reelected two years later. Though Barbara learned to enjoy the excitement of campaigning and found Washington a fascinating place to live, her husband's long absences on congressional business began to bother her. They moved to New York City in 1971 when George was appointed ambassador to the United Nations, then back to the capital in 1973 after Bush accepted President Richard Nixon's request to head up the Republican National Committee. Barbara managed to keep busy by volunteering at a local nursing home and by playing lots of tennis (she'd always been the athletic type), but she continued to see less of her husband than she would've preferred. The kids were growing up and moving out, George always had something exceedingly important to do, and Barbara began wondering what her life was really all about.

As it happened, her husband was as fed up with the status quo as she was and leapt at the opportunity offered him by President Gerald Ford to become the United States envoy to China. He and "Bar," as he called his wife, ended up spending some three fabulous years there. For Mrs. Bush it was more than just an exotic adventure; it was one long stretch of quality time with her husband. They learned Chinese together, toured the country's historic sites and beautiful countryside, and got to know each other all over again.

The dream came to an end in 1976 when George, after a great deal of deliberation with his wife, his kids, and himself, accepted the job of director of the CIA. For Barbara, the return to Washington was an utter drag. As the nation's chief spy, Bush shared even less of his life with her than he had in his earlier days. The children, of course, were all living lives of their own, and Barbara found herself alone and anxious. Jealous of all the professional women who surrounded her husband, she seriously questioned her decision to reject a college degree and become a full-time homemaker. The result was a long and very nasty bout of depression that often verged on the suicidal. Deeply troubled by his wife's grim demeanor and crying jags, Bush urged Bar to get professional help (she would later wonder why he didn't leave her). Instead, she resumed her volunteer projects, threw her energies into tennis and political entertaining, and developed a project all her own: Having once been utterly terrified of speaking before an audience, Bar developed a slide show on China, toured the country with it, and sent the proceeds on to her favorite church in Houston.

Fortunately, Barbara's self-engineered therapy began to work, for she soon found herself in a role that needed her to be at her best. After George became vice president under Ronald Reagan in 1980, Mrs. Bush took on a truly exhausting schedule. During her eight years as second lady, she hosted well over 1,000 events, logged nearly one and a half million miles of travel both here and abroad, and—most importantly—allowed herself to be hoisted by a cherry picker every December to place a star on top of the national Christmas tree. It's safe to say that she more than made up for calling Geraldine Ferraro a "stitch." (Ahem.)

During Bush's presidential campaign in 1988, Bar toured the country with a slide show of her beloved family, a presentation meant to visualize the Republican Party's emphasis on "family values." It also served to galvanize Mrs. Bush's image as a kindhearted, grandmotherly figure—she even looked the part with her pearl necklaces and mane of gray hair. But if Bar seemed naturally to put people at ease, she also had the capacity to stir up controversy. She had always been forthright. But after public remarks that indicated she differed with her more conservative husband over such issues as abortion and gun control, she quickly learned to curb her candor (at least before the media).

Of course, the new first lady's straightforward style could also be an asset. Incapable of putting on airs, Barbara Bush never took herself seriously, and virtually every one of the innumerable guests at the White House over her four-year tenure found her impossible not to get along with. Something she did take seriously, however, was her opportunity to make a difference. Literacy was her project of choice, a campaign she had embraced in her second lady days and that she now pursued even more vigorously. She supported reading programs around the country by creating the Barbara Bush Foundation for Family Literacy, did a radio program to encourage adults to read aloud to their children, and pushed the president to sign the National Literacy Act in 1991. She even wrote a couple of books about her dogs, C. Fred's Story (written during her years as second lady) and Millie's Book, whose royalties went toward funding literacy projects. Though many Americans considered her a sort of throwback to the days before feminism (as exhibited by protesters at Wellesley College who thought Mrs. Bush, whose fame rested solely on the work of her husband, was a bad choice for commencement speaker), Bar got high marks from the majority of the country—and not just for her sense of humor. When she famously embraced and kissed AIDS victims, she went a long way toward dispelling the myth that casual contact could spread the virus. And her impassioned public statements against racism helped advance the national dialogue on the challenges facing people of color.

Unfortunately for the president, his popularity wasn't quite as high as his wife's. Indeed, it would keep falling, particularly during the Gulf War. Though Barbara campaigned right along with him in 1992 for his reelection and gave a stirring speech at the Republican convention, she was getting weary of the withering criticism being heaped upon him by his opponents. His loss to Bill Clinton stung but also came as something of a relief for Barbara. By devoting herself after the defeat to refurbishing the family homes in Maine and Texas, by writing her memoirs, and by continuing to work on behalf of literacy, Bar fell into a routine typical of a former first lady. But she eventually took on a task shared by only one other predecessor. In 2000, she enthusiastically campaigned in her son's race for the White House. And when he won, she became the first woman since Abigail Adams to be both a wife and mother to American presidents. Looks like leaving college to raise a family wasn't such a bad idea, after all.

MAKING THE GRAY

Barbara Bush's gray hair became something of a symbol to Americans of the first lady's matronly appearance and demeanor (her family nicknamed her the "Silver Fox"). In fact, her brown hair went white at quite an early age, and the cause was tragic. In 1953 the Bushes' first daughter, Robin, contracted leukemia. The little girl spent eight months in a New York hospital, attended by her parents, until she died. Needless to say, the long vigil proved devastating to both Barbara and her husband. By the time of Robin's death, Bar's hair had gone white. She tried at first to color it brown but eventually gave up.

WEIGHTY ISSUES

Barbara Bush was masterful at the art of self-deprecating humor. That she was no fashion diva was as obvious to her as it was to the rest of the country, and she had no desire whatsoever to do anything about it. As she remarked upon becoming first lady, "My mail tells me a lot of fat, white-haired, wrinkled ladies are tickled pink." She once said that her "winning smile makes me look as if I'm being electrocuted." But it was her weight that Barbara joked about most often, a subject that produced some of her finest one-liners. At the beginning of her first ladyship, reporters questioned her about predecessor Nancy Reagan. "As you know, we have a lot in common," she replied. "She adores her husband; I adore mine. She fights drugs; I fight illiteracy. She wears a size three . . . so's my leg." When *Parade* magazine received a question from one of its readers about the first lady's weight, it printed an article that put her between 135 and 145 pounds. "Just for starters," she quipped in a speech shortly after the information was published, "I was born weighing 135 pounds." Then there was the trip to visit soldiers in the Gulf during Thanksgiving, in the course of which she was to sit down to no less than three holiday dinners. Her remark to reporters summed it up nicely: "You know, I was built for the job."

WILLARD

During her husband's inaugural parade in 1989, Barbara Bush broke from her Secret Service detail and ran for the barricades lining Pennsylvania Avenue. She had spotted everyone's favorite weatherman, Willard Scott, and ran over to give him a kiss.

Mock Lobster

While second lady, Barbara Bush occasionally indulged her sense of vanity by attending state dinners without her glasses. At one of them, she proceeded to dig into the first course, a lobster tail, only to be interrupted by the Australian prime minister, who was sitting next to her. "Barbara," he whispered, "that's the adornment." The lobster tail proved to be only a lobster shell. Mortified by the faux pas, she soon scheduled an appointment with an eye doctor to get some contact lenses.

38

Hillary Rodham
CLINTON

October 26, 1947–

MARRIED:
October 11, 1975

PRESIDENTIAL HUSBAND:
William Jefferson Clinton

CHILDREN:
Chelsea Victoria

FIRST LADY:
1993–2001

ASTROLOGICAL SIGN:
Scorpio

RELIGION:
Methodist

SOUND BITE:
"I am surprised at the way people seem to perceive me, and sometimes I read stories and hear things about me and I go, 'Ugh. I wouldn't like her either.'"

Hillary Rodham Clinton has racked up quite a few firsts in her storied lifetime: the first Wellesley student to be allowed to speak at commencement, the first lawyer to become first

> As first lady, Hillary Rodham Clinton proposed a byzantine health care plan that baffled many in congress—including her own supporters.

lady, the first first lady to be given an office in the West Wing right along with her husband, and the first wife of a president to be elected to the Senate. Of course, she was also the first presidential spouse to be subpoenaed by a grand jury. It's a dubious distinction, to be sure, and lies at the heart of Mrs. Clinton's evolving legacy. For all her achievements and ability, she has become forever associated with the scandals and strife that dominated her husband's presidency.

Even from a young age, Hillary Rodham was clearly going places. Born in Chicago and raised in Park Ridge, Illinois, she was infused with an appreciation for personal achievement and community service by her Methodist church and by her parents, Hugh Ellsworth Rodham and Dorothy Howell Rodham. By the time she graduated from high school, she was an honor student, voted "most

likely to succeed," and had helped fellow teens organize volunteer efforts to help the underprivileged, particularly migrant workers. Her curriculum at Wellesley College went well beyond classes in political science, and she became famous on campus for her outspoken liberalism and for boycotting classes on behalf of civil rights. She was just as active in New Haven after she entered Yale Law School in 1969, organizing protests against the Vietnam War and joining a student movement to ensure legal objectivity in the trial of Black Panther members. Women's issues were also very important to her—she fought to have tampon dispensers placed in all of Yale's ladies' rooms.

To fellow law student Bill Clinton, Hillary was the perfect woman: intelligent, dedicated, pretty, and independent. They fell in love shortly after meeting in 1970. After graduation, Hillary ended up pursuing her own course for a time by joining the legal staff of the committee that was attempting to impeach President Richard Nixon. Her relationship with Clinton, however, proved more powerful. Though her friends and associates vigorously attempted to talk her out of it, she decided to go to Arkansas to help Bill with his congressional campaign.

And help she did. While teaching law at the University of Arkansas, she lent her consummate intelligence and legal savvy to Clinton's campaign, playing a vital role in his political endeavors. After marrying him in 1975, she continued to devote time to her own career as well as his, working for Jimmy Carter's presidential campaign in 1976 and serving on the board of her friend Marian Wright Edelman's Children's Defense Fund. She helped Bill get elected Arkansas attorney general, went to work for the Rose Law Firm in 1976 (at which she would eventually make full partner), and devoted much of her time to Bill's successful run for governor in 1978. It's as if she were living two lives, and both of them were going splendidly.

Well, not quite. In fact, many Arkansans had some bones to pick with the governor's wife. Bill was a native, but his wife was anything but—and she seemed to play the outlander a bit too well. She hadn't taken Clinton's name, for instance, a fact that made her look like some sort of feminist (no!). Moreover, she displayed a galling habit of going without makeup and showing up in frumpy dresses and big glasses that made her look like a crunchy freak—or, worse, some sort of carpetbagger come to preach the liberal gospel to the uninitiated. When

Clinton lost his bid for reelection in 1982, his wife took it as a clarion call for change. Both of them immediately began working for his gubernatorial return in 1984, but Hillary went the extra mile by getting contacts, styling her hair, and replacing her decidedly unpopular duds with business suits.

Oh, yeah—she also started calling herself Hillary Rodham Clinton.

Whether because of Hillary's makeover or not, Bill got back into the governor's mansion and wouldn't leave until becoming president in 1993. As for Mrs. Clinton, she began performing her old trick of working for her husband and herself at the same time—and doing both rather well. The governor made her chair of the Arkansas Educational Standards Committee, in which capacity Hillary proved a canny legislator and efficient manager of change. But she was also bringing in more bacon than her important husband by continuing in her law practice and serving on the boards of companies like Wal-Mart. With the added responsibility of raising her daughter, Chelsea, born in 1980, Hillary had truly become the ultimate multitasker.

And one of her many tasks was coping with her husband's monstrous libido. Bill had proven incapable of resisting extramarital temptations even before they were extramarital: He was cheating on Hillary before they were married. That Clinton didn't even have the decency to be cautious about it simply made things worse, and not just because of the inevitable humiliation. Hillary had her eyes fixed on the White House as assuredly as Bill had, and his reckless womanizing was creating unnecessary trouble. The result was a promise by Clinton not to . . . er, screw up anymore and an effort on both their parts to perfect their marital image for the 1992 presidential race.

There was trouble nevertheless. When more allegations about Clinton's philandering became public during the campaign, he and Hillary decided to squelch the crisis by making a television appearance to convince the nation of their marital solidarity. "I'm sitting here," said Hillary to the cameras, "because I love him and I respect him and I honor what he's been through and what we've been through." The spot worked for the most part, though Mrs. Clinton's insistence that she wasn't "some little woman standing by my man like Tammy Wynette" invoked the wrath of the country-western singer for what she considered a misinterpretation of her lyrics. Hillary had run into similar trouble when she replied to questions about her obvious influence by saying, "I suppose I could have stayed at home and baked cookies," inspiring a firestorm of criticism from those who thought she was smugly insulting full-time homemakers. All in all, it proved a challenging campaign for both Clintons.

And yet they won. It was the realization of a dream that Hillary had entertained for years. She had been Bill Clinton's closest adviser since he began his political career, and her influence would only increase with time. Of course, there had been presidential marriage/partnerships before, but nothing like this. Hillary's enormous role in the administration would become clear just weeks after the inauguration, when the president appointed his wife chair of a task force to oversee health-care reform. If Mrs. Clinton brought enormous legal and managerial clout to the job, it only served to make her failure more conspicuous. Health care was no easy nut to crack, to be sure. But the first lady's byzantine recommendations left Congress utterly befuddled, and the program was defeated. Critics of the administration were already making noise about what they considered Hillary's inappropriate power in the White House; the health-care debacle just made things worse.

The inevitable result was a retreat into something like a more traditional first lady role. For the rest of her husband's stint as president, Hillary would devote her efforts to issues that had long been dear to her: child welfare and women's rights. In addition to publishing a book entitled It Takes a Village (1996), which outlined a program for fashioning communities that could allow children to make the most of their potential, she spoke widely both in America and abroad on feminist issues and the need for children's legal protection. Most people, however, were paying close attention to the legal battles that had overtaken the administration. Though Clinton won reelection in 1996, his reputation had been souring since 1994, when the attorney general began an investigation of the Clintons' alleged illegal dealings back in Arkansas with a real estate scam run by the Whitewater Development Corporation. Hillary herself was in hot water over missing billing records from her old employer, the Rose Law Firm. Written off by the first lady as attacks by a "vast right-wing conspiracy," neither accusation would result in conviction (or, for that matter, illumination of the real facts). The Whitewater investigation, however, did end up prying into an area of profound vulnerability for the president: his extramarital affairs. When the president was caught on tape lying about his White House affair with intern Monica Lewinsky, the stuff really hit the fan, resulting in an impeachment trial. Clinton escaped conviction, but the whole mess put a decidedly foul patina on the remainder of his second term.

Of course, it also left a foul taste in Hillary's mouth. For years she had been trying to overlook her husband's transgressions and welcoming him back into the marriage after he strayed. Her devotion to him will perhaps always remain a matter of conjecture. What seems more certain, however, is that she'd been riding his coattails for too long, offering the best of her mind in exchange for wayward behavior. The result was probably inevitable, if somewhat controversial: After offering conspicuous clues about her intentions in 1999, Hillary formally announced in 2000 her intention to run for senator from New York. (New York?) Yes, New York. The residency issue was settled when the Clintons bought a huge house in Westchester County, New York. The rest was settled by . . . well, women. If Hillary Clinton was thought by many to be a mouth-off and an opportunistic enabler, she was considered a fighter for feminism and a female icon by plenty of New York's women—sixty percent of them ended up voting for her in the Senate race, giving her a fairly large victory.

In many ways, therein lies the conundrum of Hillary Rodham Clinton. As a highly educated and intensely motivated woman, she inspires the hottest of emotions—to Americans, she is either a marvelously capable heroine of the women's movement or a conniving and manipulative witch on wheels. Whatever the truth may be, Mrs. Clinton may well be on her way to achieving yet another first: the first woman to run for president. Hey, it may never happen. But can you imagine the voter turnout?

SPACEY

As a child, Hillary Rodham dreamed of becoming an astronaut. NASA wasn't exactly supportive. When she wrote a letter to the agency looking for advice as to how she should proceed, they responded simply that she shouldn't and that space was the province of the male gender. Needless to say, she was appalled.

ABOUT-FACE

Hillary Clinton has long been a favorite target of the right wing. But she wasn't always a Democrat—in fact, it wasn't until her college days that she began leaning to the left. Back in high school, she was an ardent supporter of severe rightwing Republican Barry Goldwater.

FOSTER CARE

When White House adviser Vince Foster committed suicide in 1993, it focused the sort of attention on the Clinton administration that every presidential couple dreads. Vince Foster was a fellow Arkansan who, by all accounts, was something of a golden boy—he was handsome, intelligent, and one heck of a lawyer. He was also, according to some, more than just a friend to Hillary Clinton—and had been since they both worked for the Rose Law Firm. Though definitive evidence of the alleged affair may never come to light, numerous Clinton friends and cronies have attested to the unusually close relationship Hillary shared with Foster before his death. Considering her husband's profligate habits with other women, the possibility that Mrs. Clinton may have sought comfort in the arms of a man such as Foster can hardly come as a shock. Based on his interviews with Clinton insiders for his book *State of a Union: Inside the Complex Marriage of Bill and Hillary Clinton*, former *National Enquirer* reporter Jerry Oppenheimer offers the possibility that Foster, upon joining the Clintons in Washington after Bill's election, suffered from a profound malaise brought on by the shift that White House realities brought to his relationship with Hillary. Whatever the truth may be, Hillary Clinton was loath to even discuss Vince Foster whenever his name was brought up again.

Photo Op

Like most first ladies, Hillary Clinton was concerned with maintaining whatever privacy she could. Hence her concern when, while riding a bike one day along the Potomac, she was waved off the trail by Japanese tourists. It looked as if they were intent on getting a photo of the first lady and that her disguise of sunglasses and a baseball cap had failed. In fact, the opposite was true: they were merely looking for someone to take their picture. After doing so, she calmly rode off without anyone the wiser.

ROUGH START

That Hillary Clinton ended up winning a Senate seat at all in 2000 may seem extraordinary when you consider how poorly her campaign went at first. The trouble stemmed from two things: the fact that she was the first lady and that she was a person seeking political office. The result was a conflict of interest that at times could become a genuine predicament. When her husband the president decided to offer clemency to sixteen Puerto Rican nationalists who'd been jailed for committing crimes on behalf of the Fuerzas Armadas de Liberacion Nacional, it became apparent to some (especially those who had been victims of FALN's violent crimes) that Bill was currying favor with the Latino vote on behalf of his wife. The accusation was a stretch, but Hillary just complicated things later by coming out against the decision—and disappointing many in the Hispanic community who thought the pardon was long overdue. Then there was the trip she made to Israel. In fact, she made the journey as first lady, not senatorial candidate, a fact lost on many Americans. While visiting Ramallah in the occupied territories, she calmly sat next to Suha Arafat, Yasir Arafat's wife, while Suha accused the Israeli army of using tactics involving poison gas. After failing to respond to the allegation, Hillary got up and warmly kissed Mrs. Arafat on the cheek. Back in America, the embrace was viewed as incredibly irresponsible. Mrs. Clinton emphasized her support of the Middle East peace process and claimed not to have heard the translation of Suha Arafat's words. But the damage was done—particularly with the Jewish vote in New York State.

39

Laura BUSH

November 4, 1946–

MARRIED:

November 5, 1977

PRESIDENTIAL HUSBAND:

George Walker Bush

CHILDREN:

Barbara Pierce and Jenna Welch

FIRST LADY:

2001–

ASTROLOGICAL SIGN:

Scorpio

RELIGION:

Methodist

SOUND BITE:

"Parents need to be involved and support teachers, whether it's providing a quiet space where their children can learn or baking cupcakes for Valentine's Day."

hen reporters asked Laura Bush what her concerns were upon becoming first lady, she replied, "It's a major life change. I'm not particularly worried about safety. Privacy. I'm very worried about privacy." And she wasn't kidding.

Despite her experience as a librarian, First Lady Laura Bush had no problem with her husband's Patriot Act, which gave the government access to patron accounts and borrowing histories.

If there's one thing Laura Bush has done well since moving into the White House, it's maintain a low profile. Few of her twentieth-century predecessors were ever so good at avoiding controversy.

She grew up an only child amidst the oil-spawned wealth of Midland, Texas, where her father, Harold Welch, made a good living in housing development. The placid idyll of her youth literally came to a screeching halt when, at the tender age of seventeen, she was involved in a car accident that instantly killed a friend and classmate of hers. Understandably, the tragedy served to pull her back within herself. She had always been a bright and intellectually curious kid; now, hurled into adulthood overnight, she developed a thoughtful earnestness that went hand in hand with a growing love for the written word.

That connection to books shaped the next decade of her life. Laura was a serious student at Southern Methodist University, too busy with scoring high grades to join the protests that increasingly consumed her generation. After graduating with a teacher's certificate, she taught elementary school children in Dallas and Houston for a few years, went back to school at the University of Texas at Austin to get her master's degree in library science, and ended up working as a librarian in Houston and Austin. She had found her calling, and she warmly embraced it.

It wasn't long before she was also warmly embracing George W. Bush. After meeting at a barbecue in 1977 arranged by a mutual friend, the two hit it off almost right from the start and began a relationship that fired up very quickly into a mutual desire to get married—which they did just a few months after first setting eyes on each other. The explosive progress of their courtship seemed proof that opposites attract—if Laura was serene, deliberate, intellectual, and introspective, her new husband was an outgoing, restive partyer-turned-businessman who liked to jaw and joke more than read. But if members of both families were bemused by the young couple's differences in temperament, they were just as impressed by the obvious electricity between them.

Laura had fallen deeply in love, but at a price. A Democrat who once voted for the liberal-minded Eugene McCarthy, she now found herself part of the Texas Republican juggernaut that was the Bush clan. They welcomed her with open arms; but it was also clear that burying her own political views was in everybody's best interest. In fact, it was a reality to which the retiring Laura could easily adjust. Politics were George's province, not hers, and her sense of devotion led easily to unconditional support.

The first test came almost immediately after they were married, when George made a run for Congress. Laura performed admirably as a public speaker (only when she had to, for she had no desire to do it) and campaign helper. When her husband lost the election, it was back to the oil business. For Laura, the life of a housewife proved rewarding—she continued to read her treasured books and volunteered in local charities and civic organizations. One area of her life, however, remained unfulfilled. Both she and George had raced to wedlock partly because they both wanted children so badly. But like many young couples, they soon discovered that pregnancy was easier said than done. In 1981, they were in the midst of dealing with an adoption agency when, quite unexpectedly, Laura discovered she was pregnant. And with twins no less. By the time Barbara Pierce and Jenna Welch were delivered by cesarean section on November 25, 1981, their poor mother had suffered a debilitating pregnancy, lengthy hospitalization, and the frantic fear of kidney failure.

The pregnancy may have been hard going, but the Bushes had their eagerly anticipated children. And nobody was prouder than granddad, George H.W. Bush, then vice president of the United States. In fact, the senior George Bush would go a long way toward fostering his daughter-in-law's political education by enlisting her husband's help in his campaigns. Laura caught her political stride as a relative of the vice president and eagerly joined her husband in 1988 to help in George H.W.'s successful presidential campaign. Though just as intent as always on keeping her life and interests to herself, her beauty, vivacity, and simple charms seemed to personify the Bush clan's obsession with "family values."

She had definitely become an asset to the Bushes and especially to her husband. In 1994, after moving his family to Dallas and making a killing as managing partner of the Texas Rangers baseball team, George made a successful run for governor. Laura soon proved herself as a popular (and always discreet) political wife. Though she became active as a fund-raiser for everything from breast cancer to the arts, it was toward her cherished subject of reading that Laura—like her mother-in-law, Barbara—devoted most of her energies in Texas. In addition to promoting state literacy programs, she created the annual Texas Book Festival, a popular and successful event that raised plenty of cash for local library systems.

But if being the governor's wife was a good old time, becoming first lady was another matter altogether. As George bounced his presidential ideas off friends and advisers, Laura came out against the idea (in private, of course). Becoming the object of national scrutiny was a tailor-made example of the sort of thing she feared. Her husband went ahead with it anyway, and, as always, Laura supported him 100 percent. She even delivered a rousing speech at the 2000 Republican National Convention. It ended up being one of the closest, most controversial elections in American history, but George won.

And Laura found herself immediately challenged by privacy issues as never before. If she had different opinions from the president about topics like abortion rights, she wasn't going to make them explicit, especially in public. "If I differ from my husband," she once said to a reporter, "I'm not going to tell you about it. Sorry." It became something of a mantra. The first lady maintained her sense of mystery even when her daughters, particularly Jenna, displayed a taste for college partying that threatened to put their notorious dad to shame. Her relationship with her daughters was a private matter, period, as was her belief that they had just as much of a right to act like young libertines as any other co-ed. Laura had her causes, of course. In addition to eventually turning her Texas Book Festival into an all-American event on the National Mall, she continued to act on her passion for literacy and learning by holding literary salons in the East Room of the White House (in which writers and scholars were invited to discuss various genres) and by launching a national initiative to boost teacher recruitment.

The "New Teacher Project," as it was called, was shoved aside after September 11, 2001 by the efforts of a government at war. In the wake of the terrorist attacks against the World Trade Center and the Pentagon, the first lady displayed heroic composure, purpose, and empathy. While the president attempted to shore up a stunned American people with bellicose rhetoric, his wife waded into responsibilities that may have been "softer" but were just as vital. Laura wrote open letters to the youth of the nation, imploring them to confront their confused and horrified feelings; she went on the air to remind parents that turning off their television sets at a time like this might not be such a bad idea; she visited those who had been wounded by the attacks; and in Pennsylvania she consoled those who had lost loved ones on Flight 93, which had crashed in that state, thwarting the plans of the terrorists who'd hijacked it. Concerned about her husband's image, she even played a role in reminding him to turn down the saber rattling a bit (though she wasn't always successful). After U.S. forces invaded Afghanistan to take on the Taliban, Laura became the first presidential spouse to deliver an entire presidential radio address, an opportunity she used to discuss the rights of oppressed Afghan women. And while traveling abroad, she went on European airwaves to tackle the insanity of terrorism and its nefarious influence on helpless children.

Clearly this was a first lady who had risen to the occasion, who was leveraging the influence granted her by the position. After her effective public appearances and speeches on behalf of women's rights and children's security, the country got a taste of her compassion and eloquence. They wanted more. And they were not to get it. The first lady's forays into opinionated discourse were more the product of desperate times than anything else and were quickly to become a thing of the past. Laura Bush had long ago become a silent partner, and things weren't going to change now. As the administration launched its controversial war in Iraq to destroy Saddam Hussein's sadistic Baathist regime, she faded even further into the background. And no amount of questioning by eager reporters could possibly pull her out. A perfect example was President Bush's Patriot Act, one of whose stipulations was that government officials could investigate which books a particular reader in the United States had borrowed from public libraries. It's telling that Laura, a librarian with a keen appreciation for the freedom of intellectual curiosity, offered no comment beyond "We are in a special time right now, where we need to do everything we can to avoid another attack."

When Laura decided that her February 12, 2003, East Wing salon was to focus on poetry, it marked perhaps the most dramatic clash between her husband's policies and what she considered the separate world of her comfortable first ladyship. It soon became obvious that most of the poets she was inviting to the event were vehemently opposed to the administration's war in Iraq; in fact, many of them were contributing to an antiwar anthology meant to highlight the symposium's agenda. The first lady's reaction was simple and abrupt: she canceled the whole thing altogether, insisting that the salons were an inappropriate forum for political conflict. And that was that. She had striven rather mightily to avoid the controversial arena that dominated her husband's job—so mightily, in fact, that she had ironically become the subject of controversy.

And so it goes. In the end, Laura Bush seems to have brought the first ladyship full circle, adopting a role as the wife of our elected president—no more, no less. In being the very antithesis of her predecessor, Hillary Clinton, she has certainly proved at least one thing: that a first lady's silence, however convenient or welcome, can sometimes be just as difficult as a first lady who makes a ruckus. Is this job a catch-22 or what?

THE ACCIDENT

It was just a few days after her seventeenth birthday when Laura Welch borrowed her parents' car in Midland to go to a party and, after blowing by a stop sign at fifty miles per hour, slammed into a car being driven by her friend Michael Douglas. Laura's friend Judy Dykes had been in the passenger seat of the Welches' car and was raced to the hospital along with Laura. Michael Douglas, however, was killed instantly in the collision. (In a horrifying twist of fate, Michael's father had been driving behind him at the time and witnessed the accident.) The police report is not clear as to whether Laura's blood-alcohol level was tested. What is certain is that no ticket was issued to her for going through the stop sign.

SMOKIN'

There's an old story told by members of the Bush clan that goes something like this: At their first meeting, Laura Welch was asked by the imperious Bush matriarch Dorothy Walker Bush what she did. "I read, I smoke, I admire," is what Laura is reported to have replied. Though Laura denies having said exactly that, it was the sort of response that, according to her in-laws, endeared her to all and sundry—especially the smoking part. In fact, Laura Bush smoked cigarettes regularly until the early 1990s.

Laura the Librarian

George Bush often joked that his wife's idea of oratory amounted to saying, "Shh-hhh!" Laura usually bristled at the ribbing she got from her husband for being a librarian—perhaps because it struck a little too close to home. When they first met, Laura had already adopted the practice of organizing the books in her bedroom by the Dewey decimal system.

SELECTED BIBLIOGRAPHY

Anthony, Carl Sferazzza. *First Ladies: The Saga of the Presidents' Wives and Their Power 1789-1961*. New York: William Morrow, 1990.

Anthony, Carl Sferazzza. *First Ladies: The Saga of the Presidents' Wives and Their Power 1961-1990*. New York: William Morrow, 1991.

Boller, Paul F. *Presidential Wives: An Anecdotal History*. Second Edition. New York: Oxford University Press, 1998.

Bradford, Sarah. *America's Queen: The Life of Jacqueline Kennedy Onassis*. New York: Viking Penguin, 2000.

Bryan, Helen. *Martha Washington: First Lady of Liberty*. New York: John Wiley & Sons, 2002.

Bush, Barbara. *A Memoir*. New York: Scribner, 1994.

Cook, Blanche Wiesen. *Eleanor Roosevelt*. Vol. 1, 1884-1933. New York: Viking, 1992.

Cook, Blanche Wiesen. *Eleanor Roosevelt*. Vol. 2, 1933-1938. New York: Viking, 1999.

David, Lester. *The Lonely Lady of San Clemente: The Story of Pat Nixon*. New York: Thomas Y. Crowell, 1978.

Fleischner, Jennifer. *Mrs. Lincoln and Mrs. Keckly: The Remarkable Story of the Friendship Between a First Lady and a Former Slave*. New York: Broadway Books, 2003.

Foss, William O. *First Ladies Quotation Book*. New York: Barricade Books, 1999.

Gerhart, Ann. *The Perfect Wife: The Life and Choices of Laura Bush*. New York: Simon & Schuster, 2004.

Kilian, Pamela. *Barbara Bush: Matriarch of a Dynasty*. New York: St. Martin's Press, 2002.

Lash, Joseph P. *Eleanor and Franklin: The Story of Their Relationship Based on Eleanor Roosevelt's Private Papers*. New York: W.W. Norton, 1971.

Levin, Phyllis Lee. *Edith and Woodrow: The Wilson White House*. New York: Scribner, 2001.

McCullough, David. *John Adams*. New York: Simon & Schuster, 2001.

Nagel, Paul C. *John Quincy Adams: A Public Life, A Private Life.* New York: Alfred A. Knopf, 1997.

Oppenheimer, Jerry. *State of a Union: Inside the Complex Marriage of Bill and Hillary Clinton.* New York: HarperCollins, 2000.

Ross, Ishbel. *The General's Wife: The Life of Mrs. Ulysses S. Grant.* New York: Dodd, Mead & Company, 1959.

Russell, Francis. *The Shadow of Blooming Grove: Warren G. Harding in His Times.* New York: McGraw-Hill, 1968.

Russell, Jan Jarboe. *Lady Bird: A Biography of Mrs. Johnson.* New York: Scribner, 1999.

Saunders, Frances Wright. *Ellen Axson Wilson: First Lady Between Two Worlds.* Chapel Hill, North Carolina: The University of North Carolina Press, 1985.

Schneider, Dorothy and Schneider, Carl J. *First Ladies: A Biographical Dictionary.* New York: Facts on File, 2001.

Sheehy, Gail. *Hillary's Choice.* New York: Random House, 1999.

Tomasky, Michael. *Hillary's Turn: Inside Her Improbable, Victorious Senate Campaign.* New York: Free Press, 2001.

Truman, Margaret. *First Ladies: An Intimate Group Portrait of White House Wives.* New York: Fawcett Columbine, 1995.

Wead, Doug. *All the Presidents' Children: Triumph and Tragedy in the Lives of America's First Families.* New York: Atria Books, 2003.

INDEX

NOTE: *Page numbers in bold refer to illustrations.*

A

Adams, Abigail, 18–23, **19**

Adams, Charles, 23

Adams, John, 18, 20, 21, 22, 23

Adams, John Quincy, 21, 23, 37, 39, 40–41, 42, 43

Adams, Louisa Catherine, 37–43, **38**

Adams, Nabby, 22, 23

adultery accusations

    Carter, Jimmy, 257

    Clinton, Hillary Rodham, 280

    Clinton, William Jefferson, 277, 279

    Coolidge, Grace, 187

    Eisenhower, Dwight D., 214–15, 216

    Garfield, James, 115–16, 117–18

    Harding, Warren G., 176–77, 178, 179

    Jackson, Rachel, 44

    Johnson, Lyndon Baines, 229, 232

    Kennedy, John Fitzgerald, 218, 225

    Roosevelt, Eleanor, 203

    Roosevelt, Franklin Delano, 199, 203

    Wilson, Woodrow, 164

advertising, 58–59, 124, 126

alcohol

    Eisenhower, Mamie Doud, 216–17

    Ford, Betty, 246, 248, 249

    Harding, Florence Kling, 179–80

    Hayes, Lucy Webb, 9, 106, 110–11

    Polk, Sarah Childress, 65

    Roosevelt, Edith Kermit, 144, 149, 150

    Tyler, Letitia Christian, 53

    Wilson, Edith Bolling, 171

Anderson, Marian, 203, 216

Arafat, Suha, 281

art talent, 134

Arthur, Chester, 119

Arthur, Ellen Herndon, 119

assassination attempts, 104, 118, 265, 266

assassinations

    Garfield, James, 117, 118

    Kennedy, John Fitzgerald, 223

    Lincoln, Abraham, 87, 89, 95, 104

    McKinley, William, 140, 142

automobiles, 157, 233, 282, 288

B

Bacall, Lauren, 210

Ball, Lucille, 217

Boxer Rebellion, 190, 194

Bush, Barbara, 266, 267–73, **268**

Bush, George Herbert Walker, 267, 269, 270, 271, 272

Bush, George Walker, 284–85, 287, 288

Bush, Laura, 282–88, **283**

Bush, Robin, 272

C

Calhoun, Lucia Gilbert, 115–16

Carter, Jimmy, 251, 253, 254, 255, 256, 257

Carter, Rosalynn, 251–57, **252**

cherry trees, 158

Civil War

    Grant, Julia Dent, 101, 104

    Harrison, Caroline, 130

    Hayes, Lucy Webb, 115

    Johnson, Eliza McCardle, 94, 96, 97

    Lincoln, Mary Todd, 88

    Pierce, Jane, 81, 82

    Polk, Sarah Childress, 64

    Tyler, Julia Gardiner, 57–58, 59–60

Cleveland, Frances, 120–27, **121**

Cleveland, Grover, 120–25, 126–27

Cleveland, Ruth, 126–27

Clinton, Hillary Rodham, 274–81, **275**

Clinton, William Jefferson, 276, 277, 278, 279, 280, 281

Cockburn, Sir George, 30

cooking, 232–33

Coolidge, Calvin, 181, 183–84, 185, 186, 187

Coolidge, Grace, 181–87, **182**

Crauford-Stuart, Charles, 172

Custis, Daniel Parke, 13, 16

Custis, John, IV, 16, 17

D

dancing, 59, 243, 245, 247, 250

Dandridge, John, 15

Daughters of the American Revolution, 132, 133–34, 203

De Wolf, Henry, 173–74

DePriest, Mrs. Oscar, 195

Douglas, Michael, 288

drugs, 246, 248, 249, 262, 263

E

Eisenhower, Dwight D., 127, 211, 213, 214, 215, 216, 217

Eisenhower, Mamie Doud, 211–17, **212**

entertaining

  Adams, Louisa Catherine, 40, 42

  Coolidge, Grace, 184–85

  Eisenhower, Mamie Doud, 214, 215–16, 217

  Grant, Julia Dent, 102, 103, 104–5

  Harrison, Caroline, 132–33

  Hayes, Lucy Webb, 111

  Lincoln, Mary Todd, 85, 89

  Madison, Dolley, 27–28, 29, 30, 31

  Monroe, Elizabeth, 35

  Pierce, Jane, 80, 81, 82

  Polk, Sarah Childress, 63, 64–65

  Roosevelt, Eleanor, 200, 202

  Taft, Helen Herron, 158

  Tyler, Julia Gardiner, 54, 57, 59

  Tyler, Letitia Christian, 52, 53

Equal Rights Amendment (ERA), 247, 248, 249

F

Fairfax, Sally, 13–14

fashion

  Bush, Barbara, 273

  Cleveland, Frances, 126

Grant, Julia Dent, 105

Lincoln, Mary Todd, 89, 90

Madison, Dolley, 27, 28, 29, 31

McKinley, Ida Saxton, 136, 142

Reagan, Nancy, 259, 262, 263, 266

Roosevelt, Edith Kermit, 149

Washington, Martha, 14

Fillmore, Abigail, 71–76, **72**

Fillmore, Caroline Carmichael McIntosh, 77

Fillmore, Millard, 71–73, 74, 75, 76, 77

finances

  Carter, Rosalynn, 251, 253, 256

  Cleveland, Frances, 125

  Coolidge, Grace, 184, 185

  Grant, Julia Dent, 100, 101, 102–3

  Hayes, Lucy Webb, 117

  Johnson, Eliza McCardle, 92, 94, 97

  Lincoln, Mary Todd, 85, 86, 88, 89–91

  Madison, Dolley, 31

  McKinley, Ida Saxton, 136, 142

  Polk, Sarah Childress, 61, 63, 64, 65

  Reagan, Nancy, 261, 262–63, 266

  Roosevelt, Edith Kermit, 144, 147–48

  Tyler, Julia Gardiner, 57–58, 59

  Tyler, Letitia Christian, 52, 53

firearms, 163, 202–3

First Lady

  as job, 9–10

  as term, 25

Ford, Betty, 10, 243–50, **244**

Ford, Gerald R., 243, 245–46, 247, 248, 249, 250

Foster, Vince, 280

France, 34, 36, 43

G

Gacy, John Wayne, **252**, 257

Galt, Norman, 165, 167

Garfield, James, 113–18

Garfield, Lucretia, 112–18, **114**

Goldwater, Barry, 280

Goodrich, Arthur, 163–64
Grant, Julia Dent, 98–105, **99**
Grant, Ulysses S., 98, 100–101, 102, 104, 105
Great Depression, 192–93
Grey, Lord, 172
Guiteau, Charles, 117, 118
H
"Hail to the Chief," 59
Haley, Jim, 187
Harding, Florence Kling, 173–80, **174**
Harding, Warren, 173, 175, 176–77, 178, 179–80
Harrison, Anna, 46–49, **47**
Harrison, Benjamin
    and Harrison, Anna, 49
    and Harrison, Caroline, 128, 130, 131, 132, 133, 134
    and Harrison, Mary, 135
Harrison, Caroline, 128–34, **129**
Harrison, Mary, 134, 135
Harrison, William Henry, 46, 48–49
Hayes, Lucy Webb, 9, 106–12, **107**
Hayes, Rutherford B., 108, 109, 110, 111
Hickok, Lorena, 203
Hoover, Herbert, 188, 190, 191, 193, 194, 195
Hoover, J. Edgar, 203
Hoover, Lou Henry, **187**, 188–95
I
illegitimate children, 123
illness
    Adams, Louisa Catherine, 42
    Bush, Barbara, 270–71, 272, 273
    Cleveland, Frances, 127
    Coolidge, Grace, 185, 186, 187
    Eisenhower, Mamie Doud, 213, 214, 216, 217
    Fillmore, Abigail, 74, 75
    Ford, Betty, 245, 246, 247, 248, 250
    Harding, Florence Kling, 176, 178, 179, 180
    Harrison, Anna, 49
    Harrison, Caroline, 131, 132
    Hayes, Lucy Webb, 110, 113, 115, 117, 118
    Johnson, Eliza McCardle, 94, 95, 96, 97
    Johnson, Lady Bird, 232
    Kennedy, Jacqueline Bouvier, 221, 223, 224
    Madison, Dolley, 25, 27
    McKinley, Ida Saxton, 136, 138–42
    Monroe, Elizabeth, 32, 35, 36
    Nixon, Pat, 234, 240
    Pierce, Jane, 80, 81, 82
    Reagan, Nancy, 263–64, 265
    Roosevelt, Eleanor, 199, 201, 202
    Taft, Helen Herron, 155–56, 158
    Taylor, Margaret, 68, 69–70
    Truman, Bess, 207, 209
    Tyler, Letitia Christian, 52–53
    Wilson, Ellen Axson, 161, 162, 163
insanity, alleged, 87–88, 90–91
Iran hostage crisis, 256
J
Jackson, Andrew, 44
Jackson, Rachel, 44
jealousy, 88–89, 210
Jefferson, Martha, 24
Jefferson, Thomas, 24
Johnson, Andrew, 92–94, 95, 96
Johnson, Charles, 96, 97
Johnson, Eliza McCardle, 92–97, **93**
Johnson, Lady Bird, 226–33, **227**
Johnson, Lyndon Baines, 226, 228, 229, 230, 231, 232, 233
Johnson, Robert, 97
K
Kelly, Grace, 224
Kennedy, Jacqueline Bouvier, 218–25, **219**, 230
Kennedy, John Fitzgerald, 218, 220–21, 222, 223, 224, 225, 229–30
Kitt, Eartha, 231–32

L

Lafayette, Marquis de, 35–36

League of Nations, 169, 170

Lincoln, Abraham, 83, 85–86, 87, 88–89, 91, 104

Lincoln, Mary Todd, 83–91, **84**

Lincoln, Robert, 90–91

Lincoln, Willie, 86, 91

M

Madison, Dolley, 24, 25–31, **26**, 54

Madison, James, 27, 28, 29, 30, 31

Marcia, Madame, 179

McKinley, Ida Saxton, 136–42, **137**

McKinley, Katie, 138, 141

McKinley, William, 136, 138, 139, 140, 141, 142

Mercer, Lucy, 199, 203

Mexican-American War, 68, 80, 100

Monroe, Elizabeth, 32–36, **33**

Monroe, James, 34, 35, 36

Mount Vernon, 14

"Mulatto Jack," 16–17

murder rumors, 70, 180

musical talent, 24

N

Native American heritage, 170–71

needlework, 136, 139, 142

Nesbitt, Henrietta, 202

Nixon, Pat, 234–42, **235**

Nixon, Richard Milhous, 234, 236, 237, 238, 239, 240, 241

O

Onassis, Aristotle, 223

P

Peck, Mary, 164, 168

pensions, 49, 64, 88, 103, 117, 135

Phillips, Carrie, 176, 179

Pierce, Benjamin, 80, 81, 82

Pierce, Franklin, 80–81, 82

Pierce, Jane, 9, 78–82, **79**

Pochahantas, 170–71

Polk, James Knox, 61–63, 64–65

Polk, Sarah Childress, 61–65, **62**

privacy

   Bush, Barbara, 282, 286

   Cleveland, Frances, 125–27

   Clinton, Hillary Rodham, 280

   Coolidge, Grace, 186

   Harrison, Caroline, 131

   Kennedy, Jacqueline Bouvier, 201, 223, 224, 225

   Truman, Bess W., 210

psychic abilities, 60, 103–4

Q

Quakerism, 25, 27, 28, 29

Quigley, Joan, 265–66

R

racism, 150, 195, 203, 216, 272

Reagan, Michael, 265

Reagan, Nancy, 259–66, **260**, 273

Reagan, Patti, 265

Reagan, Ronald, 258, 261–62, 263, 264, 265, 266

religion

   Hayes, Lucy Webb, 106, 108, 109–10, 111–12

   McKinley, Ida Saxton, 141

   Pierce, Jane, 82

   Polk, Sarah Childress, 64–65

   Taylor, Margaret, 68–69

Revolutionary War

   Adams, Abigail, 18, 20

   Harrison, Anna, 48, 49

   Madison, Dolley, 24

   Washington, Martha, 17

   Robards, Lewis, 44

   Roosevelt, Alice Lee, 143, 146

   Roosevelt, Edith Kermit, 143, 144–50, **145**

Roosevelt, Eleanor, 9, 194, 196–203, **197**

Roosevelt, Franklin Delano, 150, 196, 198, 199, 200–201, 202, 203

Roosevelt, Theodore, 144, 146–47, 148, 149, 150, 157

Russia, 40, 42–43

S

Scott, Willard, 273

Secret Service, 149, 187, 202, 210

September 11 terrorist attacks, 286–87

slavery
    Adams, Louisa Catherine, 41
    Fillmore, Abigail, 74
    Grant, Julia Dent, 104
    Hayes, Lucy Webb, 108, 109
    Lincoln, Mary Todd, 87, 88
    Madison, Dolley, 25, 29–30
    Pierce, Jane, 82
    Polk, Sarah Childress, 65
    Tyler, Julia Gardiner, 59–60
    Tyler, Letitia Christian, 53

smoking
    Bush, Laura, 288
    Coolidge, Grace, 187
    Eisenhower, Mamie Doud, 217
    Ford, Betty, 250
    Grant, Julia Dent, 105
    Madison, Dolley, 29
    Taylor, Margaret, 70

spiritualism, 9, 82, 86, 91, 179, 265–66

Stover, Daniel, 96, 97

Summersby, Kay, 214–15, 216

superstitions, 178–79

T

Taft, Helen Herron, 151–58, **152**

Taft, William Howard, 153, 154–55, 156, 157

Taylor, Margaret, 66–70, **67**

Taylor, Zachary, 25, 66, 67–70

Teapot Dome scandal, 180

Thomas, F. W., 59

Todd, John, Jr., 25, 28, 29, 30, 31

Todd, John Payne, 27, 31

Truman, Bess, 204–10, **205**

Truman, Harry S., 206, 207–8, 209, 210

Truman, Mary Margaret, 209

Tyler, John, 50, 52, 53, 54, 56, 57, 60

Tyler, Julia Gardiner, 54–60, **55**, 65

Tyler, Letitia Christian, 50–53, **51**

V

Van Buren, Hannah, 45

Van Buren, Martin, 45

Vietnam War, 231–32, 239

vision problems, 103, 127, 257, 273

W

War of 1812, 28, 30–31

Washington, Booker T., 150

Washington, George, 11, 13–15

Washington, Martha, 11–17, **12**, 23

Watergate scandal, 239, 240, 242

White House
    Adams, Abigail, 23
    Fillmore, Abigail, 76
    Ford, Betty, 247 250
    Harrison, Anna, 48, 49
    Harrison, Caroline, 131, 133, 134
    Johnson, Eliza McCardle, 97
    Kennedy, Jacqueline Bouvier, 218, 221–22
    Lincoln, Mary Todd, 89
    Madison, Dolley, 30–31
    Nixon, Pat, 242
    Roosevelt, Edith Kermit, 147–48
    Truman, Bess, 204, 208–9

Wilson, Edith Bolling, 9, 165–72, **166**, 178

Wilson, Ellen Axson, 159–64, **160**

Wilson, Woodrow, 159–60, 162, 163, 164

World War I, 169–71

World War II
    Eisenhower, Mamie Doud, 214, 215, 216
    Nixon, Pat, 236
    Reagan, Nancy, 264
    Roosevelt, Eleanor, 201
    Truman, Bess, 207

Wyman, Jane, 258

ACKNOWLEDGMENTS

Those interested in discovering the fascinating lives of America's presidential spouses need look no further than Carl Sferrazza Anthony's two-volume masterpiece, *First Ladies: The Saga of the Presidents' Wives and Their Power*, which offered me an invaluable introduction to the subject. I also found Paul F. Boller, Jr.'s *Presidential Wives: An Anecdotal History* to be an interesting and entertaining guide.

I am indebted as always to Jason Rekulak for his patience, enthusiasm, and editorial prowess; to designers Susan Van Horn and Andrea Stephany, who've produced a wonderfully attractive package; and to Monika Suteski, the talented illustrator without whose vision this book would be half as interesting.